CIRCUIT RIDER CONNEXION

Passing the Baton of Faith

D. Gregory Van Dussen

Asbury Theological Seminary Series in Pietist/Wesleyan Studies

EMETH PRESS
www.emethpress.com

CIRCUIT RIDER CONNEXION: *Passing the Baton of Faith*

Copyright © 2025 D. Gregory Van Dussen
Printed in the United States of America on acid-free paper

All rights reserved. No part of this book may be reproduced, or stored in a retrieval system or transmitted in any form or by any means, electronic, mechanical, photocopying, recording, scanning or otherwise, except as permitted by the 1976 United States Copyright Act, or with the prior written permission of Emeth Press. Requests for permission should be addressed to: Emeth Press, P. O. Box 533, Jackson, Georgia 30233.   http://www.emethpress.com.

Library of Congress Cataloging-in-Publication Data

Names: Van Dussen, D. Gregory, author.
Title: Circuit Rider Connexion : passing the baton of faith / D. Gregory Van Dussen.
Description: Jackson : Emeth Press LLC, [2025] | Summary: "This book examines some of the ways Wesley's movement kept its vision fresh and handed it on to new generations of leaders. How did the Methodist revival cross an ocean and sweep across a continent? How were its leaders able to recruit and equip an army of preachers to multiply and mobilize new leaders and followers, even across formidable barriers of culture and geography? How did they launch a spiritual relay race in which an endless procession of runners could receive and pass their baton of faith across American and Canadian frontiers and subsequent communities experiencing constant social change? What can we learn from the culture of mentoring in which each circuit rider played a vital part?"-- Provided by publisher.
Identifiers: LCCN 2024055995 (print) | LCCN 2024055996 (ebook) | ISBN 9781609472122 (paperback) | ISBN 9781609472139 (kindle edition)
Subjects: LCSH: Methodist Church--United States--History. | Circuit riders--United States--History.
Classification: LCC BX8235 .V35 2025 (print) | LCC BX8235 (ebook) | DDC 287.0973--dc23/eng/20250110
LC record available at https://lccn.loc.gov/2024055995
LC ebook record available at https://lccn.loc.gov/2024055996

All Photos are in the public domain

Endorsements

Greg van Dussen's most recent book, Circuit Rider Connexion: Passing the Baton of Faith, offers readers a powerful lens from which we may observe the history of Methodism, John Wesley's remarkable movement. This lens focuses our attention on the sharpness of the founder's vision and the ways in which Wesley's Methodist followers continued to see clearly how they could participate in spreading God's sanctifying grace throughout the world. It will do us well to appropriate Van Dussen's foresighted perspective so that we may also perceive our future ministry through God's eyes.

—Dr. Douglas M. Strong, Paul T. Walls Professor of Wesleyan Studies and the History of Christianity, School of Theology, Seattle Pacific Seminary

Van Dussen's study tracks the continuity of ministry values and practices from New Testament times to the modern setting. It focuses on those emphasized by John Wesley, the founder of Wesleyan Methodism in Great Britain that then moved across the Atlantic to make such a great impact in North America during the eighteenth and especially the nineteenth centuries.

Van Dussen's book is loaded with citations and narratives of the ministry habits, work, and thinking of American Methodism's first luminaries, most of whose names have been forgotten, but who, in their time, made Methodism a powerful force in the new world.

The book is not a quick read; it is not intended to be. It is chock full of extended quotations from the heroes of the faith who committed themselves to constant study of the Scriptures, wide reading, intrepid movement, preaching, letter writing, and ceaseless visitation.

It is well worth the time spent to mull over this rich resource of the thinking, habits, and results of these ministers of the Gospel who made such a difference in their world.

—Dr. Paul Webster Livermore, Northeastern Seminary, Retired

Dedication

To The Rev. Wayne and Sue West, who welcomed and oriented me to the Connexion.

Acknowledgements

My sincere gratitude to all who have encouraged me in this project. Special thanks to the Rev. Karen McCaffery, Rev, Duane Priset, Rev. Alice Priset, and Millennium Computers, Batavia, New York, for technical assistance.

Table of Contents

A Foreword / xi

Chapter 1

The Baton of Faith Begins its Journey / 1
"To the very end of the age ... to the ends of the earth:"
(Matthew 28: 20; Acts 1:8, NIV)

Chapter 2

The Baton of Faith in the New Testament Letters / 17
"For I received from the Lord what I also passed on to you...."
I Corinthians 11:23, NIV)

Chapter 3

The Baton of Faith in Wesley's Revival / 57
"The way to heaven"
(Albert C. Outler, ed. The Works of John Wesley. Nashville, TN: Abingdon, 1984, 1:105)

Chapter 4

The Baton Crosses the Atlantic / 84
"Light and power to my soul" (William Phoebus, ed.
Memoirs of the Rev. Richard Whatcoat (etc.). New-York, NY: Joseph Allen, 1828, 10.)

Chapter 5

The Baton of Faith Reaches North America / 105
"the real importance of early Methodism arises from the fact that it was the dawning of a glorious day, the beginning of a great work of God, the opening of a portion of the divine plan

for the renovation and salvation of the world." (George Peck. Early Methodism within the Bounds of the Old Genesee Conference (etc.). New York, NY: Carlton & Porter, 1860, 4.)

Chapter 6

The Baton of Faith Crosses a Continent / 119

"...to spread Scripture-Holiness over these lands...." (*The Doctrines and Discipline of the Methodist Episcopal Church*, Philadelphia, PA; Henry Tuckniss, 1797, iii.)

Chapter 7

Passing the Baton from Here / 149

"...always aiming at perfection, standing on the shoulders of those who have lived before us, and seeking the advantage of our former selves...." (The Doctrines and Discipline of the Methodist Episcopal Church, Philadelphia, PA: Henry Tuckniss, 1797, iv.).

A Foreword

While reading through the Reverend Dr. D. Gregory Van Dussen's *CIRCUIT RIDER CONNECTION: Passing the Baton of Faith*, I found myself imagining a bold theme laid against the background of a relay team competing in an important track and field event. But for the circuit riders, the outcome is far greater than a group of notables engaged in a fierce competition to win a trophy.

In terms of the circuit rider, the passing of the baton draws upon an endless line of many who faithfully, persistently, kept keeping on, passing the message of faith and love to so many for whom God would make a lifelog and eternal difference.

So it is that D. Gregory Van Dussen, a retired pastor of many years of church experience, a thoughtful researcher, and a thorough historian, mines the depths of truth and story to reflect upon the witness of faith in the flow of life.

From ancient times and on to the present day, a work of history is both storytelling and truth-telling. Essentially, Greg comes to the topic with a deep sense of faith and a firm grasp of ministry, of which mentoring and being mentored are integral parts, to draw upon many examples in Methodist, church, and American history.

Amidst all of story- and truth-telling, there are many choice quotations I cite from Greg which challenge, guide and nurture the readers as they puzzle through the various backgrounds and stages of the circuit-rider's lives. Some of these differences are in background and style. Some of these differences are in serious theological engagements.

As Van Dussen puts it, in terms of background and style, "the stories shared on a frontier might come across as outlandish to an urban pastor. A backwoods preacher might become impatient with an urban colleague's unfamiliar illustrations. Yet there is an underlying truth in all of them, and a need for each to value the distinctiveness of the others' experiences" (28).

According to Van Dussen, "there is a mysterious mutuality between truth and love, *alethea* and *agape*, that is set forth in 1 John and other letters . . . One sees love as preparation for a united witness; the other sees truth as a conducive context for love. There is a profound interdependence here that values both" (53). Then, drawing attention to 1 Timothy 1:3&5, Dr. Van Dussen points out: "Leaving people afloat on a sea of misinformation, or under the sway of unscrupulous or misguided teachers does not do them any favors" (59). There is serious business here!

Considering the debate between predestination and Arminianism, Van Dussen raises the matter: "Providing for all who believe is very different from determining who will believe" (84). Then, elaborating upon another concern: "Antinomianism is a belief that Christians are saved by grace, not works, and are not obligated to obey God's commandments. At first this comes across as good Reformation theology, or liberation from legalism, but there is something thoroughly unbiblical about its use" (88-89).

Then, "Wesley's dealings with false teaching did not relate so much to other Christian denominations, but to schools of thought, often within the churches, that veered in directions which denied or subverted important Christian doctrines. He [Wesley] did have considerable controversies with Calvinism and Roman Catholicism, where he found serious differences, but never wrote them off as non-Christian" (93).

From the beginning of this book, CIRCUIT RIDER CONNECTION is a volume rich in Scriptural references and underpinnings to which Van Dussen points the readers' attention to what also appears as an underlayment upon which is founded much for the reader's enrichment.

While reading through Greg's manuscript, I found myself redmarking a share of various thoughts that struck me as moving, fascinating, and helpful, as well as underlining a number of informational pieces among the many striking sentences, for future recall and reflection – some of which I have cited I this foreword.

Fascinating are Greg's descriptions of study conditions for which the circuit rider relied while away in the backwoods of frontier ministry. By Chapter 3, and throughout the whole, he draws out refreshing insights from early Methodist voices such as with Wesley, Asbury, Coke, Bangs, Peck and countless others among the known and unknown early circuit riders. With this, one gains an appreciation that one may not have to be the superstar to make a significant spiritual impact on people's lives.

Drawing our attention to Adam Clarke's classic Preacher's Manual: Clarke begins a part of his manual, called "A Letter to a Preacher," by saying, "'My dear friend – You are engaged in the most important work in the universe.' The world has often tried to downplay this importance, contributing to the load of discouragement too many pastors carry. We need apostolic voices to counter these negative messages and replace them with hope, energy, and inspiration" (128).

Again, citing Adam Clarke, "Shun all controversies about politics: and especially that disgrace of the pulpit, political preaching. I have known this to do much evil; but though I have often heard it, I never heard an instance of it doing good. It is not the bread which God has provided for his children; and from the pulpit, it is neither profitable for doctrine, for reproof, nor for instruction in righteousness" (129).

Throughout this treatise and other writings of his, Van Dussen demonstrates a wide and well-focused grasp of Scriptural, theological, historical, and biographical information, as, for instance, he shows his take on how various writings in the New Testament came about:

"The book of Acts shows Luke, its author, to be highly conversant in the geography, customs, and organization of the places where Peter, Paul, and others ministered. Paul's letters reveal a sophisticated use of language, ideas, and rhetoric of Gentile society, to which he is called to preach. Revelation uses a vast array of symbols and allusions, carefully chosen to offer hope to a persecuted church. All the Biblical writers had the capacity to receive and transmit God's inspired word, in their own time and for all time, not robotically, but with the Spirit working through their distinctive personalities, experiences, and gifts" (148).

With some good and honest insight, there is Van Dussen's take on "the surprising role of camp meetings in bringing together indigenous people and people of European ancestry in North America. While relationships of this kind were fraught with difficulties and were unable to stop racist violence, abuse, injustice, and systematic expropriation of native lands, they could, for a time and in limited situations, demonstrate the unifying and transforming capability of Christ" (170).

Citing circuit rider, James Finley, on how one could not look upon the camp meeting and escape getting caught up in the sights, sounds, feel and flavor, without being moved by the whole affair: "The long ranges of tents surrounding a large area, in each corner of which fires are lighted up, and then from tent and tree to see innumerable lamps hung out, casting their lights among the branches and illuminating all the ground . . . Then the sound of the trumpet, and the gathering together of thousands, who pass to and from with lights and torches, all has a tendency to awaken the most solemn reflections. And when the holy song rises from a thousand voices, and floats out upon the stillness of the night, the listener must feel that surely such a place is holy ground. These camp meetings were scenes of special mercy to thousands, and many who came to curse remained to pray" (179).

Among some other practical pieces, Van Dussen draws upon advice from Bishop Thomas Morris regarding the danger of "loquacity." It comes in terms of a question – "What is the first thing you would do in your new appointment?" The answer: "listen and learn" (200). And yet, at the opposite extreme to loquacity, according to Morris, is taciturnity. And, "between the two [is the] happy medium: that of speaking on a sensible topic, at the right time, and in a proper manner, so as to accomplish some good purpose" (201).

Analyzing the difference between John Wesley's ministry and George Whitefield's ministry, Nathan Bangs posed the description: "Whitefield was a burning and shining light, but the people rejoiced in his light for a short season; while Wesley blazed in the symbolical heavens as a star of the first magnitude" (203).

Finally, drawing from Margaret K. Henrichsen's *Seven Steeples*, published in 1953, Van Dussen picks up on what might strike as a choice and tender piece: "These Down East folk are very slow to give encouragement. Many and many a week has passed without indication that my efforts to be a good pastor meant anything to anyone. Of all instruments the devil has at his command – and he certainly has quite a bag of tools – this one of making a person feel that he isn't really needed or wanted is the most dangerous, I verily believe. When sermons seemed flat and trite to me, and my spirits [sic] grew as brown as the mud and fog that were everywhere as the winter began to break up, the best cure was to go and call on someone like Effie. Yet even there self-distrust got in my way. I wondered if I were exploiting her helplessness because of my own need to be useful. But the glow in her dark eyes and the flush of pleasure on her face was reassuring" (245).

Bishop Samuel P. Spreng, of the Evangelical Association, once pointed out: "We can be saved if we will. We can be lost if we will. God does all that even God can do for us but he does not force us. He does not invade the rights of human will. He leaves us free to choose" (246).

Furthermore, Van Dussen poses an often missed, maybe ignored, question: "how could ecumenism be a problem? The difficulty comes when our efforts to minimize conflict cause us to under value or disregard our distinctive identities, traditions, convictions, and commitments in order to achieve what may pass for unity" (249).

All in all, the Reverend Dr. D. Gregory Van Dussen, as pastor and historian, provides a sensitive and skillfully researched treatise chock full of helpful insights, colorful story, a sense of frontier evangelism, a bit of theological debate, and challenging advice – something we all need for the daily enrichment of our faith and the strengthening of our souls.

Duane W. Priset

Lord, you have been our dwelling place
>throughout all generations.
...from everlasting to everlasting, you are God. (Psalm 90:172, NIV)

O God, our help in ages past,
>Our hope for years to come.... (Isaac Watts, "O God Our Help In Ages Past,")

In every age, O God, you have been our refuge.
>In every age, O God, you have been our hope.

In Every Age © 1998, Janèt Sullivan Whitaker. Published by OCP. All rights reserved. Used with permission.

Chapter I

The Baton of Faith Begins its Journey

In all our human experience it is well to remember the past. All of us are bundles of varied experiences and half-forgotten memories. We are debtors for good or for ill to the past. So a church facing a world in crisis can do nothing better than seek first of all an understanding of its tradition. From it we may expect to find reservoirs of courage and power, a sense of direction and, one might add, dangers to be guarded against. Let us, therefore, first of all consider the importance of the fact that we are members of a tradition. (Gerald Kennedy, Heritage and Destiny. New York, NY: Board of Missions of the Methodist Church, 1953, 15&16.)

Can a movement, even one that begins with a compelling purpose and explosive energy, survive the twin onslaught of inner malaise or exhaustion and outer opposition or outright attack? When that movement, on its journey through time, encounters new visions and challenges, can its people find enough power in its origin to recover or rediscover its purpose and successfully engage its new environment? Winfield Bevins, in *Marks of a Movement*, shows how the Wesleyan revival rose above the spiritual malaise and ecclesiastical decline of eighteenth-century England to ignite a deep and successful renewal that grew quickly and spread to other lands, especially North America. (Winfield Bevins. *Marks of a Movement: What the Church Today Can Learn from the Wesleyan Revival*. Grand Rapids, MI: Zondervan, 2019.)

In this book, I would like to look at some of the ways Wesley's movement kept its vision fresh and handed it on to new generations of leaders. How did the Methodist revival cross an ocean and sweep across a continent? How were its leaders able to recruit and equip an army of preachers to multiply and mobilize new leaders and followers, even across formidable barriers of culture and geography? How did they launch a spiritual relay race in which an endless procession of runners could receive and pass their baton of faith across American and Canadian frontiers and subsequent communities experiencing constant social change? What can we learn from the culture of mentoring in which each circuit rider played a vital part?

At its origin in the first century Mediterranean world, and its North Atlantic context many centuries later, Christianity was able to overcome negative inertia and countervailing forces by immersion in its divine grounding, multilevel organization, and "contagious" way of life. Neither lethargy nor hostility could prevent "the spreading flame" of the gospel from turning the world "upside down." (George G. Hunter III. *The Contagious Congregation: Frontiers in Evangelism and Church Growth*. Nashville, TN: Abingdon, 1979; F.F. Bruce. *The Spreading Flame: The Rise and Progress of Christianity from its First Beginnings to the Conversion of the English*. Grand Rapids, MI: Eerdmans, 1980; Acts 17:6, NIV).

Charles Wesley, in a well-known hymn that has often been sung in Methodist gatherings, especially of clergy, describes dangers faced by participants since their last time together:

What troubles have we seen,
what mighty conflicts past,
fightings without and fears within,
since we assembled last!

Charles Wesley

What were/are these "troubles" and "conflicts?" They have included economic distress, loneliness, discouragement, distractions, exhaustion, theological disputes, persecution, ethnic and political conflict, disease, weather and geography, personal shortcomings, and the constant challenge of formal and informal learning, mentoring, and spiritual growth. Formidable as these and other obstacles and challenges have been, they could be overcome or transformed by the outpouring of grace:

> Yet out of all the Lord
> hath brought us by his love;
> and still he doth his help afford,
> and hides our life above.

Wesley's hymn has reminded the preachers of their destiny, the ultimate goal of the way of salvation, which is, or can be theirs "by power divine." (Charles Wesley. "And Are We Yet Alive," *Our Great Redeemer's Praise*. Franklin, TN: Seedbed, 2022, #386 .) Recalling Jesus' incarnation and great commission, we rejoice with John Wesley, who said at the end of his life, "the best of all is, God is with us. "

When Jesus sent his apostles "to the ends of the earth" on their humanly impossible mission, he promised to accompany them wherever their journeys would take them, even "to the very end of the age." (Acts 1:8; Matthew 28:18-20, NIV) His accompaniment helped them overcome the discord they would inevitably face. The Lord of space and time sent them into every intersection of space and time, not as fearful, empty servants of "the weak and beggarly elements" of this world, but fully empowered for their kingdom-building role (Galatians 4:9, KJV). They would carry with them a power greater than any to be found in the world, the power of the Holy Spirit. This promise and reality could be realized in any generation, "because the one who is in you is greater than the one who is in the world (I John 4:4, NIV)." Their wisdom, love and power would be replenished by returning to their Source (Acts 1:8; John 16:13-15). This pattern of return and renewal has proven itself again and again in the Church's pilgrimage.

In every time and place there have been essential guideposts along the roads pilgrims have traveled. John Wesley called them means of grace. Among them are the Word and Sacraments at the heart of Christian worship. While the list of these extends beyond Word and Sacraments narrowly defined to include any practice or experience in which God dwells in our midst, unites us in love, and empowers us to grow and serve, Scripture and Sacrament are essential and reliable parts of God's way of bringing grace into our lives. Together they serve as a kind of vehicle or delivery system that takes us beyond ourselves and more fully into his presence. Through them we are renewed, equipped, encouraged and energized for ministry.

John Wesley

Among the many affirmations of Scripture's importance in first century Christian life are Paul's words in I Timothy: "All Scripture is God-breathed, and is useful for teaching, rebuking, correcting and training in righteousness, so that the servant of God may be thoroughly equipped for every good work (II Timothy 3:16&17, NIV)." Scripture holds God's revelation of himself and his vision for humanity. In it also are essential truths needed by all of us whose lives are futile and empty without him. First among these is the reality and promise of the resurrection: "For I delivered to you as of first importance what I also received: that

Christ died for our sins in accordance with the Scriptures, that he was buried, that he was raised on the third day in accordance with the Scriptures...." (I Corinthians 15:3&4, ESV). This is the "tradition," which he goes on to "deliver" in a long and pivotal chapter, the essence and anchor of Christianity's ongoing life and mission. In the time following the New Testament, Christian writings continued to reflect a theological culture saturated with Scripture. That kind of saturation has appeared in other times and places, including the beginnings and early generations of Methodism.

The Mystical Supper, Traditional Byzantine Icon

The importance of Sacraments is well represented by similar words of Paul in I Corinthians: "For I received from the Lord what I also passed on to you: the Lord Jesus, on the night he was betrayed, took bread...." (I Corinthians 11:22-26, NIV). Here he is handing on the tradition he himself had received, as a way of perpetuating the ongoing presence of Christ in their midst. In the Book of Acts, Luke shows us the place of both Scripture and Communion in the worship of the earliest Christians: "They devoted themselves to the Apostles teaching and to fellowship, to the breaking of bread and to prayer." (Acts 23:42, NIV)

Christianity in general, and Methodists in particular, have also been fed by *extraordinary* means of grace, especially those practices that became extremely important to the great revival of the eighteenth and nineteenth centuries. These included camp meetings, class meetings, and the explosion of gospel music that continues in various forms today. The roots of these reach back to the Old and New Testaments. They existed alongside core means of grace, as when early Methodists broke bread (in the Eucharistic sense) as part of their camp meetings. Other extraordinary means were the love feast, covenant prayer, and the outward shape and inner experience of conviction, repentance, conversion, and sanctification in revivals. Grace itself has been evident in radically changed lives and communities, caught up in and mobilized by the outpouring of the Spirit, "welling up to eternal life." (John 4:14, NIV)

The importance of fellowship in early Christianity has reappeared at other times and places, not least of which is the Methodist movement from the Wesleys on. Although some of the strength of early Methodist fellowship may have waned over time, much of it survives and remains available as a gift and resource originating in the Holy Spirit (Romans 5:5).

Several personal experiences have made this clear to me. I once shared coffee and conversation with a pastor of a different tradition. As I was relating important experiences in my ministry, this neighboring pastor interrupted by observing that I "talked a lot about fellowship;" that fellowship must be important to me and my church. I was stunned to hear that this was not the case with him, and that he found it hard to understand. In a very different setting, where pastors of a Methodist denomination had gathered for several days of workshops and worship, a guest from another tradition expressed his appreciation for the depth of genuine fellowship he had experienced among us. He had seen nothing like this among colleagues in his own denomination and wanted to be very sure we did not overlook it or take it for granted. His spiritual perception shook many of us to a deeper gratitude for this mark of our tradition.

One further experience, called New Room, involves pastors and lay leaders from a variety of Methodist denominations and related churches. This kind of fellowship happens among seminary students and veteran and retired pastors, across local communities and international boundaries. There is, or can be, a mutual recognition of shared identity and purpose, which transcends institutional labels and treasures the richness of our connections. Whatever caused our separation cannot erase our fellowship.

This was abundantly clear when representatives of six denominations met at Roberts Wesleyan University to celebrate World Communion Sunday and share in a historical symposium. Three bishops led in the Lord's Supper. Worshipers and musicians came from The African Methodist Episcopal Church, The Wesleyan Church, The African Methodist Episcopal Zion Church, The Free Methodist Church, The Christian Methodist Church, and The United Methodist Church. Those who took part expressed a special kind of joy in celebrating together.

The power of this kind of pan-Methodism is strengthened tremendously by common vision, purpose, spirituality, and theology, when people share a deep and abiding connection with Wesleyan, evangelical orthodoxy over time. Yet there remains a surprisingly strong fellowship even among those who, while sharing little in common theologically, still recognize each other as having lived and ministered together. But while this kind of residual fellowship can have real meaning for those who have walked parallel paths, its lack of a common substance of faith moves in the direction of superficiality and fails to stand amid countervailing "wind[s] of doctrine." (Ephesians 4:14, NIV) To stand on and for the truth requires that we be equipped with "the full armor of God" (Ephesians 6:11, NIV) so as to withstand opposition from every kind of evil. But, as in football, defense is not our entire role. We are also called to "contend for the faith" (Ephesians 4:14; 6:11;

Jude, v. 3, NIV). The New Testament Letters show the Church both defended and proactive.

Jesus established a pattern of mentoring with his disciples. His mentoring employed different goals and methods for individuals as well as groups of varying size and character. For example, his conversations with Nicodemus and Zacchaeus were very different from those times when he taught his close circle of traveling Disciples. He spoke with a family of friends differently than he did at a meal hosted by a skeptical Pharisee. He even called Peter, James, and John away from his other disciples to go "up onto a mountain to pray" and to witness his transfiguration. (John 3:1-21; Luke 19:1-10; Luke 19=0:38-42; Luke 7:36-50; Luke 9:28-36, NIV) The disciples, those who became apostles or ambassadors of Christ, and the wider circle of his followers, became a community, formed by his example, his instruction, and his Spirit.

Most of what Jesus said and did during his ministry can be seen as mentoring. Some of his words and actions, like the feeding of multitudes or teaching of crowds who anxiously sought his help, were meant for large numbers of people. Others were intended for specific individuals, families, or small groups. His teachings, signs, and miracles were never haphazard or without purpose. Even when they appear random or scattershot, they are reaching out to people he knows and loves in order to accomplish an intended part of his rescue mission for humanity. Their meaning applied immediately to the moments they first took place, but also to the learning process of disciples. Many teachings, actions, and events in the Gospels served to mentor his disciples, to prepare them for their own ministries, or rather, *their* extensions of *his* ministry.

John the Baptist appears early in the Gospels to set the stage for Jesus' ministry. He baptized Jesus, but also made it clear that he, John, was not the Messiah. "He himself was not the light; he came only to bear witness to the light." (John 1:8, NIV) Early Methodist preachers took John as a model for their own ministry, since, like John, they were not merely speaking for or about themselves, or representing an institution. Like the apostles, they knew they had been sent out as ambassadors. They represented Jesus.

Their job was to prepare the way for him to take first place in the hearts and lives of their hearers. Their voices cried out, not in the "wilderness" of the Judean desert, but the great forests, prairies, mountains, lakes, and coastal regions of North America's wilderness. They announced his coming and sought to "prepare the way for the Lord." (Matthew 3:3, NIV) They thought of themselves as proclaiming, in their own way and time, "Behold the Lamb of God!" (John 1:35, KJV) They would often say of a respected colleague who had passed from this life, that like John, "he was a burning and a shining light." (Jesus' words in John 5:35, KJV)

John's Gospel contains teachings that Jesus disciples and anyone else hearing them must have found difficult, if not baffling. Yet deep within those teachings was a promise so precious that a least some grabbed hold of it and would not let go: "Very truly I tell you, whoever hears my word and believes him who sent me has eternal life and will not be judged but has crossed over from death to life." (John 5:24, NIV) His point is repeated in chapter 6, where he says, "Very truly I tell you, the one who believes has eternal life." Some reached their limit when he spoke about his flesh being "real food" and his blood "real drink." (John 6:55, NIV) When people, including some of his disciples, began to walk away because his sayings were so hard, Jesus said "to the twelve" who had been with him through so much, "You do not want to leave too, do you?" Peter's response showed how deeply he had taken in Jesus' words: "Lord, to whom shall we go? You have the words of eternal life. We have come to believe and to know that you are the Holy One of God." (John 6:68, ESV) He may have been as bewildered as those who were walking away, but he, and others, trusted Jesus and held fast his "words of eternal life," and in so doing, became an extension of Jesus' mentoring for our sake.

Jesus' ministry to individuals included responding to perplexing questions, healing devastating illnesses, driving out demons, and even raising the dead. He taught both Jews and gentiles; in cities and in the country, in the Jerusalem Temple and in Galilean synagogues; in private and in public. His miracles took place on busy highways and private homes; in the presence of large crowds and within a small circle of disciples. Because these things were widely proclaimed and retold; remembered and shared in worship; eventually written and copied; translated and taken to new lands and generations, Jesus' words and actions continue to find and inspire new audiences.

Because Jesus' teachings and example were relevant to their mission, all he said and did was mentoring. But there were times they shared, and things he said, that made the fact and importance of that mentoring especially clear. These were times of recruitment and preparation of disciples and apostolic leaders for the tasks ahead. At such times, he not only modeled the ministry he sought from them, but indicated in some way that this was exactly what he was doing. One early example of this was his initial call for particular individuals to leave whatever they had been doing in their occupation as fishermen in order to follow Jesus and learn from him "to fish for people." (Matthew 4:19, NIV) To these four, Peter, Andrew, James, and John, he would add the tax collector Matthew, the insurrectionist Simon, and six more. (Matthew 9:9; Luke 6:15&16, NIV) While his circle of close followers went far beyond these twelve, this small group played a vital, central role in building his kingdom. Starting as disciples (= students, those who were learning from him), they would become apostles (= representatives, those who were sent by him) at the time when the Church, its way of life, and the shape of its witness would be formed, tested, and propelled into action. Unlikely as those first disciples may appear as candidates for the part they would play, and even though our sources of knowledge about some of them are very limited, Jesus did/does not share those limitations. His choices, to which he would eventually add Paul, Barnabas, and others, were thankfully based on his vision and what he knew he could accomplish through them. So the Gospel accounts of Jesus choosing and calling disciples to be his apostles, provide a beginning for his work of mentoring followers for the building of his Church: "Jesus went out to a mountainside to pray, and spent the night praying to God. When morning came, he called his disciples to him, and chose twelve of them, whom he also designated as apostles." (Luke 6:12&13, NIV)

From the beginning, it was Jesus' intent to send the twelve, and later others, out into the world as apostles – after their time of intense mentoring. Part of that mentoring involved their going out on short term missions, where they would try preaching, healing, and casting out demons. This would follow a time of traveling together, mulling over his words, and watching what he did. When the time was right, the disciples became apprentices. First he sent the twelve.

> Then Jesus went around teaching from village to village. Calling the twelve to him, he began to send them out two by two and gave them authority over impure spirits. ... They went out and preached that people should repent. The drove out many demons and anointed many sick people with oil and healed them. (Mark 6; 6&7, NIV)

After this the Lord appointed seventy-two others and sent them two by two ahead of him to every town and place where he was about to go. (Luke 10:1, NIV)

Their initial experiences revealed both their potential and their limitations. When the seventy-two returned, they "returned with joy and said, Lord, even the demons submit to us in your name." Jesus' responded by telling them that greater things awaited them down the road. Yet he acknowledged and rejoiced in their success: "At that time Jesus, full of joy through the Holy Spirit, said, "I praise you, Father, Lord of heaven and earth, because you have hidden these things from the wise and learned, and revealed them to little children. Yes, Father, for this is what you were pleased to do." Then he turned to his disciples and said privately, "Blessed are the eyes that see what you see, for I tell you that many prophets and kings wanted to see what you see but did not see it, and to hear what you hear but did not hear it. (Luke 10:17; 21; 23&24, NIV) Even bolder is Jesus' statement that his followers will someday do "even greater things" than he was doing. (John 14:12, NIV)

In his Sermon on the Mount, Jesus made clear what he was expecting from his followers. In John's Gospel, Jesus calls himself "the light of the world." (John 8:12, NIV) He was the "light" that "shines in the darkness" of this world, light which "the darkness has not overcome..." But in Matthew he says, "You are the light of the world," (Matthew 5:14, NIV) indicating that Jesus' followers and ambassadors have a share in his mission. He later returned to this theme, placing their ministry in its higher context, when he said, "the righteous will shine like the sun in the kingdom of their Father." (Matthew 13:43, NIV) Here he echoes a theme from Daniel, which we find later in Philippians:

> Those who are wise will shine like the brightness of the heavens, and those who lead many to righteousness, like the stars forever and ever. (Daniel 12:3, NIV)

> Then you will shine among them like stars in the sky as you hold firmly to the word of life. (Philippians 2:15&16, NIV)

These inspiring, visionary words served a similar role to that of the Transfiguration, lifting disciples to Heavenly perspective on their work and calling; revealing the ultimate importance of everything they did, and helping them transcend and conquer any lingering distractions or temptations that needed to be cast aside and left by the roadside.

Jesus words could be direct, but he also loved telling parables and using analogies and metaphors. Thus he might begin a parable with "This is what the kingdom of God is like," or compare the Holy Spirit to "rivers of living water." (Mark 4:26; John 7:39, NIV) He could speak with great tenderness and confront evil with righteous indignation. (John 8:1-11; Matthew 23:27) Whatever he said or did came from a heart of perfect love, integrity, and wisdom. He teaches us by what he commends and by what he condemns, and there is no confusion in following him. (John 12:1-8; 8:44) He is the Good Shepherd, who "guides me on the right paths" and away from danger. (John 10:11; Psalm 23:3, NIV)

Every time the disciples accompanied Jesus on his journeys, they saw in him, and learned from him, elements they could use wherever they were sent. Some of these elements prepared them for their own active outreach to outsiders and newcomers to the faith. They saw him cut through people's excuses and confront daunting social, cultural, and economic barriers. He modeled and encouraged compassion. John's Gospel records an incident that shows Jesus' compassion breaking the religious and cultural barrier between Jews and Samaritans and a conventional barrier between men and women (John 4:1-42)

This extended example of mentoring is a compelling argument for cross-cultural evangelism, in which the disciples, and all of us who read the story, see that Christ gathering people of every nation to himself is of greater importance than anything that separates us. Jesus would address the priority of compassion over Jewish-Samaritan ethnicity again in his story of the good Samaritan. (John 4:4-42; Luke 10:25-37; An incident revealing the negative attitude separating Jews from Samaritans occurs when Jesus and his disciples sought hospitality in a Samaritan village, in Luke 9:51-56)

He also taught and demonstrated what their community should be like and how such a community was possible. As he was incarnating God's love for them, they were gradually changing, being more like him in the way they interacted with each other. As he drew for them a word picture of a vine with its branches, he was showing the way they must abide in him, submit to the Gardener's pruning, and keep his commandments, especially the central one, which is love. Through that image and reality they learned the other side of his promise to be with them forever: "apart from me you can do nothing."(John 15:5, NIV) Love was to be the hallmark of their connection to the world, to each other, and to the ever-enlarging community they would build. The love at the heart of that community would be entirely genuine, uncontrived, unselfish; not something they could create within themselves, but the same love they were receiving from God, embodied in Christ, and poured out from the Spirit. "As the Father has loved me, so have I loved you."(John 15:9, NIV) As he spoke of the Vine and branches, he talked of the friendship he had for them, and the fruit they would bear because his life and love would sustain them. Everything depended on their willing, wholehearted acceptance of his all-encompassing commandment: "This is my command: Love each other." (John 15:17, NIV) Later he would make it clear that their credibility as his witnesses depended on the reflection of and conformity to that love. In what has been called his high priestly prayer, Jesus lifted his apostles, and all who would come to believe through their testimony, to his Father. Among his words were these:

> "As you sent me into the world, I have sent them into the world." ... "My prayer is not for them alone. I pray for those who will believe in me through their message, that all of them may be one, Father, just as you are in me and I am in you. May they also be in us, so that the world will believe that you have sent me." (John 17:18; 20&21, NIV

Part of Jesus' shepherding of his disciples was a necessary warning about false prophets or teachers who would distort his teachings or even pretend to supersede his identity as Messiah. "Watch out for false prophets. They come to you in sheep's clothing, but inwardly they are ravenous wolves." In a similar vein, he contrasts himself as the good shepherd, who "lays down his life for the sheep," with a "hired hand" who "cares nothing for the sheep." (Matthew 7:15, ESV; John 10:11-13, NIV) But interference from the outside world was not the only danger. Jesus also cautioned his followers to resist growing weary in their faith, as his disciples did in the garden the night of his arrest.

In the Last Supper, especially in the synoptic Gospels and I Corinthians, Jesus words and actions recall a past event and foreshadow a great banquet in heaven. Between those past and future events, they are a rich and meaningful part of our life as the Church. Jesus gave us both his words and actions of that night to remember and reenact, as a dramatic way not only to gratefully recall that fateful night, but to realize and share his ongoing presence in our world and in our midst. Thus the holy meal Jesus left us as the gift of himself was and remains an example of mentoring, a mysterious means of grace that continues to resource the Church and people to live the life he gives us.

When we come to the Last Supper, we find Jesus responding to a familiar argument that must have been especially irksome at this particular moment. As he so often does, he uses this incident as an opportunity to mentor. He makes the contrast between his disciples' ambition for power and position, with his own desire to serve. They will need to replace their competitive instincts by imitating Jesus' selfless humility:

> A dispute also arose among them as to which of them was considered to be greatest. Jesus said to them, "The kings of the Gentiles lord it over them; and those who exercise authority over them call themselves 'Benefactors.' But you are not to be like that. Instead, the greatest among you should be like the youngest, and the one who rules like the one who serves. For who is greater, the one who is at the table or the one who serves? But I am among you as one who serves." (Luke 22: 24-27, NIV; see Mark 10:35-45)

Apparently James and John – and how many others who pursue position and power - had not fully heard or appropriated teachings like, "the last will be first, and the first will be last." (Matthew 20:16, NIV) Another teaching on humility, also associated with Last Supper, involved a ritual action that shocked Jesus' apostles. John gives us this account of Jesus' surprise lesson, designed to render his teaching about servant leadership unforgettable. First, he acted out his teaching; then he explained what he had done: "he got up from the meal, took off his outer clothing, and wrapped a towel around his waist. After that, he poured water into a basin and began to wash his disciples' feet, drying them with the towel that was wrapped around him." Peter's reaction is well known, and Jesus overcomes his objection.

> When he had finished washing their feet, he put on his clothes and returned to his place.' Do you understand what I have done for you?' he asked them. 'You call me 'Teacher' and 'Lord,' and rightly so, for that is what I am. Now that I, your Lord and Teacher, have washed your feet, you also should wash one another's feet. I have set you an example that you should do as I have done for you. Very truly I tell you, no servant is greater than his master, nor is a messenger greater than the one who sent him. Now that you know these things, you will be blessed if you do them. (John 13:2-5; 12-17, NIV)

He walked the desolate road to his crucifixion, deserted but mysteriously glorified, and after his resurrection, he returned to his friends in a triumph he shared, with forgiveness, and with teaching that recapitulated and reinforced their life together. (Mark 16:1-8; Matthew 28:1–10; Luke 24:38-49; John 12:23; 13:31&32; 20:1-29; 21:1-19) Finally, he commissioned them for their apostleship and promised both his presence and the Spirit's power. (Matthew 28;16-20; Luke 24:48&49.)

We are among the nations to which Jesus sent his apostles, equipped with the Spirit's transforming power and the truth of God's unchanging word. In that truth and power, assisted by grace empowered faith and imagination, we join Jesus' hearers near Bethsaida to hear the Sermon on the Mount. We hear him call his disciples and realize he also has a call for us. We can almost taste the newly made wine at a wedding in Cana. We climb the mountain of transfiguration and hear the Father telling us to listen to his Son. We gasp in grateful amazement at the healing of a man who was blind from birth, and in greater astonishment as he calls Lazarus from his tomb. We hear him speak to Nicodemus about a spiritual rebirth that is offered to us today, and like those he taught long ago, we are inspired and sometimes confused by the parables we hear.

Even more amazing, we are there in Bethlehem for his birth, and in Jerusalem for the horrible bleakness of his death and the ultimate joy of his resurrection. We join his witnesses in living and proclaiming his good news "to the ends of the earth."(Acts 1:8, NIV) Because he invites us, even at this great distance, to be his witnesses, we also receive his mentoring, his gift of the Spirit, and his promise to be with us always. As we read in the Scriptures how he mentored his first disciples, and as we hear how his early followers mentored their converts and each other, we realize how essential their mentoring fellowship was, to each one personally, to their communities (local, regional, and universal), and to the overarching mission, which we are privileged to share.

Chapter 2

The Baton of Faith in the New Testament Letters

"What I Received I also Passed on to you:" (I Corinthians 11:23, NIV)

Paul, The Apostle: Traditional Byzantine Icon

When Paul wrote in I Corinthians about handing on Jesus' words, the New Testament Letters were continuing Jesus' mentoring of his followers. They sought to form early Christian communities in Jesus' image. While they contain moral teachings and discipline, instructions for worship in the life of congregations, theological and spiritual insight, wisdom and encouragement, they aim beyond any one of these to set forth a vision of our ultimate destiny in Christ and offer the grace to take us there. In Ephesians, for example, Paul gives a compelling, sweeping vision of boundless love and peace in the body of Christ, with the ultimate goal "that you may be filled to the measure of all the fullness of God." None of this is possible because of some kind of Herculean human achievement, but from "power through his Spirit in your inner being. " (Ephesians 3:16-19; 4, NIV) II Peter concludes with the desire that his readers will "grow in the grace and knowledge of our Lord and Savior Jesus Christ," growth that early Methodists knew was infinite and eternal, because God is infinite and eternal, and we are called and empowered to grow in his likeness. In Paul's case, his letters provide "a model for how he applied ... the gospel to local situations." Now, with the intervening of considerable time and space, we must make a similar interpretive connection. (II Peter 3:18, NIV; Adam Clarke. *Christian Theology*. Salem, OH: Convention Book Store, 1967, 276&27; Craig S. Keener. *1 - 2 Corinthians*. New York, NY: Cambridge University Press, 2005,6.)

Much of New Testament mentoring related to particular congregations in their original settings, while much relates equally to the universal Church in every place and time – even when individuals or specific congregations are mentioned or addressed. But some Letters were primarily aimed at the mentoring of individuals by Paul or another apostle. These include especially I and II Timothy, Titus, and Philemon. Their messages are certainly relevant to the whole Church, not just to the individuals and situations that form their original contexts and reasons for being. But the personal nature of these Letters takes us to some different dimensions of life in the churches. There is an unmistakable intensity and immediacy in the mentoring embodied in them. They reveal something of the special pastoral relationship between sender and receiver, and the culture of mentoring which was forming the Church's way of life. Here we see a kind of reciprocity in mentoring that values the energetic, gifted commitment of youth as well as the experience and accumulated wisdom of older Christians.

In I Timothy we see the way leadership flowed outward from an apostle, through "my true son in the faith," to that son's teaching of essential truths and modeling of the Christian way. (I Timothy 1:2, NIV) Paul openly admits his dependence on grace for all that has value in his ministry, thus establishing an essential equality in the ground on which they both stand. He offers "grace, mercy and peace from God the Father and Christ Jesus our Lord" as necessary resources for Timothy's ministry. He is clear about the dangers that have taken too many off course, and equally clear that God "wants all people to be saved...." (I Timothy 2:4, NIV) He writes about practical matters Timothy must address, always in the context of God's way of salvation. Paul has come to respect and rely on Timothy, in spite of their difference in age, and he wants Timothy to act on that authority for the sake of the Church: "Command and teach these things. Don't let anyone look down on you because you are young, but set an example for the believers in speech, in conduct, in love, in faith and in purity."(I Timothy 4:11&12, NIV)

In the very different, shorter, and more focused Letter to Philemon, we see another mentoring relationship – two of them, actually – in which issues of discipleship and entrenched secular social custom clash within one of the apostle's churches. Here Paul takes an important step forward in a matter that would one day yield to the Spirit and teachings of Christ. This was the issue of slavery in the Christian movement, where in the spirit of the Golden Rule, "there is neither slave nor free," (Galatians 3:28, NIV) and where economic prejudice and division militated against the Great Commandment. (Galatians 3:28; NIV; I Corinthians 11:17-22; James 2:1-9)

What we see in these mentoring Letters to individuals, and similar portions of more general Letters, is a necessary part of building a multifaceted movement that could teach, live, grow, and reproduce over vast stretches of time and space. Jesus' words in the Great Commission and his parting words in Acts, together with the multicultural realities of Pentecost and the Apocalypse, indicate that God was and is building a kingdom designed to last and to withstand any form of compromise, opposition or decline. This communal dimension to discipleship was discovered and rediscovered by such disciples as Francis of Assisi:

> In the Bible, Jesus directs his words to his disciples - all twelve, not just one. Francis sensed immediately that Jesus' call was not for him alone. Other youth would follow. Jesus had sent out many, not just one,"to proclaim the kingdom of God and to heal." (Matthew 28:16-20; Acts 1:8 & 2:1-12; Matthew 16:18; Revelation 7:9; Howard A. Snyder. Francis of Assisi: Movement Maker (etc.) Maryknoll, NY:Orbis, 2024,36.)

That is not to say that a church or movement within a church cannot flourish and then wander off course, lose its initial direction, or fragment into competing organizations. In fact, this has very often been the pattern across the panorama of organized Christianity. Long before the Reformation, Eastern Christianity splintered into a variety of Orthodox churches, followed by the major schism that divided what we know as Eastern Orthodoxy from Roman Catholicism, and further divisions have followed. Howard Snyder's new book on St. Francis shows how difficult it has been for the Franciscan movement to remain united and consistent with its origins, in spite of the appeal of its founder, its roots in the Gospel, its resilience over time, and its ability to leap across cultural barriers. (Howard A. Snyder. *Francis of Assisi, Movement Maker: The Unconventional Leadership of a Simple Saint*. Maryknoll, NY: Orbis, 2024. The appeal of Francis and the durability of the movement bearing his name are exemplified by the fact that Snyder is a Free Methodist historian and his book comes from a Catholic publisher.)

Protestantism has been notorious in its tendency to divide, to the point where an already lengthy catalog of denominations continues to proliferate, with formal, institutional splits alongside countless independent, "non-denominational," or community churches.

But these divisions should not obscure the mutual attraction of separated churches and their people, which we see in organizational mergers, ecumenical cooperation, and mutual enrichment of pastors, scholars, and many others. Examples are readily available in the diversity of authors read by seminarians, pastors, and congregations; shared efforts in evangelism and service, and overlapping resources for worship and music. Protestant ministers and seminary students often seek spiritual renewal in Catholic monasteries, such as Gethsemane in Kentucky or the Abbey of the Genesee in New York. Not long ago I spoke with a Protestant seminary professor who had been deeply moved and blessed during a retreat at a Russian Orthodox monastery. Over a period of more than fifty years, I have made and led retreats at Mount Saviour Monastery in Pine City, New York. Meanwhile, Catholic and Orthodox readers have long appreciated the writings of the Anglican lay theologian C.S. Lewis. People of many backgrounds now pray with icons. I once attended a Coptic Orthodox festival where Egyptian food was accompanied by evangelical, contemporary Christian music. Leaders from a wide variety of churches in the Wesleyan tradition, along with some Anglicans and Pentecostals, worship, learn, and teach together at conferences sponsored by Asbury Theological Seminary. The fellowship experienced in places and events like these flows from one Spirit and testifies to a unity that lives on in the divided body of Christ. For ultimately, as Paul said to the Ephesians, "There is one body and one Spirit, just as you were called to one hope when you were called; one Lord, one faith, one baptism; one God and Father of all, who is over all and through all and in all." (Ephesians 4:4-6, NIV) We can see and experience this seemingly counterintuitive reality when we find it in God and live it in humility. Therefore, "Be completely humble and gentle; be patient, bearing with one another in love. Make every effort to keep the unity of the Spirit through the bond of peace." (Ephesians 4:2&3, NIV)

From the beginning, Methodism sought to be a way of life, rooted in Scripture and the life and teachings of early Christianity, and organized to live and spread what Wesley called Scriptural holiness. Leaders in this movement would instruct and mentor newer, often younger leaders, in the doctrines (beliefs and principles) and discipline (manner of life and organization) which formed and implemented the vision of Wesley and subsequent leaders. This instruction and mentoring covered the entire content and ethos of the movement. Far from building a closed, inwardly directed community, secluded and protected from the outside world, this movement and its leaders (preachers, scholars, class leaders, etc.) were designed to reach and transform the world. The transformation they were seeking was radically personal and available to all who would accept it. Its power source was the same One who guided, motivated, and inspired the early Church. Its end was the realization of a new creation in each person and finally in the world itself. Key to this realization was the shaping of leadership and its larger society to conform to God's own purpose and vision for a redeemed and sanctified humanity, led and modeled by a vanguard of redeemed and sanctified ministers.

This vanguard would be a community within the community, built up and perpetuated by teaching, modeling, and mentoring the doctrines and discipline to which they were all committed. How else would their mission be clearly articulated and passed on to new generations? How else could preachers grow in the exercise of their gifts for ministry? How would the movement as a whole be equipped for its distinctive ministries?

Like Jesus' and his apostles' mentoring of different kinds and numbers of people in different circumstances, the mentoring we will see in early Methodism takes different forms to suit people with different gifts, experiences, personalities, and callings. The advice of a bishop to a newly ordained preacher might well differ from what that same bishop might say to a senior appointee on his tenth circuit. A conversation among superannuated (retired) veterans might take a direction different from one among new exhorters. The stories shared on a frontier trail might come across as outlandish to an urban pastor. A backwoods preacher might become impatient with an urban colleague's unfamiliar or highly intellectual illustrations. Yet there is an underlying truth in all of them, and a need for each to value the distinctiveness of the others' experiences.

Mentoring among early North American Methodists was formal and informal, planned and spontaneous, written and oral.

The greatest single fact about this mentoring was its universality. Virtually every part of the structure and life of Methodism *required and lent itself* to mentoring. Its universality matches, among Methodist preachers, the universal eagerness to learn and grow. There could be no end to this eagerness, for it paralleled and reflected the quest for Christian perfection, planted within by God, empowered by grace, and extending to eternity. Bishop Gerald Kennedy understood well the character of tradition as a living process of handing on, a relay race through time and space: Note what he says about giving and receiving as part of our Wesleyan tradition:

> A tradition is in reality an agreement. It is the older generation placing its hand on the shoulder of the new generation to steady and encourage it. It is a covenant between fathers and sons, [mothers and daughters,] that the values achieved in the past will not be lost today and that we shall not forget that eternal vigilance and constant effort are necessary to keep life good.
>
> The inheritance is ours. What must we do now to accept it? ... The more important the gift the more significant the quality of the receiver. The Wesleyan heritage can only be passed along if Methodists of any particular generation are able to comprehend and receive it. (Gerald Kennedy. Heritage and Destiny. New York, NY: Board of Missions of the Methodist Church,1953, 19; 29.)

When Paul relayed Jesus' commands regarding Holy Communion and the Resurrection, he was taking a next step in the relay race of faith. Here is the heart of what tradition is all about. Tradition is not the dry, lifeless repetition of practices from long ago that have lost their meaning for a new generation. A Tradition is something handed on because of its timeless value. Tradition is also the process of handing it on. Thus when Paul says "What I have received from the Lord what I have also handed on to you..." (I Co, 11:6, NIV) he gives us one of the earliest examples of passing the baton of faith, a single step in the process of traditioning, a hand off from Jesus to Paul, followed by another hand off from Paul to the Corinthians, and still others from the Corinthian church to everyone who has heard or read the Letter, through many generations, all the way to God's people today. The "baton," in this case, is the Lord's Supper, given so we could better remember, so it would fulfill its purpose as a present means of grace, and so through it we would "proclaim the Lord's death until he comes." The tradition is more than a story, for it comes to us with a command to "Do this in remembrance of me." (I Corinthians 11: 24&26, NIV) It comes to life in us and strengthens the body of Christ. Then, having established this foundation, he goes on to correct misuses of this sacred meal.

Paul's traditioning takes a similar form as he hands on the fact and significance of Jesus' resurrection, which he calls a matter "of first importance." Here is the foundation upon which the Church was built, and the message it went forth to proclaim. The resurrection is not just an article of faith – a line in a creed (important as that is) - but the bedrock upon which the Church's life stands. The authority behind this teaching is Jesus himself, speaking through this apostle. The rest of chapter 15 spells out its importance for the Church's life, in thunderous and inspiring words, in which the Spirit speaks, then and now, through this masterful writer. Paul's resurrection chapter makes clear what is at stake for the body of Christ and each member of that body.

There are differences in scholarly opinion about authorship of some of the Letters. This study accepts the traditional attribution, including the Pastoral Epistles, but not Hebrews, which is almost universally regarded as non-Pauline. Many well regarded scholars have argued for traditional authorship. For much of Methodist history, traditional authorship has been accepted for sound reasons or assumed. In any case, we are concerned with the way the Letters address situations facing the churches and how they help form communities over time.

GRACE AND PEACE

New Testament Letters offer spiritual resources, essential blessings from God to their readers. Because they function as Scripture, they *seek to convey*, rather than merely wish these blessings. They begin and end most of the Letters, serving as bookends for the body of each Letter, and empowering readers to live the message each one contains. We often use these words as greetings and benedictions in worship and in our own letters, with a similar purpose. Neither an apostolic Letter nor Sunday worship service should end without an assurance that we gather seeking grace; nor should it end without offering the grace needed to face and walk the road ahead. Several of Paul's greetings are identical, or nearly so. The greetings and benedictions in the non-Pauline Letters are quite distinctive. They are blessings and good words, linked to the reality and power of God's word, written and incarnate.

The long introduction to Romans leads to a typical greeting: "Grace and peace to you from God our Father and from the Lord Jesus Christ," and ends (though followed with a lengthy series of personal messages) with "The God of peace be with you all. Amen." (Romans 1:7; 15:13, NIV) The same greeting is found in I Corinthians, and the letter closes, in part, with "The grace of the Lord Jesus be with you." That closing follows a harsh anathema: "If anyone does not love the Lord, let that person be cursed! Come, Lord!" At the very end, Paul returns to a more pastoral tone: "My love to all of you in Christ Jesus. Amen. (I Corinthians 1:3; 15:22-24, NIV). II Corinthians contains the same initial greeting as Romans and I Corinthians, but closes (uniquely) with the "apostolic," Trinitarian benediction: "May the grace of the Lord Jesus Christ, and the love of God, and the fellowship of the Holy Spirit be with you all." (II Corinthians 13:14, NIV) Its Trinitarian form and content may convey completeness. Craig Keener suggests "fellowship created by the Spirit" to clarify the last phrase. (Craig S. Keener. *1-2 Corinthians*. New York, NY: Cambridge University Press, 2005, 247.)

Galatians begins with the same greeting as the others we've seen so far, and adds, "who gave himself for our sins to rescue us from the present evil age, according to the will of our God and Father, to whom be glory for ever and ever. Amen." Paul then goes into a warning to and about false teachers, including an anathema like the one in I Corinthians, and finally ends with a blessing. Ephesians opens with the same blessing we have seen but ends with a longer benediction. Philippians includes the same opening and similar closing benediction. Colossians' greeting is very brief:

"Grace and peace to you from God our Father." Its closing blessing is also quite brief; "Grace be with you." (Colossians 4:18, NIV)

The opening greeting in I Thessalonians is simply, "grace and peace to you," where II Thessalonians returns to the fuller pattern we have seen in other Letters. The closing to I Thessalonians elaborates on "peace' in a way which makes it stronger: "Now may the Lord of peace himself give you peace at all times and in every way. The Lord be with all of you." (I Thessalonians 1:1 & 3:16, NIV.) While it can be helpful to isolate some closing benedictions from surrounding verses, it seems fitting, especially in a Wesleyan context, to include some of the fuller material from II Thessalonians: "May God himself, the God of peace, sanctify you through and through. May your whole spirit, soul and body be kept blameless the coming of our Lord Jesus Christ. The one who calls you is faithful, and he will do it. ... the grace of our Lord Jesus Christ be with you." (II Thessalonians 5:23&24, NIV)

I and II Timothy add "mercy' to the familiar greeting, resulting in "Grace, mercy and peace from God the Father and Christ Jesus our Lord." I Timothy ends with "grace be with you all." II Timothy is abbreviated: "The Lord be with your spirit. Grace be with you all." Titus begins, "Grace and peace from God the Father and Christ Jesus our Savior." The closing of Titus is like that of I Timothy. Philemon has the familiar greeting, "Grace and peace to you from God our Father and the Lord Jesus Christ," and ends with 'the grace of the Lord Jesus Christ be with your spirit."

James stands out among the New Testament Letters in its extremely simple opening, "To the twelve tribes scattered among the nations: Greetings." The sender is identified as "James, a servant of God and of the Lord Jesus Christ." (James 1:1, NIV) James is filled with wisdom linked with several of Jesus' teachings, some applied to specific situations in the churches being addressed. There is no closing benediction. However, James features many strong lessons on peace and clearly wants peace to be the way of life for his readers.

I Peter begins,"Grace and peace be yours in abundance." (I Peter 1:2, NIV) I & II Peter and Jude all use the expression, "in abundance." The usual (for Paul) closing benediction is omitted. The theme of II Peter's opening greeting –"Grace and peace be yours in abundance through the knowledge of God and of Jesus our Lord," carries through to the benediction: "But grow in the grace and knowledge of our Lord and Savior Jesus Christ. To him be glory both now and forever! Amen." (II Peter 1:2; 3:18, NIV) Jude opens with "Mercy, peace and love be yours in abundance." (Jude 1:2, NIV) Jude has a closing doxology, but no blessing: "To him who is able to keep you from stumbling and to present you before his glorious presence without fault and with great joy - to the only God our Savior be glory, majesty, power and authority, through Jesus Christ our Lord, before all ages, now and forevermore."(Jude 1:24&25)

I John begins and ends with the Letter's theological substance (love), adapted to open and close the Letter. The beginning of II John includes this traditional greeting: "Grace, mercy and peace from God the Father and from Jesus Christ, the Father's Son, will be with us in truth and love." "the common acknowledgement of the eternal Truth is the certain foundation of love."(Brooke Foss Westcott, *The Epistles of St. John.* Grand Rapids, MI: Eerdmans 1966, 225, orig. 1883.) This distinctive 'in truth and love" matches the same expression later in the Letter. The confidence that God's blessing *"will* be with us" also sets it apart by giving it added confidence. There is a closing greeting, apparently from the sender's church to that of the recipient. (II John 1:3&13, NIV) III John has a greeting unlike most of the Letters, yet identifying both sender ("the elder") and recipient ("my dear friend Gaius, whom I love in the truth"). The letter closes with greetings from "the friends here" to "the friends there." The warmth of John's Letters, with their constant stress on the love at the heart of Jesus' teaching and the heart of the Church and the churches, conveys authenticity and reinforces that love as we read them.

SCRIPTURE, STUDY

Parallel to this is the place of Scripture in the apostles' teaching and leadership. In Romans 1:2, the prophetic writings in the Old Testament proclaim in advance the Gospel Paul is preaching. He roots the Gospel deep in Judaism, which through Christ is now also offered to the Gentiles, who are the chief focus of Paul's ministry. (Romans 1:5&6) It is often pointed out that the Scripture for New Testament Christians meant what we call the Old Testament. But the books of the New Testament were increasingly regarded with an importance and authority that amounted to Scripture in formation for a community in formation.

The formative role of both kinds of Scripture is perhaps most clearly stated in II Timothy. Here Paul commends his younger colleague's lifelong knowledge of "the Holy Scriptures, which are able to make you wise for salvation through faith in Christ Jesus." The ultimate purpose of Scripture is not to accumulate arcane information, but to lead each of us to become "a new creation" in Christ. (II Corinthians 5:17, ESV) "The path of life" set forth in Scripture is meant to be lived in fellowship with Christ and his people. Scripture guides us into and within that way. (Psalm 16:11, NIV) So Paul offers these memorable words on the divine origin of Scripture and the part it must play in Timothy's ministry: "All Scripture is God-breathed and is useful for teaching, rebuking, correcting and training in righteousness, so that the servant of God may be thoroughly equipped for every good work." (II Timothy 3:15-17, NIV) On the basis of these words, Paul gives Timothy "this charge:"

> Preach the word; be prepared in season and out of season; correct, rebuke and encourage – with great patience and careful instruction. For the time will come when people will not put up with sound doctrine. Instead, to suit their own desires, they will gather around them a great number of teachers to say what their itching ears want to hear. They will turn their ears away from the truth and turn aside to myths. But you, keep your head in all situations, endure hardship, do the work of an evangelist, discharge all the duties of your ministry. (II Timothy 4:1-5, NIV)

These words, without alteration, applied equally to early Methodist preachers, no matter where their road might lead. Today's seminary graduates, ordination classes, and anyone else called to some form of ministry should find these words equally pertinent and powerful.

II Peter's reference to Paul's Letters as Scripture, indicate the fluidity in the way the New Testament was formed and received. II Peter refers to the challenge of reading Paul's Letters, but also the wisdom they contain. "His letters contain some things that are hard to understand, which ignorant and unstable people distort, as they do the other Scriptures, to their own destruction." (II Peter 3:16, NIV) This classification of Paul's Letters with "the other Scriptures" is part of the process of canonization that would continue for a long time before settling on our familiar list.

II Peter contrasts the credibility of Scripture with the unreliability of the sources used by false teachers. The apostolic focus on knowledge and growing in knowledge stands over against "fabricated stories."(II Peter 2:3, NIV)

HUMILITY

New Testament Letters, especially those of Paul, often express an honest admission of sinfulness, inadequacy, and reliance upon grace in order for the writer to live up to his calling and justify his authority. This same openness is expected of the recipients, making this feature of the Letters a deep and admirable form of mentoring. The writer may admonish the recipient, but will often go to great lengths to offer praise and encouragement. Nearly always the Letters begin, and often end, with words of grace and peace.

In I Timothy, Paul readily admits, as no doubt he had in past conversations, that his qualification to be an apostle is an undeserved gift: "Christ Jesus came into the world to save sinners - of whom I am the worst." God's purpose in showing grace to "a blasphemer and a persecutor and a violent man," was so that "in me, the worst of sinners, Christ Jesus might display his immense patience as an example for those who would believe in him and receive eternal life." I Timothy 1: 13, 15&16, NIV)

In his Second Letter to Timothy, Paul refers, without explanation, to a conversation they once had. This young pastor was struggling with temptation, opposition, or false doctrine. The context suggests that Timothy was having trouble bearing some part of his responsibility and needed encouragement. Whatever the precise reason, Paul referred back to it as unfinished business:

"Recalling your tears, I long to see you, so that I may be filled with joy." At a challenging time in Timothy's ministry, this mentoring relationship clearly meant a great deal to both of them. There is nothing superficial in these words. Not long after them we come to other words of Paul, written to bolster Timothy's strength in leadership; "I remind you to fan into flame the gift of God, which is in you through the laying on of my hands. For the Spirit God gave us does not make us timid, but gives us power, love and self-discipline." From this point on, it is clear that the conversation centers on persecution: "So do not be ashamed of the testimony about our Lord or of me his prisoner. Rather, join with me in suffering for the gospel by the power of God." II Timothy 1:6-8, NIV)

The passage goes on to speak of their ministry and his imprisonment in the context of God's way of salvation. Timothy is being humiliated for his connection with the prisoner Paul. "Yet this is no cause for shame, because I know whom I have believed, and am convinced that he is able to guard what I have entrusted to him until that day." (II Timothy 1:12, NIV, words reminiscent of Romans 1:16: "For I am not ashamed of the gospel, because it is the power of God that brings salvation to everyone who believes.") Paul writes candidly about those who have worked against him and those who have come to his aid, including Onesiphorus, who "was not ashamed of my chains." (Ii Timothy 1:16. NIV) Timothy is well aware of these things: "You, however, know all about my teaching, my way of life, my purpose, faith, patience, love, endurance, persecutions, sufferings…. Yet the Lord rescued me from all of them." Then he makes it clear that "everyone who wants to live a godly life in Christ Jesus will be persecuted…." (Ii Timothy 3:10-12) With all this in mind, Paul writes the unforgettable words, "I have fought the good fight, I have finished the race, I have kept the faith." (I Timothy 4:7, NIV) Far from a sense of shame or disgrace, he conveys a triumphant sense of work accomplished.

Another indicator of the level of cooperation between Paul the mentor and Timothy the protégé is found in Paul's requests in preparation for a future meeting. Near the end of the Second Letter, Paul includes this detail: "When you come, bring the cloak that I left with Carpus at Troas, and my scrolls, especially the parchments."(II Timothy 4:13, NIV) These may seem like simple, almost trivial matters – necessary clothing and necessary materials for writing. But for an apostle, whose life was lived on the road, often in less than friendly company, for whom Letters were his lifeline, these were vital. Timothy, of all people, would understand, both because so much of his own ministry was fed by Paul's Letters, and because he sometimes joined Paul in sending Letters. Timothy appears in opening greetings with Paul in II Corinthians, Philippians, Colossians, and Philemon. His exact role in each of these could be as co-author, but the overwhelming similarity of the Letters suggests either that Timothy served as a secretary for all or part of a Letter, or that he was united with Paul's intent, who included his name as support. The presence of his name in solidarity with Paul may well have strengthened the Letter in the minds of recipients.

LOVE, THANKSGIVING

Paul anchors his relationship to the people he addresses in love, gratitude, and prayer. Most importantly, this love flows ultimately from God. As in most apostolic letters, Romans begins with God's grace and peace. (Romans 1:7-10) Even in Galatians, which has an urgency that moves the writer quickly into the painful issue at hand, there is no bypassing the usual greeting, though there is no thanksgiving or extended personal greetings. These samples of thanksgiving at the beginning of Colossians, II Thessalonians, and Philippians, demonstrate the importance and flavor of this element:

> We always thank God, the Father of our Lord Jesus Christ, when we pray for you, because we have heard of your faith in Christ and of the love you have for all God's people – the faith and love that spring from the hope stored up for up in heaven.... (Colossians 1:3-5, NIV)

> We ought always to thank God for you, brothers and sisters, and rightly so, because your faith is growing more and more, because the love all of you have for one another is increasing. (II Thessalonians 1:3, NIV)

> I thank my God every time I remember you. In all my prayers for all of you, I always pray with joy because of your partnership in the gospel from the first day until now, being confident of this, that he who began a good work in you will carry it on to completion until the day of Christ Jesus.
>
> It is right for me to feel this way about all of you, since I have you in my heart and, whether I am in chains or defending and confirming the gospel, all of you share in God's grace with me. God can testify how I long for all of you with the affection of Christ Jesus.
>
> And this is my prayer: that your love may abound more and more in knowledge and depth of insight, so that you may be able to discern what is best and may be pure and blameless for the Day of Christ, filled with the fruit of righteousness that comes through Jesus Christ – to the glory and praise of God. (Philippians 1:3-11, NIV.)

This lengthy expression of thanksgiving in Philippians reveals the depth of love between Paul and this particular congregation, built up over time through shared blessings and trials. Portions of this passage have provided the words for pastors to their congregations as they leave for retirement or a new appointment.

> One of the shortest of Paul's letters, it is perhaps the most beloved by the church. No doubt, this is due in part to its high concentration of memorable passages that constantly challenge and encourage the people of God. ... What is more, the letter glows with affection and joy. The imprisoned Paul who writes Philippians is not hard to love. (Dean Flemming. Philippians (etc.) Kansas City, MO: Beacon Hill, 2009, 21.)

These thanksgivings contain elements in a church's life. Paul commends the Colossian church for its "faith and love that spring from hope." In the Thessalonians he sees faith in God "growing more and more" and "love for one another" which is "increasing." His connection to the church at Philippi comes through in specific references to a long and fruitful "partnership in the gospel," that has yielded impressive spiritual results. Paul and the Philippians have been through a lot and accomplished a lot together, so that he "long[s] for all of [them] with the affection of Christ Jesus." He sees even greater things ahead, complete with abundant love that produces growing "knowledge and depth of insight, so that [they] may be able to discern what is best and may be pure and blameless..., filled with the fruit of righteousness." He remains positive, encouraging, and appreciative throughout this Letter, which "contains little ... correction of beliefs (unlike 1 Corinthians) ... or detailed syllogisms proving a point with logic. Paul is able to rely on his well-established ethos and pathos shared with the audience...." (Ben Witherington III. *Paul's Letter to the Philippians (etc.)*. Grand Rapids, MI & Cambridge, UK: Eerdmans, 2011, 112.)

Paul's love for his churches is sometimes mixed with pain and frustration, either within a particular congregation or more generally, as in II Corinthians 4; 6:3-13, part of which reads: "We have spoken freely to you, Corinthians, and opened wide our hearts to you. We are not withholding our affection from you, but you are withholding yours from us. As a fair exchange – I speak as to my children – open wide your hearts to us." (II Corinthians 6:11-13, NIV) The pain and passion of such passages speak clearly after twenty centuries and indicate the depth of emotion binding these people to, and sometimes holding them back from each other. Love always seeks the best for others, and risks misunderstanding and even rejection in doing so. For this reason it is so important for the apostolic leader to have the resources of grace in a rock-solid relationship with God, so as to be shielded from the destruction of too much pain and constantly replenished and encourage by the God who is love. (I John 4:8.) A Scripture that reflects and conveys this truth is Psalm 46:1 – "God is our refuge and strength, an ever-present help in trouble."(NIV) Sadly, though not surprisingly, a particular church may not yield readily, even to the wisest and most caring admonition, which was the case with persistent disunity in the church at Corinth. (I Corinthians 1:10-17; 3:1 - 4:19)

THE TWO WAYS

To these characteristics of a spiritually healthy church, we can add both confirmation and additional elements from the Letters. There are, for instance, lists of shared values, which the apostles commend or recommend, depending on the situation. No doubt the best known of these is in I Corinthians 13, where the overarching category of love is shown to contain many important ingredients, including patience and kindness. The chapter also tells us what love is not. Love excludes envy, boastfulness and pride. "It does not dishonor others, it is not self-seeking, it is not easily angered, it keeps no record of wrongs." Love is forgiving, honest, protective, trusting, hopeful, and persevering. (I Corinthians 13:4-7, NIV)

To these we should add the fruit of the Spirit in Galatians: "But the fruit of the Spirit is love, joy, peace, forbearance, kindness, goodness, faithfulness, gentleness and self-control. Against such things there is no law." (Galatians 5:22&23, NIV) New Testament Letters often contain lists of evil or spiritually unhealthy characteristics, such as this one in Galatians:

> The acts of the flesh are obvious: sexual immorality, impurity and debauchery; idolatry and witchcraft; hatred, discord, jealousy, fits of rage, selfish ambition, dissensions, factions and envy; drunkenness, orgies, and the like. I warn you, as I did before, that those who live like this will not inherit the kingdom of God (Galatians 5:19-21)

Another pair of lists is in Colossians 3. Introducing them is a call to focus on what matters in life and base our actions; indeed the whole course of our lives on that:

> Since, then, you have been raised with Christ, set your hearts on things above, where Christ is, seated at the right hand of God. Set your minds on things above, not on earthly things. For you died, and your life is now hidden with Christ in God. When Christ, who is your life, appears, then you also will appear with him in glory. (Colossians 3:1-4, NIV)

Since our priorities and our destiny are beyond the petty, transient concerns Paul designates as "earthly things," our thoughts should be "on things above," preparing us for an eternity with Christ "in glory." Our lives must reflect that destiny, which requires the rejection of everything that stands opposed to Christ, and the acquisition of everything consistent with Christ:

> Put to death, therefore, whatever belongs to your earthly nature: sexual immorality, impurity, lust, evil desires and greed, which is idolatry. Because of these, the wrath of God is coming. You used to walk in these ways, in the life you once lived. But now you must also rid yourselves of all such things as these: anger, rage, malice, slander, and filthy language from your lips. Do not lie to each other. Since you have taken off your old self with its practices and have put on the new self, which is being renewed in knowledge in the image of its Creator. (Colossians 3:5-10, NIV)

All the old divisions of humanity are now obsolete, as Christ supersedes them all.

> Therefore, as God's chosen people, holy and dearly loved, clothe yourselves with compassion, kindness, humility, gentleness and patience. Bear with each other and forgive one another if any of you has a grievance against someone. Forgive as the Lord forgave you. And over all these virtues put on love, which binds them all together in perfect unity.
>
> Let the peace of Christ rule in your hearts, since as members of one body you were called to peace. And be thankful. Let the message of Christ dwell among you richly as you teach and admonish one another with all wisdom through psalms, hymns and songs from the Spirit. And whatever you do, whether in word or deed, do it all in the name of the Lord Jesus, giving thanks to God the Father though him. (Colossians 3:12-17, NIV)

Lists like these have a good deal in common among themselves and with teachings of Jesus. But this is hardly useless repetition. It is exactly what is required by people and congregations who are prone to losing their way and redefining their purpose to suit their own misguided self-interest. Thus Paul wrote, "It is no trouble for me to write these things to you again, and it is a safeguard for you." (Philippians 3:1, NIV) Their importance has not diminished in the centuries since they were written.

In I Corinthians 12 and Romans 12, Paul uses the allegorical image of the body of Christ to show how Christians live and their churches function when their life is truly in Christ. This image gives us a way to visualize and measure how well we are doing in living up to the expectation and promise of Christ for God's people. For example, there are lists in both these chapters that illustrate how diverse people can work together in community to the benefit of all. Then just as I Corinthians does in chapter 13, Romans 12 goes on to delineate ways in which love perfects unity in the body. In doing this Paul gives us another list of elements of love's character, which must become the character of the Church. Notice the depth of love and its connection to related virtues, such as humility, and the practical applicability to pastoral and congregational dynamics:

> Love must be sincere. Hate what is evil; cling to what is good. Be devoted to one another in love. Honor one another above yourselves. Never be lacking in zeal, but keep you spiritual fervor, serving the Lord. Be joyful in hope, patient in affliction, faithful in prayer. Share with the Lord's people who are in need. Practice hospitality.
>
> Bless those who persecute you; bless and do not curse. Rejoice with those who rejoice; mourn with those who mourn. Live in harmony with one another. Do not be proud, but be willing to associate with people of low position. Do not be conceited.
>
> Do not repay anyone evil for evil. Be careful to do what is right in the eyes of everyone. If it is possible, so far as it depends on you, live at peace with everyone. Do not take revenge.... (Romans 12:9-19, NIV)

A Christian or congregation that lives in this way, fulfills Paul's intention "not [to] conform to the pattern of this world, but be transformed by the renewal of your mind," so that they will "not be overcome by evil, but overcome evil with good." (Romans 12:2&21, NIV) One further observation from Romans: Much like Jesus' Great Commandment (Matthew 22:36-40), Paul writes about God's commandments being fulfilled by love. (Romans 13:8-10)

Life under the Lordship of God means a life under the structuring power of grace. That power transforms not only individuals, but the individuals' relationships to the community around them. Living by the power of the Spirit, and accepting the gracious Lordship of God, the Christian's world has been made new. (Paul Achtemeier. Romans. Interpretation, Louisville, KY: John Knox, 1985,195.)

James contrasts false "wisdom," which "does not come down from heaven but is earthly, unspiritual, demonic," with "the wisdom that comes from heaven." The first shows itself in "bitter envy and selfish ambition," leading to "disorder and every evil practice." But real wisdom produces "deeds done in humility" ... "the wisdom that comes from heaven, is first of all pure; then peace-loving, considerate, submissive, full of mercy and good fruit, impartial and sincere. Peacemakers who sow in peace reap a harvest of righteousness." (James 3:14-18, NIV)

II Peter gives us another list of Christian virtues, empowered in believers by grace, with the capacity to grow us, even to the point where we can "participate in the divine nature." In this arrangement, the virtues of faith, knowledge, self-control, perseverance, godliness, mutual affection, and love seem to build on each other. We are encouraged to grow in these virtues "in increasing measure" to avoid becoming "ineffective and unproductive" disciples. (II Peter 1:3-8, NIV)

In I John 3, the two ways are defined as life and death, experienced as love and hatred of people; love of God vs. love of the world:

> "We know that we have passed from death to life, because we love each other. Anyone who does not love remains in death." (I John 3:14, NIV)

> "Do not love the world or anything in the world. If anyone loves the world, love for the Father is not in them. (I John 2:15, NIV) "without explicit utilization of the 'two ways' language found in postapostolic sources ... John reflects a comparable viewpoint. His summons to love continues to grow out of a combined critique of evildoing and commendation of agapic attitudes and actions." (Robert W. Yarbrough. 1 - 3 John. Grand Rapids, MI:

Baker,2008, 199.)

The Didache, a very early outline of the Christian way of life, (nearly as old as the New Testament), contains long lists called "The Way of Life" and "The Way of Death." Thomas O'Loughlin believes the Didache was written during the New Testament era. (Thomas O'Loughlin. *The Didache: A Window on the Earliest Christians*. Grand Rapids, MI: Baker, 2010.) Similar lists appeared in other early Christian documents, including The Letter of Barnabas. The introduction to the Two Ways in the Didache reflects the document's Scriptural grounding and the seriousness with which it was read and used in disciplining the Christian path. (Huub van de Sandt & David Flusser. *The Didache: Its Jewish Sources and its Place in Early Judaism and Christianity*. Assen, Netherlands: Royal Van Gorcum & Minneapolis, MN: Fortress, 2002, 59-70. The widespread use of these lists indicates their usefulness in providing clear guidance for a Jewish or Christian subculture within the Roman Empire. (See also Aaron Milavec. *The Didache: Text, Translation, Analysis, and Commentary*. Collegeville, MN: Liturgical, 2003.)

The two ways idea is reminiscent of the ways Israel could keep or break their covenant with God. Moses summarizes this extended promise/warning with these dramatic words: "This day I call the heavens and the earth as witnesses against you that I have set before you life and death, blessings and curses. Now choose life...." (Deuteronomy 30:19, NIV)

In Romans, Paul elaborates at length on "life according to the flesh" and "life in accordance with the Spirit." (Romans 8:5, NIV) Here he reflects theologically on how much is at stake in our flawed humanity, in the moral decisions we make, the way of life that flows from those decisions, and the ultimate results of living in Christ or in "the flesh." In a powerful statement of the eternal consequences of our life in or apart from Christ, Paul writes,

> You, however, are not in the realm of the flesh but are in the realm of the Spirit, if indeed the Spirit of God lives in you. And if anyone does not have the Spirit of Christ, they do not belong to Christ. But if Christ is in you, then even though your body is subject to death because of sin, the Spirit gives life because of

righteousness. And if the Spirit of him who raised Jesus from the dead is living in you, he who raised Christ from the dead will also give life to your mortal bodies because of his Spirit who lives in you. (Romans 8:9-11, NIV)

One specific way the New Testament Letters addressed their own and subsequent generations, was to draw lessons from the Old Testament. Such lessons could be derived from positive or negative examples. In one of the latter, "Now these things occurred as examples to keep us from setting our hearts on evil things as they did." (I Corinthians 10:6, NIV) Another was to apply Biblical wisdom, from either testament, to concrete situations that might arise or had already arisen in the everyday life of a church or its members. In James, for example, there are passages cautioning against careless or harmful speech (James 1:19&20; 26; 2:12&13; 3:1-12; 4:11-17; 5:12.).

Another way was for the Letters to offer mentoring by the apostolic writers themselves and others whose examples are worthy of imitation. Paul wrote to the Philippians, "Whatever you have learned or received or heard from me, or seen in me, put it into practice." (Philippians 4:9; NIV: See also, Philippians 3:17-21) This can be read as boasting, but instead we should see it as part of his sacrifice for the Church – offering an alternative to the values of the pagan culture surrounding them. It was a mentoring role he was ready to share: "You became imitators of us and of the Lord, for you welcomed the message in the midst of severe suffering, with the joy given by the Holy Spirit. And so you became a model to all the believers in Macedonia and Achaia...." (I Thessalonians 1:6, NIV)

Better yet, Christ is the ultimate example, as in Philippians:

> Do nothing out of selfish ambition or vain conceit. Rather, in humility value others above yourselves, not looking to your own interests but each of you to the interests of the others. In your relationships with one another, have the same mindset as Christ Jesus:
>
> Who, being in very nature God,
>   did not consider equality with God something to be used
>   to his own advantage;

rather, he made himself nothing,
By taking the very nature of a servant,
Being made in human likeness.
And, being found in appearance as a man,
He Humbled himself
by becoming obedient to death –
even death on a cross!
Therefore God exalted him to the highest place
and gave him the name that is above every name,
that at the name of Jesus ever knee should bow,
In heaven and on earth and under the earth,
and every tongue acknowledge that Jesus Christ is Lord,
to the glory of God the Father. (Philippians 2:3-11, NIV)

"Far from being a power move, the call to imitation of Paul as he imitates Christ is a call to step down, to humble oneself...." - Ben Wiitherington III. *Paul's Letter to the Philippians (etc.).* Grand Rapiids, MI & Cambridge, UK: Eerdmans, 2011, 128.)

All of these address the culture of life in Christ, in and of itself as well as in relationship to life or the world in general. Romans 1:11&12 shows Paul's desire to mentor the Roman Christians face to face, but also his awareness that he needs what they can share with him: "I long to see you so that I may impart some spiritual gift to make you strong – that is, that you and I may be *mutually encouraged* by each other's faith." (N.T. Wright, Romans, *New Interpreter's Bible*. Nashville, TN: Abingdon, 2002, 10: 422.)

ENCOURAGEMENT

For everything that was written in the past was written to teach us, so that through the endurance taught in the Scriptures and the encouragement they provide we might have hope. May the God who gives endurance and encouragement give you the same attitude of mind toward each other that Christ Jesus had, so that with one mind and one voice you may glorify the God and Father of our Lord Jesus Christ. (Romans 15:4-6, NIV)

Paul notes that Scripture was written to teach believers (!5:4).

He believed that the events actually happened partly for later generations to learn from (1 Cor 10:6, 11), but here emphasizes more precisely that they were written for this purpose. He does not treat them as symbols of later realities, but indicates that one may learn by analogy from examples. The Scriptures were meant to sustain hope.... (Craig S. Keener. Romans. Eugene, OR: Cascade, 2009, 171.)

A Christian community animated by God's love is one in which leaders and members alike encourage each other, and all are inspired by the encouragement of Scripture and the "great cloud of witnesses." (Hebrews 12:1) Paul closes his Second Letter to the Corinthians, with this message: "encourage one another, be of one mind, live in peace. And the God of love and peace will be with you." (II Corinthians 13:11, NIV) The participants in this kind fellowship – this culture of deeply rooted, mutual encouragement – have a powerful resource for overcoming the inevitable obstacles they encounter. Their victorious way of life will bring them joy and glorify their Lord.

Such encouragement should not flow in one direction only. Paul was thankful for the ways members of the various churches encouraged him. One important source of encouragement for him came when he found people living the gospel they professed; where he could see the fruit of his apostolic labor. Thus he writes to Philemon, "Your love has given me great joy and encouragement because you, brother, have refreshed the hearts of the Lord's people." (Philemon 1:7, NIV) Paul is taking a difficult route through this Letter, in which he hopes to bring together in the equality of Christian fellowship two friends who are separated by the commonly accepted practice of slavery. His was not an easy task, yet he was encouraged by the generosity of spirit Philemon usually showed in his interactions with fellow Christians, and he knew from other conflicts that fellowship could overcome the disorder of troubled relations in the body. (II Corinthians 7:13)

The Letters are filled with inspired words of encouragement whose force has outlasted the times and situations that first prompted them and to which they first spoke, including these examples from Philippians:

> ...being confident of this, that he who began a good work in you will carry it on to completion until the day of Christ Jesus. (Phi-

lippians 1:6, NIV)

> ...it is God who works in you to will and to act in order to fulfill his good purpose. (Philippians 2:13, NIV)

> But our citizenship is in heaven. And we eagerly await a Savior from there, the Lord Jesus Christ, who, by the power that enables him to bring everything under his control, will transform our lowly bodies so that they will be like his glorious body. (Philippians 3:21, NIV)

> Do not be anxious about anything, but in every situation, by prayer and petition, with thanksgiving, present your requests to God, and the peace of God, which transcends all understanding, will guard your hearts and your minds in Christ Jesus. (Philippians 4:6&7, NIV)

In prayer and sermons; in public worship and personal correspondence, words like these have continued to convey their inspired message, no matter how much our world changes in other respects. In every generation there are those who gratefully receive and generously hand on the baton of faith.

REAFFIRMING SHARED BELIEFS, VALUES, PURPOSE

Paul addressed one of his Letters, "To Titus, my true son in our common faith."(Titus 1:4, NIV) When it came to essential Christian teachings and values, it was important that Christians be "like-minded, having the same love, being one in spirit and of one mind." On the basis of eyewitness testimony, John's First Letter is written to confirm the truth and purpose of the incarnation, so that the church will know the joy of fellowship:

> That which was from the beginning, which we have heard, which we have seen with our eyes, which we have looked at and our hands have touched – this we proclaim concerning the Word of life. The life appeared; we have seen it and testify to it, and we proclaim to you the eternal life, which was with the Father, and has appeared to us. We proclaim to you what we have seen and heard, so that you also may have fellowship with us. And our fellowship

is with the Father and with his Son Jesus Christ. We write this to make our joy complete. (I John 1:1-4, NIV)

There is a mysterious mutuality between truth and love, *alethea* and *agape,* that is set forth in I John and other Letters; a necessary reciprocity in which God's people more and more resemble their Lord. (Romans 15:6; II Corinthians 15:11; I Peter 3:8; II John 1:2&4.) One illustration from the history of worship is an exchange that introduces the Nicene Creed in Orthodox churches. Here a deacon says, "Let us love one another, that with one accord we may confess," to which the choir responds, "Father, Son, and Holy Spirit, the Trinity one in Essence and undivided." (Liturgy of St. John Chrysostom, in Isabel Florence Hapgood, ed. Service Book of the Holy Orthodox-Catholic Apostolic Church. Englewood, NJ: Antiochian Orthodox Christian Archdiocese, 1975, 99.) Another comes from a song called "Irish Day," recorded by the band Iona: "Love can heal when truth is found." (copyright BMG Rights Management, Universal Music Publishing Group and quoted by permission.) One sees love as preparation for a united witness; the other sees truth as a conducive context for love. There is a profound interdependence here that values both.

The Letters often argue important theological, spiritual, or ethical principles that deserve a reminder. These are designed to give strength and clarity to beliefs and values the apostle and readers share. Especially important are calls to remember and renew the Church's original purpose. Perhaps someone has sown doubt or confusion in the minds of the people and their leaders, but it may just be that a celebration is needed in order to bolster confidence and gratitude. Examples of the latter include the celebration of the resurrection in I Peter 1:3-9, and lessons extoling humility and condemning favoritism in James 1:9-11; 2:1-7; 3:13; 4:10.

II John reaffirms a central teaching - Jesus' command to love - commends those who are living by that teaching, but warns against those who are undermining the church with false teaching. John rejoices that "some ... are walking in the truth," but rails against those who are deceiving people with a view of Christ that casts doubt on his divinity. He tells the faithful part of the congregation, "If anyone comes to you" with false teaching about Christ, "do not take them into your house or welcome them. Anyone who welcomes them shares in their wicked work." (II John vs. 10&11, NIV) This must have seemed a hard teaching when juxtaposed with Jesus' command to love, since it places a limit on hospitality, certainly an important Christian virtue. But it stands with others (such as Galatians, II Peter, Jude) that recognize the destruction caused by misguided welcome and the importance of standing for the truth.

I John balances positive teaching on love with clear condemnation of its opposite. In this letter, John identifies the ultimate source of love as God, his communication of love to us in Christ, and the relationship of hatred and evil to the evil one. The considerably greater length of I John in comparison with II John also allows him to elaborate on the Christological heresy addressed in the Second Letter.

> Dear friends, do not believe every spirit, but test the spirits to see whether they come from God, because many false prophets have gone out into the world. This is how you can recognize the Spirit of God: Every spirit that acknowledges that Jesus Christ has come in the flesh is from God, but every spirit that does not acknowledge Jesus is not from God. This is the spirit of the antichrist, which you have heard is coming and even now is already in the world. (I John 4:1-3, NIV)

But John is at his most eloquent and most moving when he writes triumphantly about God's love for us and in us:

> Dear friends, let us love one another, for love comes from God. Everyone who loves has been born of God and knows God. Whoever does not love does not know God, because God is love. This is how God showed his love among us: he sent his one and only Son into the world that we might live through him. This is love: not that we loved God, but that he loved us and sent his Son to be an atoning sacrifice for our sins. Dear friends, since God so loved us, we also ought to love one another.

I Howard Marshall summarizes this point well. Commenting on I John 4:8, he says:

> a person who does not love does not know God. His lack of love

demonstrates that he does not belong to the divine sphere, since God is love. The implication is that knowledge of God leads men to love one another. A person cannot come into a real relationship with a loving God without being transformed into a loving person. (I. Howard Marshall. The Epistles of John. Grand Rapids, MI: Eerdmans, 1978, 212.)

John's First Letter also wants us to see something of our destiny in Christ if we remain true to Christ's teaching in word and action: "Dear friends, now we are children of God, and what we will be has not yet been made known. But we know that when Christ appears, we shall be like him, for we shall see him as he is." (I John 3:2; see also: 5:18-20 NIV). The transformation of believers by God's grace working within is also a significant theme in other Letters, by different authors:

And we all, who with unveiled faces contemplate the Lord's glory, are being transformed into his image with ever-increasing glory, which comes from the Lord, who is the Spirit. (II Corinthians 3:18, NIV)

His divine power has given us everything we need for a godly life through our knowledge of him who called us by his own glory and goodness. Through these he has given us his very great and precious promises, so that you may participate in the divine nature, having escaped the corruption in the world caused by evil desires. (II Peter 1:3&4, NIV)

II Peter makes very clear the need to restate and confirm the doctrinal content of the faith: "So I will always remind you of these things, even though you know them and are firmly established in the truth you now have." He does not want people's recall or understanding of these things to weaken over time. "I think it is right to refresh your memory as long as I live in the tent of this body.... And I will make every effort to see that after my departure you will always be able to remember these things." (II Peter 1:12-15, NIV)

The New Testament Letters are rooted in first hand, apostolic testimony. This grounding in Christ sets their testimony apart from lesser sources. Peter's example is the presence of three apostles on the mount of transfiguration:

> For we did not follow cleverly devised stories when we told you about the coming of our Lord Jesus Christ in power, but we were eyewitnesses of his majesty. He received honor and glory from God the Father when the voice came to him from the Majestic Glory, saying, "This is my Son, whom I love; with him I am well pleased." We ourselves heard this voice that came from heaven when we were with him on the sacred mountain. (II Peter 1:16-18, NIV)

Apostolic reliability is also rooted in prophecy, which "never had its origin in the human will, but prophets, though human, spoke from God as they were carried along by the Holy Spirit." (II Peter 1:21, NIV) Inspired, Biblical prophecy is "a light shining in a dark place." The contrast could not be starker between apostolic credibility and the deception and confusion coming from false teachers. (II Peter 1;19, NIV; 2:1-22.)

In these Letters, Scripture serves to teach enduring truth and to encourage Christians to remain steadfast amid challenging times (Romans15:4). The Bible is common ground in a divided church and "a light on my path." (Psalm 119:105, NIV) Study of Scripture keeps Christians and their churches firmly connected with the truth, and with the One who is the Truth.

WARNINGS: COUNTERFEIT TEACHING, LETHARGY

Just as these Letters reaffirm elements of the truth, they often give warnings about teachings and teachers that seek to modify or replace the truth in order to gain control or substitute something more to their liking. In Galatians, the Apostle is appalled that some of those converted under his ministry were "turning to a different gospel." Then he tells them "even if we or an angel from heaven should preach a gospel other than the one we preached to you, let them be under God's curse. (Galatians 1:6&8, NIV) Paul tells Timothy to "command certain people not to teach false doctrines any longer" not out of a desire for raw control. "The goal of this command is love, which comes from a pure heart and a good conscience and a sincere faith." (I Timothy 1:3&5, NIV) Leaving people afloat on a sea of misinformation, or under the sway of unscrupulous or misguided teachers does not do them any favors. II Peter goes to great lengths to show the damage being done to the Church:

> But there were also false prophets among the people, just as there will be false teachers among you. They will secretly introduce destructive heresies, even denying the sovereign Lord who bought them – bringing swift destruction on themselves. Many will follow their depraved conduct and will bring the way of truth into disrepute. (II Peter 2:1, NIV – II Peter's condemnation continues through the end of the chapter.)

In a similar passage, Jude says, "For certain individuals whose condemnation was written about long ago have secretly slipped in among you. These are ungodly people, who pervert the grace of our God into a license for immorality and deny Jesus Christ our only Sovereign and Lord. (Jude, v. 4, NIV)

John's First Letter warns that "many false prophets have gone out into the world," people who deny that "Jesus Christ has come in the flesh" and that he "is from God." Who are they? "They are from the world and therefore speak from the viewpoint of the world, and the world listens to them. We are from God, and whoever knows God listens to us; but whoever is not from God does not listen to us. This is how we recognize the Spirit of truth and the spirit of falsehood." (I John 4:1,3 &5, NIV)

Lethargy in faith may come when someone begins to take God's love and salvation for granted. In time it is possible to lose energy for ministry or succumb to burn out or compassion fatigue. Faith may weaken and spiritual senses lose their sharpness and clarity. Scripture indicates that we have a responsibility to keep fresh and to guard against lethargy. Lethargy is not something that just happens to us while we remain passive. Thus Paul exhorts his readers in Romans, "Never be lacking in zeal, but keep your spiritual fervor, serving the Lord. (Romans 12:11, NIV) The same message occurs memorably in two of the letters to the seven churches in Revelation:

> To the Church in Ephesus

"you have forsaken the love you had at first. Consider how far you have fallen! Repent and do the things you did at first."

To the Church in Laodicea

"I know your deeds, that you are neither cold nor hot. I wish you were either one or the other! So, because you are lukewarm – neither hot nor cold – I am about to spit you out of my mouth." (Revelation 2:4&5; 3:15&16, NIV)

While we are responsible and called upon to repent, as with any other facet of Christian life, we rely on grace and the means of grace to identify the need and access God's remedy.

"I HOPE TO SEE YOU SOON, AND WE WILL TALK FACE TO FACE:" THE LIMITATIONS OF LETTERS

Couples who love each other know painfully well the value and limitations of written communication. Today the separation they experience can be mitigated through several forms of technology, yet even when they shorten the distance using e-mail, texting, or social media, still something is missing. Families who are scattered because of college or career moves can be held together by texts and phone calls, often enhanced by video communication, yet they still travel great distances to see each other face to face. Coworkers and workplaces, disrupted by pandemic, were often held together by their computers. The same is true of teachers and their students, pastors and their congregations. But while this substitute for in person classes, worship, and meetings was appreciated for its benefits, it also showed its limitations. Even when distance meetings result in cost savings, allow for students to attend universities far from their homes, and congregations to stay connected during public heath emergencies, the experience is not the same and, many would argue, loses considerable value.

In the New Testament era, apostolic supervision and coordination of local congregations was greatly assisted by letters. However, as valuable as these letters were at the time, and remain today, both senders and recipients acknowledged their limitations and longed for times when at last they would be together again. At those times their fellowship would be renewed, problems would be more effectively addressed, missionary work would be accomplished, and encouragement would be shared.

We see this in the closing of the Second Letter of John where the writer says, "I have much to write to you, but I do not want to use paper and ink. Instead, I hope to visit you and talk with you face to face, so that our joy may be complete." (II John 1:12, NIV)

John's Third Letter ends in a similar way, and also refers to a problem in the recipient's community, which the writer will deal with in person on a future visit. But for the moment, he closes in this way: "I have much to write you, but I do not want to do so with pen and ink. I hope to see you soon, and we will talk face to face." (III John 1:13&14, NIV)

In other Letters, we see the same hope or promise of face to face encounter. Here we see it at the beginning and end of Romans:

> I pray that now at last by God's will the way may be opened for me to come to you.
>
> I long to see you so that I may impart to you some spiritual gift to make you strong – that is, that you and I may be mutually encouraged by each other's faith. I do not want you to be unaware, brothers and sisters, that I planned many times to come to you (but have been prevented from doing so until now in order that I might have a harvest among you, just as I have had among the other Gentiles.
>
> I am obligated both to Greeks and non-Greeks, both to the wise ad the foolish. That is why I am so eager to preach the Gospel also to you who are in Rome. (Romans 1:10-14, NIV)
>
> ...I have been longing for many years to visit you. I plan to do so when I go to Spain. I hope to see you while passing through and to have you assist me on my journey there, after I have enjoyed your company for a while. (Romans 15:23&24, NIV)

Paul describes his duties prior to his desired travel to Rome, then,

> I know that when I come to you, I will come in the full measure

of the blessing of Christ.

> I urge you, brothers and sisters, by the Lord Jesus Christ and by the love of the Spirit, to join me in my struggle by praying to God for me ... so that I may come to you with joy, by God's will, and in your company be refreshed. (Romans 15:29-32, NIV)

PERSONAL MESSAGES

Four New Testament Letters – I and II Timothy, Titus, and Philemon - were addressed specifically to individual, named recipients. Others, while written to local or regional communities, include greetings or other messages intended for particular members. Sometimes a personal message is meant to be "overheard" by that person's community.

Romans and Colossians end by mentioning many individuals. Often they commend someone for their ministry, perhaps thanking them publicly for supporting Paul in his. They might make requests or mention hopes. Often they express encouragement and sometimes correction. They often tell us something important about the way congregations worked together and the kinds of responsibilities people carried within their larger communities. Several women are described as exercising significant leadership. These personal references also show the importance of connections that bound local communities to each other as they fulfilled the Great Commission in the great centrifugal motion of the Church.

Romans identifies Phoebe as "a deacon of the church in Cenchrae." She has been a "benefactor of many people, including [Paul]," who hopes she will be treated hospitably in Rome. (Romans 16:1&2, NIV) Paul sends greetings to Priscilla and Aquila, "co-workers in Christ Jesus," and to "the church that meets in their house," This couple is known to us from references I Acts 18, I Corinthians 16:19, and II Timothy 4:19. From these we learn that theirs was a traveling ministry and that they were teachers of the faith. Paul's greeting to their house church suggests that the Christian community at Rome was large enough to have more than one gathering place. (Romans 16;3, NIV)

He goes on to greet, and seek greetings, for a host of fellow servants, some Jews and some Gentiles, a continued mix of men and women (at least nine are women), all of them treasured friends. To these he adds those who join him in sending greetings, including Tertius, who was assisting him in writing the Letter.

He breaks into this sequence in order to address the all too familiar problem of divisiveness and false teaching in the church. About these he is clear, as he is on the need for stern discipline so that the perpetrators will not "deceive the minds of naive people." (Romans 16:18, NIV) Even so, the dominant tone of the Letter is one of mutual love and hospitality.

In Colossians we also have a long list of personal messages. First, he writes about those he is sending to Colossae to greet the church on Paul's behalf: "Tychicus will tell you all the news about me. He is a dear brother, a faithful minister and fellow servant in the Lord. I am sending him to you for the express purpose that you may know about our circumstances and that he may encourage your hearts." Here we have two important reasons for letters and visits - keeping fellowship alive and offering encouragement. A second person will come for similar reasons, but is better known in Colossae: Tychicus "is coming with Onesimus, our faithful and dear brother, who is one of you. They will tell you about everything that is happening here." (Colossians 1:7-9, NIV)

Now that he has their attention, Paul sends more greetings and personal messages. He first are from Aristarchus, Mark, and Justus, "the only Jews among my coworkers for the kingdom of God, and they have proved a comfort to me."(Colossians 4:10&11) Next he coveys greetings from, and commendation for, Epiphras, "who is one of you. He is always wrestling in prayer for you, that you may stand firm in all the will of God for you, mature and fully assured. I vouch for him that he has been working hard for you and for those at Laodicea and Hierapolis. He relays greetings from Luke, whom he identifies as "the doctor" (traditionally the writer of the third Gospel and, for some, one of the travelers Jesus met on the road to Emmaus) and Demas.

In an interesting glimpse into the life of an apostolic Letter, Paul sends "greetings to the brothers and sisters at Laodicea and to Nympha and the church in her house," to which he adds, "After this letter has been read to you, see that it is also read in the church of the Laodiceans and that you in turn read the letter from Laodicea. He then sends a somewhat cryptic message, which many have read as referring to Philemon:" Tell Archippus: see to it that you complete the ministry you have received in the Lord.

The closing of I Corinthians includes another list of personal messages. Philippians includes special mention of "those who belong to Caesar's household," an interesting part of the Church's demographics. Also in Philippians, Paul seeks reconciliation for some valued coworkers: "I plead with Euodia and I plead with Syntyche to be of one mind in the Lord. Yes, and I ask you, my true companion, help these women since they have contended at my side in the cause of the gospel, along with Clement and the rest of my co-workers, whose names are in the book of life," (Philippians 4:2&3, NIV) Philippians allows us glimpses of traveling ministers, carrying Letters and news, dispensing encouragement, distributing resources, and maintaining the momentum of a rapidly growing movement.

In Philippians, Paul describes two of these coworkers, Timothy and Epaphroditus. Timothy can be depended upon as a messenger because he "will show genuine concern for your welfare. For everyone looks out for their own interests, not those of Jesus Christ. But you know that Timothy has proven himself, because as a son with his father he has served with me in the work of the gospel." (Philippians 2:19-22, NIV)

Paul writes of Epaphroditus as, "my brother, co-worker and fellow soldier, who is also your messenger, whom you sent to take care of my needs." The Philippians have heard that Epaphroditus has been sick.

> Indeed he was ill, and almost died. But God had mercy on him, and not on him only but also on me, to spare me sorrow upon sorrow. Therefore I am all the more eager to send him so that when you see him again, you may be glad and I may have less anxiety. So then, welcome him in the Lord with great joy, and honor people like him, because he almost died for the work of Christ. He risked his life to make up for the help you could not give me. (Philippians 2:25-30, NIV)

We could quickly pass over passages like these as so much "ancient history," details whose importance has faded with time and must now be pushed aside in order to focus on what still matters. But the questions we are asking in this study demand a closer look. How did a church, at a critical moment, live out its purpose over time and against all obstacles? What role did a culture of mentoring play in creating a strong, resilient church? Surely a network or connection of deeply, even sacrificially committed people is a significant part of the answer.

II Timothy has a special word of greeting for Priscilla and Aquila, who figure prominently in Paul's ministry, and several people – Eubulus, Pudens, Linus and Claudia – add their greetings to Timothy. (II Timothy 4:19-21, NIV) Titus closes with personal references. Paul lets Titus know that he is sending Artimas and Tychicus to him, but we can only wonder about the purpose of their visit. He hopes to see Titus at Nicopolis and asks Titus to assist Apollos and Zenas. He sends further greetings from "everyone with me." (Titus 3:12&13; 15.) The Letter to Philemon is sent from Paul and Timothy to Aphia and Achippus, along with Philemon himself and "the church that meets in [his] home." It ends with greetings from Epaphras, Mark, Aristarchus, Demas and Luke." Several of these names appear in other Letters, leading to various theories as to possible and even likely connections.

At the very least, these greetings and messages reveal Paul's network of co-workers, a missionary fellowship engaged in mutual encouragement and practical, cooperative discipleship. This network, which in another time and place would be called a connexion, or connection, extended beyond any single congregation, locality, or region, joining this network to Paul and to each other. Their relationship continued over time and their purpose propelled them forward and outward in mission. The ties of prayer, encouragement, instruction, discipline, strategy and cooperation (including stewardship) bound them together and made their work possible and fruitful.

WORSHIP, FELLOWSHIP, RENEWAL

"The church is in need of perennial revival because of recurrent spiritual decline." (Earle E. Cairns. *An Endless Line of Splendor: Revivals and their Leaders from the Great Awakening to the Present.* Wheaton, IL: Tyndale, 1986, 19.) The form of revival may change with time and culture, but the fact of revival is necessary to reverse or upend decline, exhaustion, distraction, and opposition. The Church, including each local congregation and every Christian, needs to be renewed in faith directly by the Holy Spirit and indirectly as the Spirit works in the Church's life and tradition. Worship provides, or can provide, opportunities for both these pathways of inspiration in our lives. Worship reconnects us with God in prayer (including music as a form of prayer – "Let the message from Christ dwell among you richly as you teach and admonish one another with all wisdom through psalms, hymns and songs from the Spirit, singing to God with gratitude in your hearts." (Colossians 3:16, NIV; See Ephesians 5:19.) These references to Christian music continue the Old Testament emphasis on Psalms and build toward a vital, permanent part of worship in Methodism and the larger Church. Communion, Scripture and Biblically informed teaching, and fellowship, including the sharing of food, have been essential elements of worship from the beginning. Thus we can relate so easily to these four components of worship listed in Acts 2:42. The New Testament Letters play a central role in this renewal, since these Letters were read and heard during worship as a significant form of "the apostles' teaching."

The Books of Acts and Revelation include letters, or messages set forth as letters, with words of instruction, encouragement, warning, etc. Hebrews has come to us as a letter, once thought to be written by Paul. It is a valuable book of theological and spiritual instruction with parallel themes to those in the Letters we have considered. While we are here concerned with actual letters, there is obviously much to be gained from these other books, which also interact with the New Testament Letters proper. There are other documents from early Christian sources – many of them letters that can be useful in understanding their times and in some cases shed light on the Letters of the New Testament. One of these is I

Clement, or the Letter from the Church at Rome to the Church at Corinth, which tells us that, after a space of forty years, the Corinthian Church "has not made much progress toward maturity and stability; dissension and anarchy have manifested themselves within its ranks once more." (F.F. Bruce. *1 & 2 Corinthians*. Grand Rapids, MI: Eerdmans & London, UK: Marshall, Morgan, & Scott,1971, 256; Rick Brannan. I Clement, in *The Apostolic Fathers: A New Translation*. Bellingham, WA: Lexham, 2017, 11-55; See also in Brannan, Polycarp to the Philippians, 122-130.)

Chapter 3

The Baton of Faith in Wesley's Revival

"THE WAY TO HEAVEN" (Albert C. Outler, ed. The Work of John Wesley. Nashville, TN: Abingdon, 1984.)

GRACE AND PEACE

Letters were important throughout John Wesley's entire ministry, for keeping connected with preachers, but also with family, friends, fellow clergy, and public figures. His letters carry out many of the same purposes as those in the New Testament – teaching, encouragement, correction, coordination, and supervision of a constantly growing movement. Wesley served as the apostolic leader of Methodism, first in Britain and Ireland and then in North America.

The following chapters seek to follow the same outlines as those above. Dissimilarities in the kinds of material or conditions and circumstances may make it difficult to accomplish this in every case but the overwhelming similarities and parallels still justify the plan.

Because he came under so much fire from more conventional clergy, Wesley ventured into new methods, in which his preachers had to be oriented, trained, and supported. For example:

> Methodist preachers – ordained or lay – were generally denied the use of Anglican churches. They therefore followed the Wesleys' example and preached in any available house or public building and even in the open air. Their commission was to seek all who were lost, including those who failed to attend regular church services. Ultimately, field preaching became an integral part of Methodist practice by virtue of its spectacular success in drawing

large audiences and converting sinners to Christ and the Methodist cause. (Neil Semple. The Lord's Dominion: The History of Canadian Methodism. Montreal QC & Kingston, ON; London, UK & Buffalo, NY: 1996, 21&22.)

A central part of the baton of faith which Wesley received and handed on to us was his experience and theology of Holy Communion as a means of grace, an emphasis he shared with his brother Charles. This important topic will be explored in the final section of this chapter.

SCRIPTURE, STUDY

"Blessed Lord, who has caused all Holy Scriptures to be written for our learning, grant that we may in such wise hear them; read, mark, learn, and inwardly digest them; that by patience and comfort of thy holy word, we may embrace and ever hold fast the blessed hope of everlasting life, which thou hast given us in our Lord Jesus Christ. Amen. (Collect for the Second Sunday of Advent, *Book of Common Prayer (etc., 1662)*, Cambridge, UK: Cambridge University Press, 2004, 49; Adam Clarke. *Clavis Biblica (Etc.)*, generally known as *Preacher's Manual*, New-York, NY: T. Mason & G. Lane, 1837, 70.

John Wesley's well- known saying on "the way to heaven" clearly shows the place of Scripture in his theology of salvation:

> I have thought, I am a creature of a day, passing through life as an arrow through the air. I am a spirit come from God and returning to God; just hovering over the great gulf, till hence I am no more seen – I drop into an unchanging eternity! I want to know one thing, the way to heaven; how to land safe on that happy shore. God Himself has condescended to teach the way; for this end He came from heaven. He hath written it down in a book. Give me that book! At any price give me the Book of God! I have it. Here is knowledge enough for me. Let me be homo unius libri."(Albert C. Outler, ed. The Works of John Wesley. Nashville, TN: Abingdon, 1984, 1: 104 & 105.)

Wesley referred to himself as a "man of one book," which at first seems strange when we think of his Oxford education, his lifelong, extensive reading, and his prodigious writing and publishing.

Indeed, Wesley set an example for the movement he founded. Study of the Bible most of all, and of a wide range of other important literature, was something he did himself and expected his preachers to do.

HUMILITY

In the "Letter to a Preacher," in his *Preacher's Manual*, the early Methodist Bible scholar Adam Clarke strikes a note of humility before offering advice based on his own ministry: "...permit one who has learned experience on a variety of points connected with a preacher's usefulness, and at no ordinary expense, either (having had the pain to be often instructed through the medium of his own blunders) to give you the following advices." This is a remarkable statement from someone as accomplished as he.

Clarke includes in his "Letter to a Preacher" the expectations handed down from John Wesley for the conduct of Methodist preachers ("twelve rules of a helper"), some of which are still read in Annual Conferences and adapted for present day ministry. Two of the twelve rules deal with humility:

> Do not affect the gentleman. You have no more to do with this character than you do with that of a dancing master. A preacher of the gospel should be the Servant of all. (Clarke realized that this reference to "gentleman" might be misunderstood. Part of his clarification is from Wesley: "...do not pretend to be what you are not – to be nobly descended, when you are not- nor be above serving yourself or others, even in the meanest offices of life." A Methodist preacher who pretends in this way, "may be thought so by persons as empty as himself; but, in the sight of every man of good common sense, is a vain, conceited, empty ass; [and] is unworthy of the ministry....

> Be ashamed of nothing but sin: not of fetching wood or drawing water, if time permit: nor of cleaning your own shoes, nor those of your neighbor.

Clarke goes on to list some useful points of his own, including this one on humility: "Remember that admirable advice, given by the greatest preacher God ever made, to a young man just setting out in the work: 'The servant of God must not strive, but be gentle toward all; apt to teach; patient; in meekness instructing those who oppose themselves," (2 Timothy ii, 24, 25.)

He further echoes Paul's words, this time from I Corinthians:

> In this work, God often "chooses the foolish things of the world to confound the wise; and the weak things of the world to confound the things that are mighty; and the base things of the world, and the things that are despised, and the things that are not, hath he chosen to bring to naught the things that are, that no flesh might glory in his presence." (I Corinthians 1:27-29)

Again regarding humility, Clarke cautions preachers to "avoid the error of those who are continually finding fault with their congregations because more do not attend." This kind of chastising, which may be a temptation in any generation, is, for one thing,

> *unjust*, it being contrary both to reason and equity, to scold those who come, because others do not attend. I have known this conduct [to] scatter a congregation, but I never knew it [to] gather one. Indeed it savours too much of pride and self-love. It seems to say, "Why do you not come hear ME? Am I not a most excellent preacher? What a reproach is it to your understanding that you keep away when I am here!" Bring Christ with you, and preach his truth in the love thereof, and you will never be without a congregation, if God have any work for you to do in that place, (Adam Clarke, Clavis Biblica (etc.), generally known as Preacher's Manual. New-York, NY: T. Mason & G. Lane, 1837, 79-81; 83; 85.)

Humility was a part of Methodist memoirs, where it took the form of testimonies, the before and after stories of lay people and preachers alike. These became powerful statements of saving faith, designed to persuade outsiders and confirm believers. They would be especially important in strengthening the faith of believers at love feasts, which were central to the camp meeting experience. Biographies and autobiographies of prominent Methodists would be incomplete without such episodes. Testimonies fostered humility by putting everyone on the same footing as flawed human beings, saved by God's universally available grace.

An example from England is that of Richard Whatcoat, who would later become a Methodist Episcopal bishop. While his background lacked "the gross sins of the age," the spiritual contrast between earlier and later periods in his life was clear and serious.

> ...in July, 1758, when I was about twenty-one years and five month old, I attended Methodist preaching regularly, and soon found the word was made light and power to my soul; for when the preacher was describing the fall of man, I thought he spoke as if he had known every thing that was in my heart. When he described the nature of faith, I was conscious I had it not; and though I believed all the Scriptures to be of God, yet I had not the marks of a Christian believer: and I was convinced that if died in this state, wherein I then was, I should be miserable for ever. Yet I could not conceive how I, that had lived so sober a life, could be the chief of sinners. But this was not long; for I no sooner discovered the spirituality of the law, and the enmity that was in my heart against God, than I could heartily agree to it. The thoughts of death and judgment now struck me with terrible fear. I had a keen apprehension of the wrath of God, and of the fiery indignation due to sinners: so that could have wished myself to be annihilated, or to be the vilest creature, if I could but escape judgment.

After a bleak, dark time, when, he said, "I could find no rest, day or night, either for body or soul: so that life was a burden," there came a breakthrough. Whatcoat had been reading Scripture, in search of some indication of God's love and forgiveness.

> When I came to those words, "The Spirit itself beareth witness with our Spirit [sic], that we are the children of God," as I fixed my eyes upon them, in a moment, my darkness was removed, and the Spirit did bear witness with my Spirit [sic], that I was a child of God. In the same instant I was filled with unspeakable peace and joy in believing; all fear of death, judgment, and hell, suddenly vanished. Before this, I was kept awake in anguish and fear, so that I could not get an hour's sound sleep in a night. Now I wanted no sleep, being abundantly refreshed by contemplat-

ing the rich display of God's mercy, in adopting so unworthy a creature as me, to be an heir of the kingdom of heaven! (William Phoebus, ed. Memoirs of the Rev. Richard Whatcoat etc. New-York: Joseph Allen, 1828, 10.)

Methodist testimonies were as unique as the people who gave them, yet they followed a familiar pattern, similar to these familiar lines from John Newton's "Amazing Grace:"

I once was lost, but now I'm found,

Was blind, but now I see. (John Newton, "Amazing Grace," African Methodist Episcopal Zion Hymnal. Charlotte, NC: A.M.E. Zion Publishing House, 1957, #195, v. 1.

LOVE, THANKSGIVING

Wesley expressed his love and thanksgiving in the way he wrote his letters. Letters took valuable time out of an already daunting schedule, remembering the content of conversations in order to maintain dialog over time, often providing insights or questions; all of this requires time, study, and attention. Praying for one's coworkers and correspondents in some depth, was implied by the letters themselves. These he gave freely and generously helping cement his relationship with those he served and to preserve the living connection of his movement.

THE TWO WAYS

Wesley differed from many Protestant theologians and churches in that he was an Arminian, one who believed in people's need and ability (because of prevenient grace) to respond to God's offer of salvation. He wrote a great deal about the issues raised by Calvinism, particularly related to predestination. While there were elements of Calvin's thought, including his Eucharistic theology, with which Wesley would agree, he argued vigorously against this important doctrine in order to accurately convey the teaching of Scripture. Those teachings and that argumentation were essential to his ministry and became a central part of his enduring legacy. When Abel Stevens wrote his commemorative history, *The*

Centenary of American Methodism, he stressed Wesley's preaching of Christ's universal offer of salvation, by grace through faith and not through any human achievement.

> He taught the absolute sovereignty of God: that, like the potter with the clay, he can make some vessels for more, some for less honor; yet he also taught that, as wisdom and beneficence are essential attributes of the divine sovereignty, God neither would nor could (any more than the wise potter with his clay) make some for the gratification of a wanton caprice in their destruction, much less in their interminable anguish. (Abel Stevens. The Centenary of American Methodism (etc.). New York, NY: Carlton & Porter, 1866,128.)

ENCOURAGEMENT

Among john Wesley's words as he was dying were these, remembered and repeated to this day: "The best of all is, God is with us." (Davis W. Clarke, ed. *Death-bed Scenes; or, Dying With and Without Religion (etc)*. New York, NY: Carlton & Porter, 1851, 164.) This was a fitting closing for a life devoted to encouraging people to live the gospel in every aspect of life and to grow in God's transforming grace. He sought for each person the love God pours out upon us and the reflected love we are commanded to share as freely as God shares his love with us.

This is one of many ways Wesley takes to point to the goal of sanctification or Christian perfection, toward which he continually shepherded anyone under his pastoral influence, especially his preachers and societies. Wesley's emphasis on Christian perfection was a gift of hope that by grace we could become all we were created to be in Christ.

REAFFIRMING SHARED BELIEFS, VALUES, PURPOSE

The baton of faith was shared in Britain and Ireland, and then in North America through the growing number of Methodists and their outreaching worship, conveying the spiritual energy and gathering momentum of their movement.

> Methodism is essentially aggressive, and one of the laws of its being is progress. It had its origin in the University of Oxford, but the island of Great Britain could not long contain its energizing spirit. It passed over the Irish Channel....
>
> Having achieved miracles in England and Ireland, Methodism crossed the Atlantic and commenced its operations in America. (George Peck. Early Methodism within the Bounds of the Old Genesee Conference (etc.). New York, NY: Carlton & Porter, 1860,15.)

One example from Ireland came from the experience of Richard Whatcoat, from the Inniskillen [Enniskillen] circuit, to which he was assigned in 1771:

> "This circuit took us eight weeks to go through it; we commonly preached two or three times a day, besides meeting the societies and visiting the sick. By this year's labours and sufferings, my strength was exhausted; but what sweetened labour, and made affliction tolerable was a blessed revival, for we had nearly three hundred souls turned to the Lord this year; most of whom found "redemption in the blood of Christ, the forgiveness of sins." (William Phoebus, ed. Memoirs of the Rev. Richard Whatcoat (etc.). New-York: Joseph Allen, 1828, 14.)

Even though many circuits did not share the same dramatic growth as Inniskillin, this account is a sample of what could happen, and supports the picture of a circuit rider's heroically hard work and its often impressive results. Whatcoat would become the third bishop of the Methodist Episcopal Church and a leading advocate for camp meetings following the explosive events at Cane Ridge, Kentucky in 1801. (D. Gregory Van Dussen. *Camp Meetings: Power for the Road Ahead*. Lexington, KY: Emeth, 2022.

THE TWO WAYS

Wesley was well aware of the false or flawed teachings available in his time, as well as those faced by early Christianity (some of the latter appear, often in an early stage, in the New Testament. John Wesley's sermons were, like the early Christian writers, soaked in Scripture. Through them Wesley sought to present Christianity in a way that was clearly consistent with Scripture itself, and in a way that spoke the language of Scripture. He gathered relevant passages together to confirm and strengthen the main Scriptural point he was making, so that his readers and hearers were deluged with compelling arguments. One example is his presentation of "Scriptural Christianity," a form of which – "Scriptural holiness"– eventually became an overarching term for the distinctive purpose and program of his movement.

John Wesley

In his sermon, "Scriptural Christianity," Wesley contrasts those whose heart and life embody the Great Commandment and those whose attitudes and behavior have a different, indeed opposite source. The difference is seen in the presence or absence of God's love, which he calls, "the very essence" of a Christian's faith. Many of the Scriptures he brings to bear on the subject are from I John, for which love is a major theme. Other Scriptures, such as I Corinthians 13:4, appear also, but the preponderance of Quotations from John's First Letter set the tone for the sermon and indicate the special importance of this Letter in Wesley's thinking. Wesley not only pours out verse after verse to ground his theme; he also presents it in terms of the familiar two ways. The choice here is between faith that originates in God, nurtured in Christian worship (Acts 2:42) and the power of the Holy Spirit, and "those who lay unconcerned in darkness and in the shadow of death," a conflict between "the virtues" from God and the "reigning sins" facing God's judgement. (Albert C. Outler, ed. The Works of John Wesley. Nashville, TN: Abingdon, 1984, I:164-166.)

A second sermon, "The Way to the Kingdom," offers another, more subtle contrast. This one looks at two ways of worship; one is "outward," formal, and empty, the other is "the religion of the heart," consisting of "righteousness, and peace, and joy in the Holy Ghost." (Romans 14:17) This contrast is subtle because the outward observances or activities are not bad in themselves, but when they substitute for the religion of the heart, they reveal their limitations. Wesley specifically lists correct liturgical form, orthodox doctrine, and acts of charity. Each has, or can have, its own importance, but can become problematic when elevated to ultimacy. Any of them can become hollow when separated from a genuine, spiritual connection with God. This distinction would become extremely important in revival worship, and remains so today, though many other issues have certainly changed. Again Wesley sees the Great Commandment as the standard and goal for genuine faith. (John Wesley. "The Way to the Kingdom," in Albert C. Outler, ed. The Works of John Wesley. Nashville: Abingdon, 1984, I: 218-221.)

The most persistent, vexing issue in which "two ways" required a decisive response was the Calvinist doctrine of predestination. While Calvinism was, for Wesley, seriously flawed, he did not go so far as to banish Calvinists from the Christian fold altogether. He maintained a lifelong friendship and a shared commitment to revival with George Whitefield. He regarded parts of Calvinist theology as Biblically and theologically inaccurate and spiritually dangerous.

Actually, predestination represents a five-fold cluster of ideas with the convenient initials T.U.L.I.P. The first initial stands for the only one on which Wesleyan Arminians and Calvinists agree: total depravity. This idea acknowledges an insight from Jeremiah 17:9 that the human heart is "desperately corrupt," (Jeremiah 17:9, RSV) beyond any possibility of saving itself. But from there, Wesley moves on to prevenient grace, which God offers to meet our desperate need, opening up the opportunity for salvation. Yet Wesley places all hope for salvation in God; no hope in ourselves alone. We do not create our destiny, but we do choose whether to freely accept or reject the one he offers.

"U" stands for unconditional election. The choice as to who will be saved belongs to God alone; humans play no part (through character, works, or cooperation) in the decision. "L" is for limited atonement: Christ died not for all, but only for the elect. "I" stands for irresistible grace. Whether you are bound for heaven or left without hope, there is no appeal and no injustice. "P" is for the perseverance of the saints and is often called eternal security or "once saved, always saved." Wesley disagreed with these four, believing instead that election is for all who believe, that Jesus died for all; grace is freely and universally offered but never forced, and grace can be rejected or lost even after salvation (backsliding). (For an overview and background of Wesley's thinking on this issue, see Paul Wesley Chilcote & Kenneth J. Collins, eds. *The Works of John Wesley*. Nashville: Abingdon, 2013, 13: 203-226.) No doubt there were Calvinists who thought they were simply carrying forward Paul's teachings on the subject in Romans and elsewhere, but in his sermon "On Predestination," John Wesley sees them living out II Peter's (II Peter 3:15 &16) comment about misguided interpreters – even "many of the most learned men in the world" – having "'wrested'" these passages "'to their own destruction.'"

Wesley offers a helpful perspective on God's foreknowledge by exploring the difference between humanity's experience of sequential time and God's experience of "all things in one point of view, from everlasting to everlasting. As all time, with everything that exists therein, is present with him at once, so he sees at once whatever was, or is, or will be to the end of time." Yet this eternal knowledge in no way determines what will take place. We remain "*free*," for example, "in believing, or not believing...." (Albert Outler, ed. *The Works of John Wesley*. Nashville, TN: Abingdon, 1985, 2:415; 417.)

Wesley goes on to describe the importance of human accountability, which is destroyed as an implication of predestination as understood by Calvinists. For Wesley, instead of salvation by capricious fiat, "God decrees from everlasting to everlasting that all who believe in the Son of his love shall be conformed to his image, shall be saved from all inward and outward sin...." Providing for all who believe is very different from determining who will believe.

This saving belief is not automatic and is not empty or fruitless, but leads to a life of grace-empowered transformation to holiness, which then readies us for heaven. Holiness is not created arbitrarily. Instead it is produced in us by sanctifying grace, with our willing cooperation, so that we are "prepared for glory." (Albert Outler, ed. *The Works of John Wesley*. Nashville, TN: Abingdon, 1985, 2:418&419.)

His sermon goes on, methodically, patiently, and helpfully, explaining, clearing away debris, and offering hope in the place of fatalism.

> What is it then that we learn from this whole account? It is this and no more: (1), God knows all believers; (2), wills that they should be saved from sin; (3), to that end justifies them; (4), sanctifies; and (5), takes them to glory.
>
> O that men would praise the Lord for this goodness! And that they would be content with this plain account of it, and not endeavor to wade into those mysteries which are too deep for men to fathom! (Albert Outler, ed. 22. Nashville, TN: Abingdon, 1985, 2:421.)

Wesley's sermon on predestination is one place among many where he deals with this important issue. Arminianism, which leaves room for people's free response to grace, was part of his family's theological heritage and an inescapable part of the theological world in his day. "In the early years of the revival John Wesley was constantly watching for books that might aid him in his battle against the more harmful understandings of predestination." (Paul Wesley Chilcote & Kenneth J. Collins, eds. *The Works of John Wesley*. Nashville, TN: Abingdon, 2013, 13:227.) " He also wrote many controversial pieces to argue his point of view and clarify the exact meaning of the predestinarian position. The tone of these tends to be more aggressive than his sermon. In A Dialogue Between a Predestinarian and His Friend, he will not allow his Calvinist interlocutor to escape the harshness of his position. So the predestinarian is compelled to honestly state exactly what the Calvinist Confession claims: "God hath once for all appointed, by an eternal and unchangeable decree, to whom he would give salvation, and whom he would devote to destruction." Wesley shows, for example, the inevitable link between determinism, according to which everything that happens is caused by God, and the resulting necessity that God is responsible for sin. Finally, the predestinarian asks, "What then do you think of *absolute unconditional* election and reprobation?" Wesley answers, "I think it cannot be found in holy writ, and that it is a plant that bears dismal fruit. An instance of which we have in Calvin himself; who confesses that he procured the burning to death of Michael Servetus, a wise and holy man, purely for differing from him in opinions in matters of religion." In his sermon on "Free Grace" Wesley calls the doctrine of predestination "blasphemy." (Paul Wesley Chilcote & Kenneth J. Collins, eds. *The Works of John Wesley*. Nashville, TN: Abingdon, 2013, 233; 238.)

Wesley dealt with the issue of eternal security in his "Serious Thoughts upon the Perseverance of the Saints." Not surprisingly, he shows in various Scriptures how, sadly, it is all too possible for believers to fall away, and how urgently we are warned about that possibility. A key example is the vine and branches image and lesson in John 15.

> Those who are branches of the true vine, of whom Christ says, ["]I am thee vine, ye are the branches,["] may nevertheless so fall from God as to perish everlastingly.
>
> For thus saith our blessed Lord himself: "I am the true vine, and my Father is the husbandman."
>
> "Every branch in me that beareth not fruit he taketh it away."
>
> "I am the vine, ye are the branches. If a man abide not in me, he is cast forth as a branch and is withered, and men gather them and cast them inti the fire, and they are burned."
>
> Here we may observe,
>
> 1. The persons spoken of were in Christ, branches of the true vine;
> 2. Some of these branches "abide not" in Christ, but the Father "taketh them away";
> 3. The branches which "abide not" are "cast forth", cast out

from Christ and his Church;

4. They are not only "cast forth" but "withered", consequently never grafted in again; nay,

5. They are not only "cast forth" and "withered", but also "cast into the fire", and,

6. They "are burned." It is not possible for words more strongly to declare that even those who are now branches in the true vine may yet so fall as to perish everlastingly. (Paul Wesley Chilcote & Kenneth J. Collins, eds. The Works of John Wesley. Nashville, TN: Abingdon, 2013, 13:249&250.)

Wesley' friend and colleague John Fletcher contributed a great deal to the controversy with Calvinism. His theological writings were standard fare for the Methodist preachers in Britain, Ireland and North America. One of them was a response to a Calvinist author's *Vindication of the Decrees*, an attack on John Wesley's Arminianism. In his response, Fletcher counters, point for point, the Calvinist's claims and defends Wesley's position. Beginning with the hopeless place people are left in under predestination as understood by the Calvinists, "'the elect shall be saved, DO WHAT THEY WILL'" and "'the reprobate shall be damned, DO WHAT THEY CAN.' Mr. Wesley thinks the consequence is undeniably true. Mr. Toplady says that it is absolutely false." Fletcher takes it from there. (*The Works of the Rev. John Fletcher*. New-York, NY: John Wilson & Daniel Hitt, 1809, IV: 7. This edition, along with many others of Fletcher's books, was published on this continent. Fletcher was standard reading for preachers here.)

ENCOURAGEMENT

Whether in person or in writing, Wesley took opportunity to encourage his preachers and people. His letter to Jasper Winscom, written August 10, 1782 must have come as a welcome blessing: Winscom's ministry has not lived up to the Winscom's own expectation. Wesley wants to let the preacher know that he understands that this situation "is none of your fault" and closes on a priceless note of encouragement:

> Dear Jasper,
>
> That the work of God has not prospered in the Salisbury circuit for several years is none of your fault. I am persuaded you have his work at heart and will do all that is in your power to promote it. So will Mr. [John] Mason; so will the other preachers. Look for happy days!
>
> I am,
>
> Your affectionate brother,
>
> J. Wesley (Randy Maddox, ed. The Works of John Wesley. Nashville, TN: Abingdon, 2024, 30: 69.)

REAFFFIRMING SHARED BELIEFS, VALUES, PURPOSE

Wesley's sermons, tracts, magazine articles, and letters are filled with theological truth and spiritual wisdom. The structured activities all reinforce the movement's purpose and the application of Wesleyan beliefs and values, to the point where preachers and laity alike can discern and assess their progress in discipleship. To these we should add the importance of the hymns which poured into the societies from both Wesleys, particularly from Charles. The entire subsequent history of Methodism holds the singing of "Psalms, hymns and sacred songs" in the very highest regard. Clearly this is essential to our identity and culture. (Ephesians 5:19, NIV; *See* John R. Tyson. *Assist Me to Proclaim: The Life and Hymns of Charles Wesley*. Grand Rapids: Eerdmans, 2008.)

WARNINGS: FALSE TEACHINGS, LETHARGY

Wesley himself, and the movement he led, were conciliar and courteous to other Christians – surprisingly so for the time. But when confronted with a bellicose and unjust challenge, they were powerful apologists for Methodist doctrine and practice. The situation took on more a more aggressive tone when the challenge came from schools of thought they saw as beyond orthodoxy and undermining Christianity altogether. One such teaching was antinomianism.

Antinomianism literally opposes law in Christian life. It is a belief that Christians are saved by grace, not works, and are not obligated to obey God's commandments. At first this may come across as good Reformation theology, or liberation from legalism but there is something thoroughly unbiblical about its use. John Fletcher wrote against it and his view, which he shared with Wesley, prevailed across Methodism. (John Fletcher, *Checks to Antinomianism*. New York, NY: J. Soule & T. Mason, 1820.)

"Fletcher's Checks" was first published in England in 1788 and quickly gained a wide readership in North America. "Many have thereby been led from the mazes of a speculative and vain philosophy. And the intricacies of Calvinian subtleties, to a clear and satisfactory view of the plan of salvation as exhibited in the Holy Scriptures." (T. Spicer, ed. Introduction, *Beauties of Fletcher (etc.)*. New York: T. Mason & G. Lane, 1840, 3.)

In the New Testament church, a similar idea was used to undermine the mandate for holiness. If someone thinks they are free of restraints from the law, they are free to disregard any part of Jesus' teaching or the moral law embodied in the Ten Commandments. Some heretical groups mentioned in the New Testament tried to steer churches in this direction. Paul devotes part of Romans to this misinterpretation.

We are those who have died to sin; how can we sin any longer?

> For we know that our old self was crucified with him [Christ] so that the body ruled by sin might be done away with, that we should no longer be slaves to sin. ...

> Therefore do not let sin reign in your mortal body so that you obey its evil desires. Do not offer any part of yourself to sin as an instrument wickedness, but rather offer ... every part of yourself to him as an instrument of righteousness. For sin shall no longer be your master, because you are not under the law, but under grace. What then? Shall we sin because we are not under the law

but under grace? By no means! (Romans 6:2; 9; 12-15, NIV.)

Grace is what saves us, not to sin freely, but to be free from sin. James tells us: as the body without the spirit is dead, so faith without works is dead. Salvation is not a free pass to do what our selfish desires dictate, but the start of a radically new life of holiness. Conversion takes us somewhere, and that somewhere is very different from corrupt world sin has built.

Related to this is John's statement that God's love should be reflected in the way we live, so that "we know that we have come to know God if we keep his commands. Whoever says, 'I know him,' but does not do what he commands is a liar, and the truth is not in that person." (I John 1:4, NIV)

In Jude we read of "ungodly people, who pervert the grace of our God into a license for immorality...." (Jude v.4, NIV)

To these Scriptures, more could be added, but with this kind of Scriptural foundation, Wesley, Fletcher, and the North American preachers had necessary tools to deal with any antinomians who crossed their paths.

When the antinomians were Calvinists, the combined teaching became doubly insidious, since predestination requires nothing from its devotees, bringing us back to the place where salvation becomes a transaction for which the elect have no responsibility.

Wesley's ministry was a model of what is often called the "Puritan ethic." There was no room for laziness or the frittering away of precious time. He lived Paul's maxim from Ephesians, "Be very careful, then, how you live, not as unwise but as wise, making the most of every opportunity, because the days are evil." (Ephesians :15 &16, NIV) His approach is best summarized in two of his rules for preachers:

1 – Be diligent. Never be unemployed a moment. Never be triflingly employed. Never trifle away time. Neither spend any more time any place than is strictly necessary.

10 - Be punctual. Do everything exactly at the time. (seedbed.com/john-wesleys-12-rules-for-preachers)

"I HOPE TO SEE YOU SOON AND WE WILL TALK FACE TO FACE:" THE LIMITATION OF LETTERS

Wesley kept up a staggering pace writing letters and meeting with people on his constant travels. The expansion of his movement to North America stretched his ability to superintend in his accustomed way. Yet his exchanges with American and Canadian leaders continued to be important to senders and recipients alike His correspondence with Nova Scotia Superintendent William Black (below) includes some degree of frustration on Wesley's part because he could not always have a complete account of how the movement was faring. This was especially true in his dealing with Newfoundland. Of course, Wesley's death and changes in North American circumstances necessitated the degree of autonomy that followed. It became clear that leaders on the ground would have to take full responsibility here, just as Methodism in Britain and Ireland would need to develop in its own way. Even so, fellowship ties and cooperation would continue. Competition in Canada between the Methodist Episcopal Church and British Wesleyans would eventually end in the merger of those bodies.

PERSONAL MESSAGES

Wesley relied on letters sent and received to extend friendships and pastoral connections far beyond what he could achieve in person. In addition to those we have seen earlier, the following is another example, from December of 1756. In this case he counsels a woman on faithful discipleship while she is dealing with physical limitations.

To Dorothy Furly

> It is a happy thing if we can learn obedience by the things which we suffer. Weakness of body and heaviness of mind will, I trust, have this good effect upon you. The particular lesson which you have now to learn is to be faithful in (comparatively) little things, particularly in conversation. God hath given you a tongue. Why? That you may praise him therewith, that all your conversation may be, for the time to come, 'meet to minister grace to the hear-

ers'. Such conversation and private prayer exceedingly assist each other. By resolutely persisting (according to your little strength) In all works of piety and mercy, you are waiting on God in the old scriptural way. And therein he will come and save you. Do not think he is afar off. He is nigh that justifieth, and sanctifieth. Beware you do not thrust him away from you. Rather say,

My heart would now receive thee, Lord:
Come in, my Lord, come in!

Write as often, and as freely and fully as you please to
Your affectionate brother and servant,

J. Wesley (Ted A. Campbell, ed. The Works of John Wesley. Nashvillle, TN: Abingdon, 2015, 27:70&71.)

A shorter example is this letter to William Sagar, dated August 11,, 1782 and dealing with an entirely different matter:

My dear brother,

Certainly nothing can more effectively stop the work of God than the breaking in of Calvinism upon you. I hope your three preachers will calmly and diligently oppose it; although not so much by preaching as by visiting the people from house to house, dispersing the little tracts as it were with both hands.

Your affectionate brother,

J. Wesley (Randy L. Maddox, ed. The Works of John Wesley. Nashville,TN: Abingdon, 2024, 30: 69.)

WORSHIP, FELLOWSHIP, RENEWAL

Along with Scripture and preaching, at the heart of worship was the experience and theology of Holy Communion as a means of grace. This was so both for John and Charles Wesley, as evidenced in their Eucharistic hymns and their expectations for leaders and recruits in their movement. The meaning of Communion included the entire panorama of grace – prevenient, justifying, and sanctifying – all of which were and are conveyed into our lives in the celebration of the Lord's Supper. John's sermon on "The Duty of Constant Communion" places this sacrament in clear Biblical perspective and shows how seriously he took it as an essential part of our worship and growth in grace.

The text for this sermon is Jesus' command that we "Do this in remembrance of me."(Luke 22:19) Wesley connects disobedience with lack of appropriate self-interest in the common neglect of the sacrament in his day. Communion is both a mandate and a blessing, which is neglected at the believer's own peril. The reason for this neglect is often a misunderstanding of Paul's warning in I Corinthians about participating in the sacrament in an unworthy manner and by doing so inviting God's condemnation. Instead, Wesley wants to convince people of our need to avail ourselves of the sacrament's transforming grace as the remedy for the sin that makes us unworthy. Since this same misunderstanding is present today among those who question frequent celebration, his argument remains relevant.

Wesley says, "it is the duty of every Christian to receive the Lord's Supper as often as he can," not only because Jesus' command comes to us as "his dying words," but "because the benefits of doing it are so great...." These include the grace of forgiveness, "the present strengthening and refreshing of our souls," and the power to lead new lives. "As our bodies are strengthened by bread and wine, so are our souls by these tokens of the body and blood of Christ. This is the food for our souls: this gives strength to perform our duty, and leads us on to perfection." Therefore, "we must never turn our backs on the feast which our Lord has prepared for us." (John Wesley, "The Duty of Constant Communion," (Albert C. Outler, ed. *The Works of John Wesley*. Nashville, TN: Abingdon, 1986, III: 428 & 429.)

Again, the Eucharist is a means of grace, part of the way to heaven, because through it God changes us, making us ready for our heavenly destination. Thus he wrote, "The Lord's Supper [was] given for this very end: that through this means we may be assisted to attain those blessings which he [Jesus] hath prepared for us; that we may obtain holiness on earth and everlasting glory in heaven." From this foundation, Wesley systematically dismantles the most common objections and excuses he faced, concluding,

> If we consider the Lord's Supper as a command of Christ, no man can have any pretense to Christian piety who does not receive it (not once a month, 0but) as often as he can; secondly, that if we consider the institution of it as a mercy to ourselves, no man who does not receive it as often as he can has any pretense to Christian prudence; thirdly, that none of the objections usually made can be any excuse for that man who does not at every opportunity obey this command and accept this mercy. (John Wesley, "The Duty of Constant Communion," Albert C. Outler, ed. The Works of John Wesley. Nashville, TN: Abingdon, III: 432, 439.)

Another important source for Wesleyan Eucharistic theology comes to us in the hymns of John and Charles Wesley. Here we plummet the depths of their experience and reflection on this key area of their theology and spirituality in the context of worship and their teachings on the way of salvation.

One of Charles Wesley's Eucharistic hymns contrasts the constant Communion enjoyed by early Christians with the common practice of his own time. As he does this, he echoes key points from his brother's sermon:

> 1 Happy the saints of former days
> who first continued in the Word
> a simple lovely loving race,
> true followers of their Lamb-like Lord.
>
> 2 In holy fellowship they lived,
> nor would from the commandment move
> but every joyful day received
> the tokens of expiring love.
>
> 3 Not then above their Master wise,
> they simply in his paths remained,
> and called to mind his sacrifice
> with steadfast faith and love unfeigned.
>
> 11 Why is the faithful seed decreased,
> the life of God extinct and Dead?

> The daily sacrifice is ceased,
> and charity to heaven is fled.
>
> 27 Return, and with your servants sit,
>   Lord, of the sacramental feast,
>   and satiate us with heavenly meat,
>   and make the world your happy guest.

He then goes on in the same hymn, to give another, deeply spiritual expression of Eucharistic spirituality that takes us far beyond any tendency to bare memorialism:

> 4 From house to house they broke the bread
>   impregnated with life divine,
>   and drank the Spirit of their Head
>   transmitted in the sacred wine.

Another hymn clearly speaks of the spiritually rich banquet found at the Lord's table, and the role it plays in preparing us for our destiny in heaven:

> 1 Author of life divine,
>   who hast a table spread,
>   furnished with mystic wine
>   and everlasting bread,
>   preserve the life that thou hast given,
>   and feed, and train us up for heaven.
>
> 2 Our needy souls sustain
>   with fresh supplies of love,
>   till all your life we gain,
>   and all your fullness prove,
>   and strengthened by your perfect grace,
>   behold without a veil your face.

(S.T. Kimbrough, Jr. & Dean B. McIntyre, eds. A Theology of the Sacraments Interpreted by John and Charles Wesley. Eugene, OR: RESOURCE Publications, 2021, 27-29; 35.)

Along with other Protestants, including the Church of England, the Wesleys and their movement rejected the medieval doctrine of transubstantiation, but the Wesleys never limited their Eucharistic teaching or experience to the memorialism held by some Protestants, either. As with other areas of doctrine, they built upon the solid foundation of Scripture and the early Church, and these rich sources kept them rooted and renewable. In many ways, Methodism connects with Eastern Orthodoxy, especially in our Eucharistic spirituality. Like them, we believe in and cherish the real presence of Christ in the Eucharistic feast. Also like them, we accept a degree of mystery and a limit to precision when trying to define exactly how he is present.

However, we are also prone to a certain neglect in the actual place and priority the Lord's Supper holds in too many congregations. We need to hear the voices **of** our founders and their sources in Scripture and Tradition, and we need to learn from the Eucharistic experience of our ancestors, particularly our Wesleyan ancestors in the faith. For example, in her book on Wesleyan Eucharistic Spirituality, Lorna Khoo (following Paul S. Sanders and Gordon Wakefield and citing John Wesley's Journal) writes of staggering numbers of converts extending and responding to their revival experience by overwhelming English and Irish churches, where they were hoping to be served at the Lord's table. Wesley named several parishes where attendees numbered in the hundreds or even more than a thousand.[1] Some of these Methodists walked long distances, sometimes in unpleasant weather, to reach these churches, churches which in many cases were not accustomed to their own congregants showing great devotion to sacramental life. This was happening at a time of "laxity in eucharistic observance" was the norm across the Church of England generally. All of this testifies to the effectiveness of Wesley's sacramental instruction and example at a very early point in Methodist experience. (Lorna Khoo. *Wesleyan Eucharistic Spirituality*. Adelaide, Australia: ATF, 2005, 1-3.)

Wesley's approach to other churches and theologies was generally irenic and conciliar. He never intended to found a new church, but sought to call Christians of diverse backgrounds to a faith and life animated by the Holy Spirit. He was himself a priest of the Church of England, believing that church's theology to be sound, but he saw the possibility of Catholics and a variety of Protestant churches as very much capable of the same revitalized faith as his fellow Anglicans. His original intent was for Methodism to be a renewing force within the Church of England. As he reached out to the vast numbers of unchurched people and as members of other churches came within his influence, it became difficult to stay within the boundaries of his church. As we have seen, his encouragement of converts to attend parish churches flooded some of those churches with more people than they could handle. Eventually Methodism would need its own chapels. Later, first in North America and then in Britain, Methodism began its own denominations.

So Wesley's dealings with false teaching did not relate so much to other Christian denominations, but to schools of thought, often within the churches, that veered in directions which denied or subverted important Christian doctrines. In the case of his own Church of England, it was a matter of a church failing to uphold or live by its own tradition. He had considerable controversies with Calvinism and Roman Catholicism, where he found serious differences, but never wrote them off as without hope or as non-Christian. Instead, he looked for common ground, on which understanding and improved relations could be built. He was definitely not equivocal on matters of importance on which there were serious differences, but he was convinced that there was a core on which all open, well-meaning Christians could agree. His aim was for people from any church, operating in good faith, to look up and see. It was that heart of the faith by which Wesley wanted to Methodism to be known, beyond organization, culture, inherited prejudice, or misunderstanding. Pointing to this essence of faith, which he calls "primitive Christianity," Wesley writes, regarding Methodist and Catholics:

> Are we not thus far agreed? Let us thank God for this, and receive it as a fresh token of his love. But if God still loveth us, we also ought to love one another. We ought, without this endless jangling about opinions, the points wherein we differ stand aside: here are enough wherein we agree, enough to be the ground of every Christian temper and of every Christian action. ...
>
> In the name, then and in the strength of God, let us resolve, first, not to hurt one another; to do nothing unkind or unfriendly to

each other, nothing which we would not have done to ourselves. Rather let us endeavor after every instance of a kind, friendly and Christian behavior towards each other. ...

let us ... endeavor to help each other on whatever we agreed leads to the Kingdom. So far as we can, let us always rejoice to strengthen each other's hands in God. (Michael Hurley, ed. John Wesley's Letter to a Roman Catholic. London, UK, et al: Geoffrey Chapman; Belfast, UK: Epworth House & Nashville, TN: Abingdon, 1968, 55 & 56. This edition of Wesley's Letter was edited by a Jesuit priest, with Introductions by the President of the World Methodist Council and the President of the Vatican Secretariat for Christian Unity and published by Roman Catholic and Methodist publishers, shortly after the 1966 meeting of the World Methodist Conference.)

There will be much said about the role of small class meetings, especially as they developed in nineteenth-century North America. Class meetings nurtured in-depth fellowship as members grew in faith and practice together. These gatherings were crucial to Wesley's program. Many are saying that their restoration remains crucially important today. Often there are times when it is helpful and instructive to return to beginnings. Here we turn to Abel Stevens as he tells the story of the beginnings of the class meetings:

> At first, there was a practical need to fund "a more commodious edifice" for Methodist gatherings 'for spiritual meetings at Bristol.
>
> The debt incurred by this building rendered necessary *a plan of pecuniary contributions* among the worshipers who assembled in it. They agreed to pay a penny a week. They were divided into companies of twelve, one of whom, called the leader, was appointed to receive their pittances. At their weekly meetings, for the payment of this contribution, they found leisure for religious conversation and prayer. These companies, formed only for a local and temporary object, were afterward called *classes*, and the arrangement was incorporated into the permanent economy of Methodism. In this manner originated one of the most distinctive features of its system, the advantages of which are beyond estimation. The class-meeting has, more than any other means,

preserved the original purity and rigor of the denomination. It is the best school of experimental divinity that the world has seen in modern times. It has given a sociality of spirit and a disciplinary training to Methodism which have been characteristic of it, if not peculiar to it. (Abel Stevens. *The Centenary of American Methodism (etc.)*. New York: Carlton & Porter, 1866, 115 &116.)

Another characteristic part of Methodist worship and a further gift to the whole Church is its use of hymns, many of them written by the Wesley brothers, especially Charles, but including many others and contributing to the long tradition of evangelical music, from the singing at nineteenth-century camp meetings to the contemporary worship songs of today. As in the sharing of singing in the New Testament worship of Colossians and Ephesians, music remains an integral part of the entire ethos of Methodism (and the larger evangelical world), as well as its mechanism for handing on its faith and culture to new generations.

Chapter 4

The Baton of Faith Crosses the Atlantic

"LIGHT AND POWER TO MY SOUL"

(William Phoebus, ed. Memoirs of the Rev. Richard Whatcoat. New- York: Joseph Allen, 1828, 10.)

Among North America's earliest appointed ministerial leaders were Thomas Coke, Francis Asbury and Richard Whatcoat, all of whom would become bishops in the Methodist Episcopal Church, which they and others would organize in 1784. Whatcoat gives a brief account of the time when he, Coke, and Thomas Vasey were ordained by John Wesley and sent forth from Bristol to lead the movement in North America:

> September 1st, 1784, Rev. John Wesley, Thomas Coke, and James Creyton, Presbyters of the Church of England, formed a Presbytery, and ordained Richard Whatcoat and Thomas Vasey, Deacons. And on September 2d by the same hands &c. Richard Whatcoat and Thomas Vasey were ordained Elders, and Thomas Coke, L.L.D. was ordained Superintendent [Bishop], for the Church of God, under our care in North America. (William Phoebus, ed. Memoirs of the Rev. Richard Whatcoat (etc.). New-York, NY: Joseph Allen, 1828, 17&18. Whatcoat adds an extended note explaining the rationale for these ordinations.)

Wesley carefully implemented, under his own watchful supervision, a detailed plan for the Methodist movement on the islands of Britain and Ireland. From conferences at the larger end, to regional circuits with their local societies, to the smaller classes and bands, led by assistants, itinerant and local, he grew a disciplined body that brought salvation to countless individuals and renewal to church, communities, and society. At its heart was "Scriptural Christianity," not a new religion, but a restoration of the great tradition, deeply rooted in the Bible and the early Church, but also drawing from the Orthodox East, the Catholic West, and the Reformation, especially Wesley's own Anglican tradition. His aim was not only for that moment or those islands. Soon he would export the revival with its organizational infrastructure. He continued his personal direction and influence, as in the days of the apostles, in the form of letters and delegated leaders. (Rupert E. Davies, ed. *The Works of John Wesley*. Nashville, TN: Abingdon, 1989, 9:1-29.)

Whatcoat gives a similarly brief account of Asbury's ordinations – on three consecutive days - in conjunction with the Christmas Conference which established the Methodist Episcopal Church: "Twenty-fifth, Francis Asbury was ordained Deacon; 26th, he was ordained Elder, and on the 27th, Superintendent...."

The North American context would bring many changes to the culture, worship, and organization of Methodism. Wesley would live until 1791, and his death necessitated new leadership, especially in the newly independent States. The contrast between Bishops Coke and Asbury points to an urgency Asbury felt for the M.E. Church to be fully American, while Coke remained deeply committed to a kind of imperial Methodism. (John A. Vickers. *The Journals of Dr. Thomas Coke*. Nashville, TN: Kingswood, 2005, 11-13.) Wesley's antislavery position remained highly relevant on this continent, though his movement divided over slavery and racial injustice. Other issues brought further divisions. The frayed relationship of Canadian Methodists with those in the U.S. and their connection to the Wesleyan Church in Britain made for a distinctive history of division and merger from the experience in the states. The strong presence of German-American denominations within the Wesleyan family added another dimension, as did the frontier and the presence of indigenous Methodists. Worship tended to become less Anglican, although today there is a renewed appreciation for the Book of Common Prayer. Elements of the BCP remain in the liturgical resources of many Methodist denominations.

The combined force of all these changes and more has not made the essential, original purpose of Wesley's movement less relevant. Instead, there is a deep longing for the baton of faith at the heart of our Wesleyan identity.

GRACE AND PEACE

John Wesley maintained a strong pastoral connection with North American Methodists, through missionaries and letters, hoping to guide the movement, even through the rough waters of Revolution and Loyalism, when some in the colonies formed an independent nation, while others remained firmly British. (For an extended Methodist account of Loyalism in North America, see Egerton Ryerson. *Loyalists of America (etc.)*. New York, NY; Haskell House, 1970 (orig. 1880), 2 volumes.)

After a few decades of disciplined forward movement, Matthew Richey could write of "a new and glorious era in the history of Christianity," in which "Methodism, under the blessing of Almighty God," had produced a "moral revolution" which has not been surpassed in magnitude and rapidity since the days of the Apostles." These words of triumph may seem overblown today, but in their own time, they clearly expressed what had actually come about by the renewing energy poured out by the Holy Spirit, an outpouring of which many Methodists could see no end. (Matthew Richey. *A Memoir of the Late Rev. William Black (etc.)*. Halifax, NS: William Cunnabell, 1839, v & vi.)

Following Wesley's example and adapting it to the North American context, Francis Asbury developed a nearly ubiquitous presence across vast territories. This he did by traveling incessantly and writing letters to fill the inevitable gaps between visits. In this way Asbury set the trajectory for Methodism to go from a small fledgling network to the largest church in America. During Asbury's lifetime (he died in 1816) the Methodist Episcopal Church spanned much of the continent, (alongside British Wesleyans, with whom the M.E. Church in Canada eventually merged), linked North American Methodists from Canada to the

West Indies, and kept hIm connected with the parent church in England as well.

Not all the letters written by Asbury or other leaders were personal. Some were addressed to institutional officials, such as Asbury's correspondence with George Washington. Others dealt with matters of the Discipline, strategy, or relations with other churches. Many reported and encouraged inspiring evangelistic events like camp meetings.

In August of 1801, Asbury wrote to Thornton Fleming, presiding elder of the Ohio District. He begins by rejoicing in some good news Fleming has shared regarding the spiritual life of his district. "I am pleased to hear the glad tidings of great joy, that the wilderness and desert places are glad...." Asbury shares "pleasing hopes of a general revival" and mentions the success of one local gathering. Then he gives some advice concerning the need to keep sanctification front and center in his [Fleming's, and all the preachers'] messages:

First Methodist Meeting House, Ohio

> O, my brother, preach fully upon holiness in every sermon, where there is but one believer. I feel, seriously, that such multitudes of young converts have been born since the gospel came to the continent; and so few old people are changed, and so few old believers are sanctified. We must urge them to go on to possess the land.

To Stith Mead he wrote, in May of 1802, these words of caution concerning statistical reports from revivals: "We have great and gracious openings. I wish you to be very accurate in your accounts of the work of God and as concise, and yet let nothing of moment slip." In other words, tell the story as it actually happened, without exaggeration but with a reliable record of genuine progress.

He wrote again to Mead in 1807, giving him and us an overview snapshot of their rapidly growing movement:

> May the good will of him that dwelt with Moses in the bush (emblem of the Church and Charge) be with thee. According to this time it shall be said of our Jacob, and Israel, in America; what hath God wrought. ...
>
> Methodism began in Britain 1730. In the British Empire of Kingdoms and Islands, above 30 million of souls to operate amongst; the minutes of last year, number of members in Britain 150,974, the numbers of Methodists in the States and Canada 144,590. ...
>
> Number of preachers in the British 576, American 536. ...

[Regarding camp meetings and their effectiveness in reaching people beyond the reach of churches and even circuits,] "Do all you can by fair means to keep order in your meetings in the woods but we will not give up this ground."

Steadfast championing of camp meeting by Asbury and the other bishops contributed enormously to the spectacular growth of Methodism. Methodists wholeheartedly embraced these meetings, which became a major part of their ethos, including mentoring.

Returning to the subject of sanctification, with considerable exuberance, Asbury wrote to James Quinn in 1812:

> The God of all grace and wisdom, grant to us grace and wisdom, and eminently to rule in our Israel. ... Ye that make mention of the Lord, keep not silence. Move heaven with your prayers, and earth with your cries. Cry aloud, spare not, lift up your voice like a trumpet! Diligence, prudence, courage, perseverance. You will care for every circuit, every society, every preacher, every family, and every soul in your charge. You will be planning continually to extend and establish the Church of God in your section. You will be eyes, ears, mouth, and wisdom, from us to the people, and from the people to us. You will be in our stead to supply our absence.

Here we see also the way the bishops' presence could be enhanced by viewing the preachers as extensions of their ministry. In these samples from the hundreds of letters Asbury sent, there are elements of what we saw in the New Testament letters – elements needed in any church that thrives, and hands on the key to its thriving: grace, connection, love, wisdom, encouragement, integrity, sanctification, unrelenting evangelism (even through extraordinary means) and genuine pastoral concern. Asbury's commitment to Wesley's theology of sanctification connects both to the New Testament and to the revival of Holiness theology and practice in the late nineteenth-century. (J. Manning Potts, ed. In chief; Elmer T. Clark & Jacob S. Payton, eds. *The Journal and Letters of Francis Asbury*. London: Epworth; Nashville: Abingdon, 1958, III: 224; 239; 351; 370; 466.)

SCRIPTURE, STUDY

As with so many other circuit riders, William Black, known as "the Apostle of Methodism in the Maritimes," put his available time to good use by studying.

William Black

> He was a constant reader of Wesley's Journal and sermons. When he was travelling to the 1784 General Conference at Baltimore, he spent his time on the vessel in study, as he writes, "Most of my time since I came on board has been occupied in reading, chiefly Flavel's Treatise on the Soul, Littleton's Roman History and Knox's Essays. Lord let none of them prove improfitable!" For spiritual growth he was accustomed to read religious biography, which is an excellent study, and he found much comfort and food for serious reflection in the Lives of John Fletcher and Whitefield. But he was not forgetful of the benefits of the solid studies which are needful for the Chris-

tian minister, and he applied himself with splendid energy to the Latin and Greek languages and works of theology. ... his journal and letters show, that he was a student all his life. (John Maclean. William Black: The Apostle of Methodism in the Maritime Provinces of Canada. Halifax, NS: Methodist Book Room, 1907, 50&51.)

Black's emphasis on learning and growing as an integral part of his identity and work as a Wesleyan missionary was very much in line with the way John Wesley carried on his own ministry and his expectations for all the preachers. Wesley and Black wrote letters back and forth through the last years of Wesley's life. (Wesley died in 1791.)

> William Black poured out his heart to his venerable leader, who in turn gave him counsel in his difficulties, sent him books, and treated him as a son.... There would be a place for him at Kingswood School [which Black had been eager to attend] but he was not urged to actually attend, as Wesley laid [even] greater stress on piety than learning, such a brave and intrepid soul was William Black.
>
> It was natural that the intercourse should exact a strong and abiding influence upon the mind and heart of the missionary, who sent reports of the work, sought advice amid the difficulties which confounded him, and spoke of his spiritual yearnings with the familiarity of a little child with its parent. John Wesley became the model upon which William Black formed his habits and character, and he succeeded well, in a country with greater privations and more difficulties in travelling than in old England.

After a very different appointment to the West Indies, under Thomas Coke, Black returned to Canada to serve as "General Superintendent of the Maritime Provinces and Newfoundland." (John Maclean. *William Black: Apostle to the Maritime Provinces of Canada*. Halifax, NS: Methodist Book Room, 1907, 40-43.) Clearly the Atlantic Ocean and the differences between England and North America were no barriers to the culture of mentoring represented by Wesley and Black. Beyond that, the connection is clear between the Pastoral Letters (among others) of the New Testament and these two apostolic figures.

It is important to look at Wesley's part in this transatlantic correspondence, for its own sake, as well as indicating the nature and extent of his vast communication with the people called Methodists. To this end we will summarize several of Wesley's letters to William Black between 1783 and 1788. These, of course, make up only a tiny fraction of Wesley's total correspondence, and a partial view of all his letters to Black over a longer period. In these letters we will see many classic purposes of Christian letter writing carried forward.

In July, 1783, Wesley proclaims his own ambitious goal for this correspondence: "It is a rule with me to answer all the letters which I receive." He urges Black to overcome disappointment and hopes the books he has sent will be useful to Black as he wrestles with opposing preachers, Henry Alline in particular. He hopes Black will actively pursue fellowship with likeminded "German brethren."

In May of 1784, Wesley hopes Black will find "that some of the [Loyalist] emigrants from New York are really alive to God. And if so, they will be every way a valuable acquisition to the province where their lot is now cast. This may be one of the gracious designs of God's providence in bringing them from their native country."

Wesley responds to Black's concern about the influence of Calvinists in the Maritimes by doubting that anything short of his own demise will convince Alline of the truth. Finally, Wesley closes with two Pauline admonitions: "keep the unity of the Spirit through the bond of peace," and "Carry each other's burdens, and in this way you will fulfill the law of Christ." (Ephesians 4:3; Galatians 6:2, NIV.)

In October of 1784, Wesley hopes there can be "a close and more direct connexion between you of the north and the societies under Francis Asbury." Here we see the connectional nature of Methodism in principle and in practice. "Is it not more advisable that you should have a constant correspondence with each other and act by united counsels? Perhaps it is for want of this that so many have turned back." Then Wesley turns to his own connection with the work in the Maritimes: "I want a more particular account of the societies in Nova Scotia and Newfoundland. And I wish you would give me a full account of the manner wherein God hath dealt with you from the beginning." This request for a fuller account builds upon Wesley's earlier hope to actually meet with Black in England, a meeting which has not worked out.

Wesley wrote again to Black in November of 1785, encouraging him by recounting recent successes in Britain and Ireland, where "the work of God is continually increasing," and exhorting him, through "fasting and uninterrupted prayer" just as he (Wesley) is always praying, and so get beyond "all discouragement."

Wesley's letter of February, 1787 rejoices in recent news of the revival's prospering in Nova Scotia, and laments the hard times that have fallen upon the Methodists of Newfoundland, though partial or uncertain information makes Wesley's assessment of, and response to events in Newfoundland equally uncertain. While he has the best interests of all his people at heart, such remote work is only partly his to remedy and control. Clearly, Wesley valued this kind of supervisory, pastoral correspondence, especially when face to face conversation was difficult, rare, or impossible. This resembles not only the connections we see in the New Testament letters, but the connection felt among early Methodists across North America. "Connexion" describes the heart of our movement, not just its organizational skeleton.

In September of that same year, Wesley responds to a letter from Black, which had shared good news about the progress and promise of Black's ministry ("great things that he [God] hath done" with "still greater things than these") to be hoped for.

The bulk of this letter, however, is a fairly complete word of advice on how to respond to a recently arrived preacher from Scotland, whom Wesley assumes is a Calvinist, and to Calvinists generally. The issues at stake are important, but should not be confronted in a belligerent manner which may inadvertently discredit all parties involved. Regarding the Scottish preacher:

> I advise you and all our preachers never oppose him openly. You must use no weapons in opposing him but only those of truth and love. You must use wisdom: first, strongly to inculcate the doctrines which he denies, but without taking any notice of him

or seeming to know that anyone does deny them; secondly, to advise all our brethren (but not in public) never to hear him at the peril of their souls; and thirdly, narrowly to inquire whether anyone is staggered, and to set such a one right as sin as possible. Thus, by the assistance of God, even those that are lame will not be turned out of the way.

Wesley wants Black and other preachers to avoid being – and being seen as – contentious, hoping to keep temperatures down, yet at the same time dealing with the "miserable" preaching in a quiet, pastoral, and effective way. One might ask how universal this instruction was intended to be, in light of public and published controversy before and after this letter, but at least in this situation, and doubtless many others, this quieter way seemed the wiser course.

In March of 1788, Wesley again rejoiced at news of progress "in the glorious work in which you are called," encouraging Black "to use all diligence. For the work is great, the day is short, and lonely is the night wherein no man can work!"

Wesley comments on the news that Black now has a coworker: "for you may have many opportunities of strengthening each others [sic] hands in God." Here we see a solid principle for many kinds of collegial, cooperative ministry, one which will prove itself over and over again, even into the present day. Not long after this letter, it would be born out in the cooperative work of preachers in leading camp meetings. In a related matter, Wesley says, "I wish you would do all you possibly can for whom this is a challenge. (Randy Maddox, ed. *The Works of John Wesley*. Nashville, TN: Abingdon, 2024, 30 (Letters, 1783-1788, 156&157; 232&233; 279&280; 402&403; 540&541; 601&602; 666&667; Paul Wesley Chilcote & Kenneth J. Collins, eds. *The Works of John Wesley*. Nashville, TN: Abingdon, 2011, 13: 201-570.)

Following the principles and practice of John Wesley, Methodist preachers in Britain, Ireland, and North America saw immersion in Scripture and related study as foundational to their ministry. Richard Whatcoat's Memoirs include a detail from his ocean passage to America, describing the opportunity taken by himself and some fellow travelers to worship and study on their

1784 voyage: "The captain and sailors behaved with great civility. We had prayers morning and evening, and preaching twice on the Sabbath day. The evenings we spent chiefly in reading over the preachers' lives, the saint's rest, and other books of divinity." Here we have a picture of the baton making its way across the Atlantic. Surely this was consistent with his experience when he shared a circuit with the great scholar Adam Clarke the year before. (William Phoebus, ed. Memoirs of the Rev. Richard Whatcoat (etc.). New-York: Joseph Allen, 1828, 19&16.)

Adam Clarke was an early British Methodist Bible scholar, who wrote what became a standard *Preacher's Manual*, to provide Methodist ministers an overview and outline of the Bible and Biblical theology. This brief *Manual*, together with his massive six-volume *Commentary*, were published and reprinted for the Methodist movement in North America, giving Methodist preachers and students a solid foundation for understanding and preaching the word. (Adam Clarke. *Clavis Biblica (Etc.)*, generally known as *Preacher's Manual*. New-York: T. Mason & G. Lane 1837; *The Holy Bible, Containing the Old and New Testaments ... Commentary and Critical Notes (etc.)*. New-York: B. Waugh & T. Mason, 1833.)

Once the priority of Scripture is recognized, there remains a place for other kinds of study. Adam Clarke wrote:" But while you read the Bible as the revelation of God, and the fountain of divine knowledge, don't let your reading *end* there. I said before, read much; but take care that all your reading be directed to the increase of your knowledge and experience in the things of God." (Adam Clarke. *Clavis Biblica (etc,)*, generally known as *Preacher's Manual*. New York, NY: T. Mason & G. Lane, 1837, 117) Clarke moves from Scripture as focus and foundation, to the relevance and usefulness of other books. Among them are those that enhance one's ability to know the background and application of Scripture. Clarke's *Preacher's Manual* orients his readers to each book in the Bible. The information he provides is brief, but helpful; his *Commentary* is extensive and detailed, suited for more thorough and advanced scholarship. An example of the former is his introduction to I John:

The writer of these three epistles [the three letters of John] is the

> same as John the evangelist, of whose history we have already had a sketch in speaking of his gospel. This epistle appears to have been written before the destruction of Jerusalem, and probably A.D. 68 or 69.
>
> The design of this epistle is to inculcate the doctrine of holiness of heart and life springing from love to God and man. Indeed this love seems to be his text, and he has written the whole epistle on this text. His own soul was filled with this heavenly fire; and it shone on and warmed all around. (Adam Clarke. Clavis Biblica (etc.), generally known as Preacher's Manual. New-York: T. Mason & G. Lane, 1837, 48&49.)

Clarke's Manual covers ideas and advice on almost every subject and situation a preacher is likely to encounter or consider. While each is well worth our attention, what is more to the point is that he cared enough to write so extensively for the benefit of other, generally younger preachers. This genre, along with biographies, memoirs, journals, and letters resulted in a formidable contribution to the culture of mentoring in early North American Methodism, which in turn formed a resilient movement quite capable of passing the baton of faith to new generations.

Methodism's commitment to learning and the distribution of Christian literature was manifest in the early establishment of publishing houses, such as The Methodist Publishing House (Methodist Episcopal) in 1789, followed by many others as the church fragmented. Even with this proliferation and the passing of so much time, these efforts express a lasting purpose, though many would question how well its original mandate has fared more recently.

> Since its beginning, The Methodist Publishing House has been dedicated to "the advancement of the cause of Christianity through the printed word." In this dedication, it has furthered the attitude of John Wesley, the founder of Methodism, who constantly urged his ministers and other followers to read and study in order to lift their lives, their minds, and their spirits to higher levels. Mr. Wesley believed that a church adhering closely to good written material was on solid ground. To this end not only did he develop proficiency as a writer and editor, but also he developed

a highly effective procedure for putting books into the hands of his people. (James Penn Pilkington. The Methodist Publishing House: A History. Nashville, TN & New York, NY: Abingdon, 1968, 1: vii.)

Typical of the place of Scripture and other study among early North American preachers was the ministry of Valentine Cook. Cook was one of the few who studied at the ill-fated Cokesbury College.

> The habits which he formed during his connection with Cokesbury College were never abandoned. He continued to prosecute his literary, scientific, and theological studies, amid all the changes and vicissitudes to which he was subjected throughout the whole period of his subsequent life.

In considering this, it is important to remember that,

> The preaching of the gospel, as the accomplishment of human salvation, was his one great work. However he may have been employed, whether at the handles of his plow, in the schoolroom, workshop, or presiding over the interests of a college, the winning of souls to Christ by the proclamation of his truth was the all-absorbing theme of his meditations – the great cardinal object to which his thoughts and efforts were constantly directed.

At the center and foundation of life and ministry was Cook's abiding devotion to Scripture.

> The Bible was his constant companion, at home and abroad, in public and in private. Other books he read as opportunity served and occasion required, but the Bible he read every day. Whether found in his private study, the schoolroom, the field, or the forest, he always had the precious volume at command. (Edward Stevenson. Sketch of the Rev. Valentine Cook (etc.). Nashville, TN: Published for the Author, by J.B. McFerrin, Agent, 1858, 20; 23&34; 26.).

Whether a preacher in our tradition began, like Valentine Cook, with a strong academic foundation, or like those whose early ambition was simply to gain the ability read the Bible with profit to themselves and perhaps a class or congregation, as different as were their starting places, their trajectories were much the same.

HUMILITY

Humility was expressed through testimony, as in a letter by William Black to John Wesley, in which he reflected at length on his experience of conversion. In this letter, Black recounts a pattern very much like that which Paul expresses in Romans 7:21-25:

> I sin, and grieve; and then I sin again. Alas! What will such repentance avail. I must be holy or I cannot be happy.

> My sins were set in battle array before me. I saw myself wretched, miserable, helpless and undone. I went about from day to day, hanging my head like a bulrush, the tears frequently streaming down my face in abundance.... I thought, surely I am one of the vilest wretches on earth.

Of course, Black did not remain in such a state forever. For some time, he "felt an awful sense of God, and of my lost condition without hope from heaven." All that would change, to be replaced by forgiveness, "a sweet peace and gladness," but he would never forget or deny the pit from which God saved him. (Matthew Richey. *A Memoir of the Late Rev. William Black (etc.)*. Halifax, NS: William Cunnabell, 1839, 25&26.)

This quality of humility is referred to favorably and often in every branch of Methodism, across the continent. A later example is Bishop Walter Hawkins (British Methodist Episcopal), of whom it was said, "His self-denial, humility, and Christian character are known throughout the Province of Ontario." (S.J. Celestine Edwards. *From Slavery to a Bishopric (etc.)*. London, UK: John Kensit, 1891, 154.)

LOVE, THANKSGIVING

Asbury continued an ambitious correspondence, prayed often for the preachers and their appointments, and for the work to which they had all given their lives to prosper.

A letter Asbury wrote "to the most loving and best beloved, the servants of God in Taunton, [VA]" in 1790 gives us a window to his motivation and hope for the churches. Part of the letter reads,

> Most dear and tender friends:
>
> Whose I am, and under God I desire to serve; to build you up in holiness and comfort hath been through grace my great ambition. This is that which I labor for; this is what I suffer for; and in short, the end of my applications to you, and to GOD for you. How do your souls prosper? Are they in a thriving case? What progress do you make sanctification? ... go on in the strength of Christ, and give diligence to the full assurance of hope to the end." (J. Manning Potts, et al, eds. The Journal and Letters of Francis Asbury. London, UK: Epworth & Nashville, TN: Abingdon, 1958, III:90-92

THE TWO WAYS

Bishops in the Evangelical Church served for limited terms, yet the impress of their character upon the churches and communities they served was often formidable and lasting. One of these was Joseph Long, who articulated at length his denomination's love of learning and commitment to educational ministry. His biographer put it this way:

> We have before us a massive intellect and a mighty moral stature, struggling like a Hercules through years of adversity, and amid great responsibilities, yet all the time hampered by a feeble body, and almost constantly battling with the morbid conditions of temper and thought thus superinduced. ...

Joseph Long

Bishop Long was a staunch friend and advocate of education.

When, in 1847, Rev. John Dreisbach came forward with a proposition in General Conference to establish a "Seminary for General Sciences in the Evangelical Association," Bishop Long, who had originally drawn up the resolution, now heartily seconded this motion, and conference adopted it unanimously. ...

In 1855 the Ohio Conference resolved to purchase a seminary located at Greensburg, Ohio. This school was carried on with some success until the disturbances of the Civil War made inroads upon it.

The seminary was one example of Long's interest in education, which included the "hitherto ... too much overlooked" area of "the Instruction of the Youth in the Evangelical Association." (R. Yeakel. *Bishop Joseph Long, The Peerless Preacher of The Evangelical Association.* Cleveland, OH: Thomas & Matill, 1897, 132&133.)

ENCOURAGEMENT

Asbury wrote to encourage people to begin, continue, and complete important ministries. Letters *to* the bishop gave preachers opportunities to express frustration or celebrate victories, perhaps hoping that he would offer help, but mainly seeking reassurance from someone who would offer understanding and a word of encouragement. In one of these, (written January, 1810) he writes to the well-known circuit preacher Jacob Gruber.

My dear Jacob:

God be gracious to thee my son, the presiding elders of our Israel are always on my mind, frequently named by me, before the Lord, always twice, if not thrice a day. ...

I have felt a great concern for the lost sheep of the house of Germany, we have only you two boys, [Gruber and Henry Boehm] that

can germanize, one with me, you will expect that the superintendency [M.E. bishops] would be unwise to remove you from one field and not put you with a larger if possible to meet and serve your father's countrymen. Prepare, prepare my son, be always ready for every call of God and your guides. I lament the want of pure practical religion, family and private prayer, and fasting, reading the scriptures, teaching , instructing the children. Our presiding elders should lecture the people closely in quarterly lovefeast, about class meetings, dress, and many Christian duties.

The letter goes on to Asbury's concerns about traveling preachers "locating," ["leaving the work"], a move often necessitated by financial hardship, not to be characterized as abandoning ministry. He also describes his recent itinerary: "riding at the rate of 10,000 miles a year," leading eight annual conferences, "preaching 200 sermons, writing 100 letters." While this letter rambles a bit, it shows how his ministry functioned. It also reveals the fact that exhaustion and frustration were sometimes the lot of preachers at every level of the church. (J. Manning Potts, et al, eds. *The Journal and Letters of Francis Asbury*. London: Epworth & Nashville, TN: Abingdon, 1958, III:424 & 425.

(In 1810), he wrote to a woman named Mary, a preacher's wife, about the responsibilities she was facing:

> Grace and peace be multiplied to you and family and all the sisterhood that labor with those who labor in the word and doctrine. It was impossible for you to count the cost of being a wife and mother and a traveler. Great the care and burden you must bear but it will daily increase as your family groweth up and you will become weak. Oh, my sister, be careful of the morning, noon and evening, private moments. Speak to all the sisters, aged and young, rich and poor. Pray with them. Preach to them powerfully in companies. Do a good part in these works of God. My time is short. Old Moses has but one war and a few months to be in the wilderness till forty. (Asbury is referring to almost forty years of ministry) ... we are all mortal, let us haste to meet our God, our Christ, our Kingdom, our crown of glory, our rest from suffering and pain. I am making ready, so are you Mary I hope, now in Jesus, farewell and prosper. I am sincerely, your father, brother, servant, friend for Jesus sake.
>
> F. Asbury

(J. Manning Potts, et al., eds. The Journal and Letters of Francis Asbury. London, UK: Epworth & Nashville, TN: Abingdon, 1958, III: 431.)

REAFFIRMING SHARED BELIEFS, VALUES, PURPOSE

Asbury – like most Methodists, had an open, hopeful attitude as he looked to the future, always depending on the faithfulness and unity of Methodists to their original purpose, to their "Doctrine and Discipline:" He wrote in a general letter, on behalf of the Virginia Conference, directed "to all their official Brethren, local preachers, class leaders, and stewards, in their Quarterly Meeting Conferences in the Districts and Circuits of their charge."

> To conclude, such fields are opening, so many preachers to preach, and so many people to pray, and such multitudes to be converted, what shall we see in twenty years to come, if the travelling and local Preachers are united, preaching the same Doctrine, approving and enforcing the same Discipline, and shall seek by every lawful means, Ministerial and among themselves, and among all Christians and Societies. Thus living and working as dear Children, what will not a good and gracious God do for us?

WARNINGS: FALSE TEACHING, LETHARGY

Like Wesley, Asbury was constantly on the move, keeping the overall picture in view, even as he attended to individuals and communities. He expected a great deal from the preachers he supervised. To the challenging life of any minister was added the special hardship of life on the Appalachian frontier. No one familiar with that frontier would seek such an appointment oblivious the dangers involved.

"I HOPE TO SEE YOU SOON, AND WE WILL TALK FACE TO FACE" THE VALUE AND THE LIMITATIONS OF LETTERS

Asbury's letters reflect an acceptance of the distances involved and the sacrifices required of himself and his constantly moving preachers and presiding elders. They enabled him to carry on the church's business in far flung local situations, while at the same time attending to the needs he saw close at hand.

PERSONAL MESSAGES:

In a letter to Methodist preacher Daniel Hitt, Asbury wrote this compassionate letter (in 1803) to one he had heard was seriously ill. "Your brother says you are much weakened and dejected; as such I fear to take you into the wilderness and to leave you there. You are now in a healthy country, and among your friends; and it is there 'I wish you to stay." (J. Manning Potts, et al, eds. The Journal and Letters of Francis Asbury. London, UK: Epworth, 3: 271.)

WORSHIP, FELLOWSHIP, RENEWAL

Bishop Whatcoat recorded the fellowship he experienced with other key leaders, on his momentous journey to the great Christmas Conference of 1784. First, he mentions time spent with one of the other preachers: "I met with Michael Ellis, to whom I gave an account of our mission: he was greatly pleased: he is a member of Conference: we were greatly comforted together; we preached at several places, and met class...." Not long after this, he writes, "I preached in Hunt's Chapel, and rode to Mr. Henry Gough's; spent the evening with Dr. Coke, Mr. Asbury, and brother Vasey, in great peace." (William Phoebus, ed. *Memoir of the Rev. Richard Whatcoat (etc.)* New-York, NY: Joseph Allen, 1828, 21. Gough was a well-to-do Methodist lay person in Maryland, who welcomed preachers traveling in the area.) From the start of the movement in North America, an important part of life in the ministry were these times on the road, or gathered for conference, or serving together at a quarterly or camp meeting. Whether planning, sharing stories, praying, or studying together, such times forged and built a strong bond of common purpose and camaraderie. This bond was not limited to preachers, but was powerfully at work among them due to common experience, shared calling, and shared sacrifice. Often Whatcoat's memoirs refer to occasions of worship as he traveled, and these references describe them as times of inspiration, encouragement, and spiritual refreshment. Though his ministry in America began just prior to the earliest camp meetings, his experiences at quarterly conference were quite similar and followed the same pattern of radical encounter with God. This was his hope for the road ahead. He wrote on January 2, 1785, "May the good Lord follow our endeavours with a never ceasing shower of heart-reviving love."

Richard Whatcoat   Thomas Coke

For the next few months, he found the people he met, "ripe for the Gospel: preaching almost every day, sometimes twice a day, with the administering of the ordinances of Baptism and the Lord's Supper, kept me in full employ." At one quarterly meeting in 1789, "the Lord came in power at our Sacrament; the cries of the mourners, and the ecstasies of believers were such, that the preacher's voice could scarcely be heard, for the space of three hours: many were added to the number of true believers." At another quarterly meeting, "the power of the Lord was present, to wound and to heal." At another, "the power of the Lord came down at our love feast. The house was filled with members of our societies, and great numbers of people were on the outside; the doors and windows were thrown open, and some throned in at the latter. Such times my eyes never beheld before." In a series of quarterly meetings, "The power of the Lord spread from circuit to circuit." That kind of "spread" would typify many revivals in the century and more ahead. At one point, Whatcoat looked back over six thousand miles and more than fifteen months of travel with Bishop Asbury, through Appalachia, during which, "Most days we have had a congregation to preach to." Such a brutal itinerary was made possible and rewarding by the power and spiritual refreshment of the Lord, and the camaraderie of colleagues and others who shared their common purpose.

Whatcoat describes the quarterly meetings he took part in while appointed to his Delmarva Peninsula district 1794-1796):

> We had large congregations, and many blessed revivals in different parts of the district. Our quarterly meetings were generally comfortable, lively, and profitable. Some appeared extraordinary; while souls were suddenly struck with convictions, and fell to the ground, and roaring out for the disquietness [sic] of their souls, or as though almost dead, and after a while start up and praise God, as though heaven were come into their souls: others were as much concerned for a clean heart, and as fully delivered. I had to attend forty-eight quarterly meetings, in the space of twelve months, while on this district.

One can only imagine the conversations when Whatcoat rode to an annual conference with Bishops Asbury and Coke, or when Jesse Lee and William Mc Kendree joined him on their way to another annual conference together after such a year. At the General Conference of 1800, Whatcoat "was elected and ordained to the Episcopal office." It is important to remember that in an earlier day, conferences, including General Conference, were times for profound worship and even revival. Regarding the general conference that year, Whatcoat noted, "We had a most blessed time and much preaching, fervent prayers, and strong exhortations through the city, while the high praises of a gracious God reverberated from street to street, and from house to house, which greatly alarmed the citizens. "It was thought that not less than two hundred were converted during the sitting of our Conference. (William Phoebus, (ed..). *Memoirs of the Rev. Richard Whatcoat (etc.).* New-York: Joseph Allen, 1828, 23-25; 27-30.)

Chapter 5

The Baton of Faith Reaches North America

"...the most important work in the universe."

(Adam Clarke. Clavis Biblica (etc.), generally known as Preacher's Manual, New-York, NY: T. Mason & G. Lane, 1837, 75.)

Barbara Heck

Philip Embury

When Wesley's first emissaries came to shore on this side of the Atlantic, they brought with them the motivation, momentum, experience, and wisdom already accumulated on the other side. They entered a work already begun by Irish lay evangelists in New York and Maryland, now carried into Canada by Loyalist Methodists, some with familiar names like Embury and Heck. One of Wesley's British preachers, twenty-six year old Francis Asbury, responded to John Wesley's appeal for volunteers to help the fledgling Methodist movement. This was in 1771, at a conference in Bristol. Asbury's leadership on this continent was so effective, and so appreciated by Methodists here, that he was chosen by Wesley and elected by the North American preachers, to be one of two bishops (the other being Thomas Coke, whom Wesley had named previously) of the newly formed Methodist Episcopal Church in 1784.Through the lingering differences left over from the Revolution and subsequent Loyalist migration north, soon to be fanned into renewed flames with the border war of 1812, the Methodist Episcopal Church began its work as one organization. For decades preachers like Nathan Bangs and Henry Ryan rode circuits on both sides of the border. The British Wesleyans also sent and organized preachers for Canada. Eventually the . The M.E. Churches in the States and Canada became autonomous. Later in the nineteenth century, the Canadian M.E. Church merged with the Wesleyans, Primitive Methodists, and Bible Christians to form the Methodist Church. Other denominations in the Wesleyan family also established themselves in Canada. These included the African Methodist Episcopal Church, the Free Methodist Church, and the United Brethren in Christ. The British M.E. Church served escaped former slaves and their families who had come to Canada by way of the underground railroad.

The M.E. Church in the United States divided several times over organization and authority, slavery and racism, and/or consistency with the movement's original theology, values, and purpose – or a combination of these. Black denominations – the African Methodist Episcopal, A.M.E. Zion, and later the Christian M.E. Churches - formed because the parent bodies failed to live up to their founder's antislavery and egalitarian principles, which were also upheld in the early M.E. Disciplines. The short-lived Republican Methodist Church and the Methodist Protestant Church left over issues of authority and structure. The Wesleyan Methodist and Free Methodist Churches were abolitionists, along with other concerns.

GRACE AND PEACE

Asbury led the M.E. Church here much as Wesley had led his movement.

> Asbury was called a dictator, and in a sense the charge was not wholly unfounded ...
>
> But if he was a dictator, he exercised a benevolent dictatorship. He loved his preachers next to God. He accepted the same small salary, endured the same hardships, lived the same life, and traveled more than any of them. He asked nothing of them that he did not impose on himself. (Elmer & T. Clark, Introduction. J. Manning Potts, et al, eds Journal and Letters of Francis Asbury. London, UK: Epworth & Nashville, TN: Abingdon, 1958, I:xiv.

Like Wesley, Asbury held the connection together in person and by letter, and also like Wesley, he was a master organizer.

His letters might begin like those of the New Testament. One he sent to George Roberts 1802 began with "may grace and peace attend you," and went on to commiserate with his recipient: "in your critical and dangerous situation."

Later that year he began a letter to Thornton Fleming in a similar way:

May grace and peace attend you and yours," before rejoicing in news from the frontier:

> The God of all grace hath manifested Himself gloriously. In our Western Conference we have had in this year upwards of 3,000, and our Southern Conference will be little short of that number, from the present appearances: and I calculate, if the Lord is with us and we are with Him, we shall have general and yearly increase of 21,000 in the seven conferences.
>
> The campmeetings [sic] are as extraordinary in North and South Carolina, and Georgia, as they have been in Cumberland and Kentucky; hundreds have fallen, and many have been soundly converted.

Nothing in the way of opposition would dissuade him from his commitment to this extraordinary means of grace as God's work. "It would not be the work of God if there were not some opposition; but is not worth our notice to stand to parley with the enemies of the work."

Asbury's correspondence also enabled him and other leaders to send and receive news during times when illness, or troubles of any kind, cried out for compassion, encouragement, and the sharing of ideas, as well as for conveying practical assistance where it was needed and available. For example, in January of 1804, Asbury wrote:

> To the Treasurer of the Fund, chartered in its State of Pennsylvania for the support of its supernumerary [beyond the number actually serving] and superannuated [retired] preachers, and its orders of preachers, etc., & of its Methodist Episcopal Church in the United States of America.
>
> Pay on sight to the Revd. Ezekiel Cooper, Elder of its Methodist Church aforesaid one hundred dollars on account of its Annual Southern Conference of its said church sitting in Augusta aforesaid, this day and year above written.
>
> Francis Asbury Thomas Coke [J. Manning Potts. et al., eds. The Journal and Letters of Francis Asbury. London, UK: Epworth & Nashville, TN, 1958, III: 247; 251; 273

SCRIPTURE, STUDY

Education was a key concern of North American Methodism from the outset. "one of the first acts of the newly formed Methodist Episcopal Church was to provide for the beginning of Cokesbury College." Shortly after the Christmas Conference, on January 5, 1785, Asbury sent out a letter announcing its purpose, "education and board of the sons of the elders and preachers of the Methodist Church, poor orphans, and the sons of the subscribers and of other friends." The new school,

> is intended for the benefit of our young men who are called to preach, that they may receive a measure of that improvement which is highly expedient as a preparation for public service. A teacher of the languages ... will be provided, as also an English master to teach with the utmost propriety both to read and speak the English language; nor shall any other branch of literature be

omitted which may be thought necessary for any of the students. Above all, special care shall be taken that due attention be paid to the religion and morals of the children....

The college shall be under the presidentship of the Superintendents of the Church for the time being.... (J. Manning Potts, et al., eds. The Journal and Letters of Francis Asbury. London: Epworth & Nashville: Abingdon, 1958,III:45.)

Somehow," for the time being," Coke and Asbury were to oversee this project, along with their other responsibilities! The college opened later that year and lasted until fire destroyed it in 1795. Although its life was cut short and it was never finally rebuilt, (though there was one short-lived effort to rebuild), this first Methodist college in the world shows how important education was right from the start.

Of continuing and growing importance to nineteenth-century Methodism was the establishment of many institutions of higher education across the continent. Those who founded, led, and supported these schools sought to shape the character of their students – especially those bound for careers in ministry, the churches, and the transformation of their societies. Stephen Olin, who for a time served as president of Wesleyan University in Connecticut, felt very keenly the weight of responsibility he carried for students entering the ministry. Olin introduced the published version of his 1845 commencement address by lamenting that too often the institutional responsibilities of his position had limited the time he could give to his pastoral connection to his students. He hoped the balance between pastoral and administrative involvements would change in future years.

Stephen Olin

In the mean time, I gladly avail myself of the present occasion to place in the hands of my young friends, as well as those who are still under my watchcare as those who have gone forth into the busy world, my exhortation and advice in regard to several topics in which they are likely feel a lively and increasing interest. (Stephen Olin. Resources and Duties of Christian Young Men (etc.).New-York: Lane & Scott, 1849, 4.)

Benjamin Titus Roberts, a student and friend of Olin, felt a similar responsibility when he founded Chili Seminary, near Rochester, New York, under Free Methodist auspices, now Roberts Wesleyan University, which states as its purpose, "education for character."

Benjamin Titus Roberts

Canadian Methodism likewise developed its own institutions of higher learning, such as Victoria University, with its "young scholar-preacher," Samuel Nelles. Nelles was another Wesleyan graduate. From the start of his career he was moved, and influenced by others, toward an academic ministry. After a brief circuit ministry in London, Ontario, he accepted an appointment to Victoria and made that school his life's work. (Neil Semple. *Faithful Intellect: Samuel S. Nelles and Victoria University*. Montreal, QC & Kingston, ON, et al: McGill-Queens University Press, 2005, 58; 85-88.)

In all these efforts, Scripture remained central to preaching and preparing to preach.

HUMILITY

Humility is an essential characteristic for any Christian, one that has to be lived as well as taught. The example of Jesus in the gospels set the standard and passages such as we've seen in the second chapter of Philippians continued to drive home its importance for the Church. That importance is reaffirmed in a letter from Francis Asbury, written to Daniel Fuller on June 22, 1793:

> I fear I do not see as much simplicity in our young brethren now as in years past. The love of shining in dress and talents appears to be too prevalent. O my dear child, keep humble, watchful, simple, and walk with God, that you may live as well as preach the very spirit and practice of the Gospel. (J. Manning Potts, et al, eds. The Journal and Letters of Francis Asbury. London, UK: Epworth & Nashville, TN: Abingdon, 1958, III: 119.)

LOVE, THANKSGIVING

Francis Asbury carried on the tradition of Paul by expressing his love and gratitude for people to whom he was writing. Part of a 1796 letter to Nelson Reed conveys this well: "I am under great obligation to you and my dear Sister Reed for every expression of love and service to make life comfortable, whilst under your roof." In the same letter, he included a message to "the stationed and local ministry, leaders, and members of the Society in Baltimore," part of which reads, "My being absent or present with you cannot alter my affection for, care over, or love to you." This introduces a statement of his desire for a change he believes would strengthen their fellowship. He offers this advice as his "humble opinion:"

> I hope what I am about to write is from God and for your good. ... I most devoutly wish and desire that if not once in a week yet once in two weeks the whole body of the society should meet alone, as the church of God to participate in each others [sic] joys, and sorrows, trials, consolations, cares, fears and decisions, hopes, wishes and feelings, that you may speak, and pray, and sing together. I humbly hope it will be rendered a special blessing. ... What I have recommended is a part of old Methodism, as it is practiced at New York and was kept up by the societies in London. (J. Manning Potts, et al., eds. The Journal and Letters of Francis Asbury. London: Epworth & Nashville, TN: Abingdon, 1958, III: 153&154.)

THE TWO WAYS

The propulsion driving the Methodist Movement met a hospitable environment in North America, where anything seemed possible. Many, even in traditionally Calvinist churches, could no longer accept the determinism of Calvinism and the now dated conviction that life must go on from generation to generation pretty much unchanged. The idea that society was condemned to live without hope ran aground on a tidal wave of nineteenth-century optimism, greatly enlarging the potential for available futures. Methodism and Charles G. Finney's revival led this wave, which "placed people in charge of their spiritual universe. No longer were men and women condemned to eternal damnation through election and predestination." (David J. Fitzpatrick. *Emory Upton: Misunderstood Reformer*. Norman, OK: University of Oklahoma Press, 2017, 7.)

ENCOURAGEMENT

Clarke's Preacher's Manual, including its orientation to the study of Scripture, contained a great deal of wisdom and encouragement for his readers. One important part of this is his reminders of the high calling of ministry – the kind of message that has often been given as part of ordination services.

He begins a part of his manual called "A Letter to a Preacher" by saying, "My dear friend, - You are engaged in the most important work in the universe." The world has often tried to downplay this importance, contributing to the load of discouragement too many pastors carry. We need apostolic voices to counter these negative messages and replace them with hope, energy, and inspiration.

Notwithstanding the work is extremely *awful* [awesome] and *difficult*, you may nevertheless take encouragement from the *honour* God has conferred upon you in calling you to it, to go forward with courage and delight; and this requisite, that you may not be too much depressed by the trials necessarily attendant on an employment which will ever be opposed by the wickedness of men, and the malice of demons.

Clarke balances this encouraging statement by recognizing the need to avoid "being elated by your honour," to the point of "being unfaithful" through pride or taking God's calling too lightly. Adam Clarke. *Clavis Biblica (etc.)*, generally known as *Preacher's Manual*. New-York, NY: T. Mason & G. Lane, 1837, 75.) Bound with Clarke's Manual are "Four Discourses on the Duties of a Minister of the Gospel," by Thomas Coke, who with Francis Asbury was a bishop of the Methodist Episcopal Church. The beginning of his first discourse looks at the minister's purpose and work from an eternal perspective:

> the ministerial office is the most important to the human race of any which is exercised on earth: for, according to the order of the dispensation of grace, the preaching of the gospel is indispensably necessary to raise mankind out of the ruins of their fall, to deliver them from all the miseries which spring from an everlasting banishment from God, and to bring them to the eternal enjoyment of Him, the sovereign Good, at whose right hand are pleasures for evermore. Thomas Coke. Four Discourses on the Duties of a Minister of the Gospel. New-York, NY: T. Mason & G. Lane, 1837, 153.

Coke's lofty view of ministry helps to keep the preacher's mind "on things above, not on earthly things." (Colossians 3:2, NIV) From this perspective the preachers could "encourage one another," serve as conduits for God to inspire their congregations, and ride the road to glory themselves. (I Thessalonians 5:11, NIV) A single example from Clarke must suffice to show the usefulness of the whole:

> Shun all controversies about politics: and especially that disgrace of the pulpit, political preaching. I have known this to do much evil; but, though I have often heard it, I never heard an instance of its doing good. It is not he bread which God has provided for his children; and from the pulpit, it is neither profitable for doctrine, for reproof, nor for instruction in righteousness. If others will bring this chaff into the house of God, copy them not; you are called to feed the flock of Christ; and this you cannot do but by the sincere milk of the word and the bread of life. (Adam Clarke. Clavis Biblica (etc.), generally known as Preacher's Manual. New-York: T.Mason & G. Lane, 1837, 100.)

Encouragement comes in many forms and circumstances, requiring insight, compassion, and discernment, all guided and empowered by the Holy Spirit. For instance, there have been many times, from the early days of Methodism to the present, when leaders (and followers) have been radically divided and the future direction of the church disputed or unclear. At such times a church and its leaders can be so caught up in that day's pressing issues that the "ordinary" conduct of ministry may be relegated to the shadows. The harm done when, in the heat of controversy, "some grew prayerless and faithless," was considerable and even tragic. For this reason, it is worth noting when a leader maintains focus and follows through with ordinary responsibilities. So it was with Bishop Whatcoat, who in the midst of a vexing crisis, supported his colleague Bishop Asbury "in all his troubles" and "continued to superintend the work through the country, and to encourage the young preachers in the work of the Lord: and to hear and settle all their troubles to the utmost of his power, often supplying their wants by sparing some of his clothes, or by selling the watch out of his pocket, to help a preacher forward in the work." (William Phoebus, ed. *Memoirs of the Rev. Richard Whatcoat (etc.)*, New-York, NY: Joseph Allen, 1828, 77; 71&72.)

REAFFIRMING SHARED BELIEFS, VALUES, PURPOSE

John Wesley's letters were many and exceedingly important for maintaining his connection with lay people and preachers among the Methodists on both sides of the Atlantic. One example is the correspondence between himself and Canadian superintendent William Black. In these letters there are constant reminders of all things Methodist, as well as applications of Methodist teaching and practice to the situations that called forth these letters.

Asbury began a letter to Mary Tubb, with a great question to remind ourselves that this quickly passing life is not the Christian's final destination: "Are you heaven born, and heaven bound?" (J. Manning Potts, et al., eds. *The Journal and Letters of Francis Asbury*. London, UK: Epworth & Nashville, TN: Abingdon, 1958, III: 351 & 371.)

WARNINGS: FALSE TEACHING, LETHARGY

Asbury often encouraged his preachers with his energetic reminders of their purpose. In July of 1806 he wrote to Henry Smith. Part of his letter reads,

> O, purity! O, Christian perfection! O, Sanctification! It is heaven below to feel all sin removed. Preach it, whether they will bear or forbear. Preach it. You have never experienced the realities of heaven or hell, but preach them. Some have professed it, (perfect love) but have fallen from it; others profess, but do not possess it. They trifle away life. They seldom use the gift God hath given them. I think we ought modestly to tell what we feel to the fullest. For two years past, amidst incredible toils, I have enjoyed almost inexpressible sensations our Pentecost is come, in some places, for sanctification.

Wesley would have rejoiced in Asbury's championing Christian perfection and the perseverance he taught and practiced regarding this central part of the Wesleyan message.

I HOPE TO SEE YOU SOON, AND WE CAN TALK FACE TO FACE:" VALUE AND LIMITATION OF LETTERS

In Wesley's letters to and from William Black, we can see how necessary these letters were at a time when face to face conversations could only happen infrequently, if at all. Once the movement in North America was fully mobilized, letters continued to keep people connected, but opportunities for bishops and preachers (and others) to meet were more plentiful here than in the case of transatlantic communication. Asbury and the other bishops, especially Whatcoat and McKendree, would lead regional annual conferences and show up at camp meetings, for example, as their travels allowed. In Canada, preachers, presiding elders and missionaries went to great lengths to stay connected and current on the status of each circuit and the general picture of ministry across larger regions. One of the historian-preachers who poured himself into this kind of work was John Carroll, whose multi-volume *Case and His Contemporaries* chronicled the progress of Canadian Methodism through its formative decades, including its cross-border connections.

PERSONAL MESSAGES

It will be obvious from even a brief sampling of his letters, that Asbury was personally interested in those with whom he exchanged letters, and that his connection with them was not merely administrative. It is also clear that he looked at life and human interaction from a theological vantage point. Hence the tone of a letter he wrote to his parents in 1786:

> My dear Parents:
>
> If Providence will so dispose of us as that we shall not see each other in , time, let us live for eternity, and labour to meet in Glory . I comfort that while the Doctor [Coke] lives, and remains in England, I shall insure you a friend. O that you would each of you live to God, and press after holiness; that your title and qualification for heaven may be good. ...
>
> Remember for many years, I lived with, and, and labored, and prayed for you. I, at this great distance of time, and place, care for and send to your relief, and cease not night and day to pray for you, who am as ever your most unworthy, but dutiful son in the Lord,
>
> Francis Asbury
>
> (J. Manning Potts, et al, eds. The Journal and Letters of Francis Asbury. London, UK & Nashville, TN: Abingdon, 1958, III:45 &46.)

WORSHIP, FELLOWSHIP, RENEWAL

Outdoor worship made a natural choice for evangelism, worship, community building and fellowship across North America. Already familiar, both from necessity (when Methodists were unwelcome in Anglican churches) and design (Scottish sacramental festivals and Methodist camp meeting strategy), they also quickly proved themselves in their new context. Both indoor and outdoor revivals appealed to many denominations; the camp meeting flourished especially among Methodists. Neil Semple stressed,

> Camp meetings in British North America became almost exclusively Methodist institutions. Methodism therefore received most of the credit and the numerical gains among those who supported camp meetings. ... Camp meetings were not only under general Methodist direction, but were intimately connected with the regular work of the connexion and even semi-official branches of the denomination. They were closely associated with the church's ongoing fellowship and grew out of the regular circuit organization. (Neil Semple.; The Lord's Dominion: The History of Canadian Methodism. Montreal, QC & Kingston, ON; London, UK & Buffalo, NY: McGill-Queens University Press, 1996, 144&145.)

As frontiers developed in both countries, mutual support and cooperation among neighbors and communities grew increasingly important and multifaceted. The need and opportunity to grow in faith and reach out in mission and evangelism also required times and places for planning, organizing, and resourcing efforts – all within the group identity and shared purpose of churches and all directed and fueled by the outpouring of the Spirit.

Chapter 6

The Baton of Faith Crosses a Continent

...to spread Scripture-holiness over these lands:"

(The Doctrines and Discipline of the Methodist Episcopal Church, Philadelphia. PA: Henry Tuckniss, 1797, iii.)

The circuit, and the conference of which it was a part, became nearly universal as the way Methodism measured space, just as the conference year was how we measured time. Conference was also the place of belonging for ministers: "preachers belonged to one conference." Even when laity gained membership, there remained a significant difference. Lay members' connection to conference was temporary; clergy membership remained. Laity were primarily members of their local congregations.

From the bishops to the newest "traveling preacher," each received or created their own territory, around which they circulated for a limited time (for most early preachers, this would be only a conference year or two), after which they moved on to their next appointment. Some served in pairs, others alone. Circuits grew smaller as population density increased, to the point where a pastor might serve a single "station." Every appointment was unique, yet there were common elements they could readily recognize and share, whether to rejoice, lament, exchange ideas, or encourage one another.

Though systems varied, appointing and moving pastors has always brought hope and anxiety to preachers and their families.

The actual experience of moving has changed with time and circumstance, but there is much in the cycle of farewells and new beginnings has remained constant, if not as frequent. Two examples from different times, countries, and denominations illustrate the commonalities as well as the distinctiveness of each move.

Joseph Hilts' autobiography included a lengthy chapter on his family's experience of "changing locations" in mid-nineteenth-century rural Ontario, from which come these excerpts:

Joseph Hilts

> In these days of conveyance on land and water, run by steam power, the average citizen of Ontario cannot fully appreciate the difference between travelling now and travelling thirty or forty years ago. Then, a move of one or two hundred miles was a matter "of great importance." It involved the employment of time, the outlay of money, the endurance of hardships, the performance of labour, the smashing of furniture, the exercise of patience, and the testing of moral and physical courage, little dreamed of by the railway travelers of the present day. Only those who have tried both the old and the new methods of migration can form anything like a correct estimate of the difference there is between them.

It is important to read Hilts' account knowing that he served as a circuit preacher and presiding elder during his career. He wrote as one keenly aware of these circumstances, from his own experience and that of others, and as one who was willing to pay the price of his calling. Here he describes typical move of the older time:

> A man would be a day or two helping his wife to pack things away in boxes that they had spent two or three days in making. Then the boxes and furniture would be loaded on two or three waggons, and he would lash them on with ropes. Then he would

take his wife and as many of the children as possible in the buggy. The rest of the children, if there were any more, would be snugly stowed away in the loaded waggons. ... Then two or three days of torture would commence. Then watch those waggons as they were drawn over the uneven roads, up and down the hills, over rough corduroys, through bridgeless creeks, and sloughs, and quagmires....

On the way to their first charge at Garafraxa, Ontario,

we came to a piece of swampy bush, known as "Black Ash Swamp." The bottom of the roadway seemed to have started on a trip to China, and for half a mile the mud was almost to the hubs of the wheels. The horses were not used to that sort of work, and most decidedly objected to proceed any further in that way. They were freed from their entrapment by a neighborly farmer whose oxen provided the needed power to get the weary travelers "through the long mud hole and on the high ground once more."

All this and more created considerable worry over possible or actual damage to travellers and cargo. With this came the constant factors in moving for any generation, leaving behind friends, familiar places, and patterns of life and ministry, and facing the uncertainties of the new situation. Once again, for a time, they would be strangers, living among strangers, hoping their common faith would sustain them and open up new friendships, and knowing they would go through this process again in another year or so. In no time he would face the rigors of another move: "I had fair success on this charge, and I became warmly attached to the people, and I did not dislike the place. We stayed there one year, and then came the time to give the itinerant wheel another turn." He would also come to appreciate good friends, colleagues, and the inexhaustible spiritual resources he would come to know along the way. (Joseph H. Hilts. *Experiences of a Backwoods Preacher*. Wiarton, ON: Bruce County Historical Society, 1986 (reprint), 55-66.)

Presiding elders were assigned to presiding elder districts, while bishops rode what colloquially was called "the big circuit." In the earliest time, nobody stayed put! Francis Asbury, William

McKendree and the other early Bishops rode thousands of miles each year, keeping the connection connected.

This constant circulation was extremely effective and also caused considerable consternation, since a third organizing principle was itinerancy. In general, ministers went where they were sent by bishops and superintendents. It should not be surprising that while most accepted the system as strategically useful and even necessary or a matter of duty, others would find it burdensome or even intolerable. There were bound to be clashes between appointments and preferences; between acquiescence to authority and desire for "the right appointment." Not surprisingly, several of the early reform movements leading to separation (Republican Methodism, the Methodist Protestant Church, the Wesleyan Methodist Connexion, and the Free Methodist Church) had objections to authority and appointment making as contributing factors. (William Warren Sweet. *The Rise of Methodism in the West (etc.)*. Nashville, TN; Dallas, TX & Richmond, VA: Smith & Lamar; New York, NY & Cincinnati, OH: Methodist Book Concern, 1920; Russell E. Richey. *The Methodist Conference in America: a History*. Nashville: Kingswood, 1996, 13.

Joseph Hilts witnessed significant changes - some of them improvements – in the course of his ministry. He especially appreciated better roads and vehicles. However, lest we think the changes were universal, or that extreme hardships in the itinerancy happened only in the unimaginable world of pioneers, we have these recollections of a twentieth-century Free Methodist pastor's son in western New York. There were still difficulties and limited resources to deal with, especially since these memories came mainly from the Great Depression.

Elmer Cook and his family moved to the tiny rural community of Brooklyn in Cattaraugus County in 1929. Brother Cook had served the Brooklyn Church before, for three years. From there they had moved to Belfast in neighboring Allegany county, and then, after two years, to the village of Cattaraugus. This time their journey would be the short, familiar trek from Cattaraugus to Brooklyn. "In that era, pastors of Free Methodist Churches were moved to new appointments on the average of every two years."

Elmer's son Arnold wrote of his father's "acceptance" of this appointment, implying that "acceptance" was not automatic. "No one else would go to this circuit, the least-desirable in the entire Genesee Conference. I made the twelve-mile move with my family from Cattaraugus back to the house where I was born." The financial implications of this appointment were stark.

> When father took appointment to the Brooklyn church in the early throes of the great depression, the need to supplement the meagre income from the pastorate was apparent. For five people to live (father, mother, Grandma Willis, my brother Irving, and me) required more than the approximately six dollars per week paid by the church. This sum included the monetary equivalent of contributions in the form of meat, home-canned items, and whatever people could offer. ...
>
> At times the amount from the church was only two or three dollars instead of the targeted amount. Some of these seven years were leaner than others, the average weekly salary varying from a low of $4.35 in 1934 and a high of $7.69 in 1931. Some of this was father's own tithe. In this he set an example for both the congregation and his family. Recognizing the poverty of most parishioners, my parents never complained. Instead, they assumed responsibility for making up, through their own efforts, whatever else was needed.

Because he had experience and skill with farming, Elmer "integrated farming on a very small scale into the work of the pastorate." This was how their family could manage for seven years. It was also what made their next move especially difficult. There were many positives ahead for them. Distance would not be a problem, but the speed off their transition was another matter:

> My parents had been attending annual conference in early September of 1936. The rumors circulating made me aware that a change was in the air. With school beginning on Tuesday, I worried about where we might be moved and how this might delay my start, wherever it might be. Besides, I was ambivalent, torn between anticipation of possible change and fearing the severing of ties of friendship which bound us to the people of Brooklyn Valley. ...

My ears caught the sound of a motor which could belong to none other than our old Chevy. Before father could even turn off the ignition, I had my foot on the running board. That mother and father were both smiling seemed a good omen.

"Are we moving? Where to? How soon do we leave? My eager questions tumbled out in quick succession.

"I've been appointed to Gowanda," father answered. "I hope we can be moved by the end of the week. That depends on when we can get a truck to take our things."

The timetable for moving made for fast transition. The pastoral changes normally took place quickly so the Sunday immediately following conference found the pastors in their new pulpits. The new school term starting the day after Labor Day injected a sense of urgency in getting the families moved.

Word traveled quickly in the Brooklyn Valley. From across that community people gathered for a gigantic send-off dinner, a time to say their thanks and wish the pastor and his family well, which made for a mixture of tears and celebration. "That we were actually leaving suddenly became very real." The next day the vehicle that would carry the bulk of their possessions was a neighbor's milk truck.

"At each move, mother always wondered what permanent marks would be impressed into the wood surface of some articles of furniture to commemorate the transfer. It always happened. The only question was which of the chairs, tables, or bedsteads would bear the scars." On the road to Gowanda their driver noticed in the mirror a rocking chair in the road behind them. The driver managed to rescue the rocker before it was lost or badly damaged.

> Since Gowanda was only about twenty-five miles away by road, father had already made numerous trips with the car, transporting the items most vulnerable to breakage. Father's farming operation still further complicated the task of moving. Most of the farm-related items had to be disposed of. Parting with the farm animals was not easy, for they had become more like family members.

"Except for one milk cow and a few chickens that were given space on the farm of a new parishioner," the rest of the stock was sold – some of it to the new pastor. The Cook family welcomed many conveniences that came with the move. Arnold wrote, "I shed no tears as I was freed from servitude to the cream separator, the butter churn, the pump handle, the clothes ringer, and the manure fork. My reluctant forced relationship with them had ended. This realization brought me a sense of freedom and relief!" He expected no difficulty transitioning to his new school. In fact, he looked forward to some advantages the new school offered. Whatever the upheaval of moving brought to this family, Rev. Cook would be in his new pulpit the next morning! (Arnold W. Cook. *Of a Boy and His Valley (etc.)*. Interlaken, NY, 1991, 6&7; 56&57; 177-180.)

Today, experiences like those of Joseph Hilts and Elmer Cook will seem exotic to many, but they were very real and not without parallels. Even if they are, or seem, extreme, they reveal the dedication of past generations here in North America. Dedication to one's calling, often to heroic lengths, remained an essential part of ministry, of carrying and passing the baton of faith.

GRACE AND PEACE

Maxwell Gaddis wrote of his desire to have his "'feet shod with the gospel of peace,' and become a messenger of glad tidings to all people, O, could I only be the means, in the hands of God, of saving one perishing soul from everlasting death, I should feel amply paid for any of my toils." This was part of an introspective reflection on his own journey in sanctifying grace. It goes to the heart of and reason for Methodist preachers' loving concern for the people they served and the connection between those people and their ministry. Gaddis clearly sought to be a deliverer of God's grace and peace. (Maxwell Pierson Gaddis. *The Sacred Hour*. Cincinnati, OH, Methodist Book Concern, for the author, 1863, 82.)

SCRIPTURE, STUDY

Nathan Bangs, an American Methodist Episcopal preacher, historian, theologian, journalist, publisher, and denominational mission executive, knew well the need for preachers to be capable students and teachers of the Bible, and to have a useful, well-planned exposure to many other kinds of knowledge. As much as he valued and promoted other areas of reading, Scripture was always first. In his book of advice to young preachers, he wrote, "Now as the sacred Scriptures reveal the only method of salvation to lost sinners, the study of these has the first claim upon the attention of the ministers of Jesus Christ." (Nathan Bangs. *Letters to Young Ministers of the Gospel on the Importance and Method of Study*. New-York, NY: N. Bangs & J. Emory, 1826, 16.

Nathan Bangs

The circuit rider's Bible was a constant companion. With it he began and ended each day. Scripture brought him closer to God and deeper in wisdom. In its pages he found much to meditate and preach upon, and much to talk over with fellow workers. No matter where the road might take him, still the Bible would prove to be an inexhaustible resource for life and ministry. There he found inspiration in verses newly discovered and newly understood. Scripture enabled him to better identify and interpret signs of the times, and better critique the inflated claims of self-important demagogues. Its message provided an ever new perspective on perennial problems, and poured forth fresh inspiration through "a great cloud of witnesses" from "the pioneer and perfecter" of our faith. (Hebrews 12:1&2, NIV)

Exactly how they went about this differed with personalities, circumstances, and level of education, yet one thing remained constant and virtually universal: a driving, determined desire to "grow in the grace and knowledge of our Lord and Savior Jesus Christ," and to better equip themselves and each other to pursue their all-important calling. (II Peter 3:18, NIV) This desire would take some to university classes and others to informal study with a colleague on a forest trail or alone by a fireplace. If discipline was not mandated by a course of study or university curriculum, it took the form of personal habit and mutual encouragement. Ohio Circuit rider D.D. Davisson, in a sermon published in 1854, said about the authority and importance of the Scriptures:

> ...they were "given by inspiration of God, and are profitable for doctrine, for reproof, for correction, for instruction in righteousness." [II Timothy 3:16, KJV] They contain the doctrine of eternal life [John 6:68], bringing into view the immortality of the soul and the resurrection of the body. The Scriptures have their authority from God alone; they are a perfect, plain, absolutely supreme, infallible, and the only standard of faith and practice.

Then Davisson offers a fruitful approach to the study of Scripture:

> We should carefully search the word of God, that we may understand it. By frequent and attentive reading of the Scriptures, meditation thereon, and comparing one place with another, in singleness of heart, attended fervent prayer for, and dependence on, the instructing Spirit of God to explain and apply them to our soul, we attain what knowledge of them is necessary to our salvation and comfort.

Scripture teaches us about Christ and the difference he makes in life, death, and eternity. It shows us the way we should live and the kind of people we should become. For example, we should have a meek spirit. Christ says, "Learn of me: for I am meek and lowly in heart; and ye shall find rest unto your souls." [Matthew 11:28&29, KJV] He also says, "Blessed are the meek: for they shall inherit the earth."[Matthew 5;5, KJV] A meek spirit is of great price in the sight of God. The apostle James says, "Humble yourselves in the sight of the Lord, and he shall lift you up." [James 4:10, KJV]

Davisson continues to show how the Scriptures demonstrate, and invite us to emulate, the character of God, and the pattern he uses weaves a strong connection between the Scriptural Christianity of the Methodists and the Christianity of the Scriptures. Then he outlines the results of engaging the word in this way.

Along with gaining a better understanding of the Bible, we will find the "continual feast" of "a contented mind [Philippians 4:11]], a "living," victorious faith, "by which [we] overcome[ ] the world;"[I John 5:4] a conscience free of the burden of regret, and the peace that comes from trusting God. (W.P. Strickland, ed. D.D. Davisson, "The Word of God in the Heart," *Practical Sermons on Various Subjects*. Cincinnati, OH: Methodist Book Concern, for the author, 1854, 210-215.)

Nathan Bangs thought very highly of the resources available in his time to assist preachers in digging into the Scriptures. He went to considerable lengths to recommend those he felt would be most useful. But he never wanted these books to displace the Bible itself in the preacher's library, "Without undervaluing, in the smallest degree, the luminous and learned commentaries which have appeared in our own and other languages upon the sacred volume, and for which we cannot be too grateful, we say that the best expositor of Scripture is Scripture itself." By reading and meditating on Scripture, in the context of Scripture, with an eye to interactions in Scripture, the reader can come to an understanding of "the holy Scriptures, which are able to make one wise unto salvation" and "we can perceive their connexion, mutual dependence , and admirable harmony." Bangs does recommend the works of Wesley, Adam Clarke, and others as helpful "when difficulties occur." Wisdom is needed in selecting the most reliable sources, so as not to get buried in an unmanageable stack of superficially understood works. "In the mean time I must remind you again, if you would succeed, you must turn commentator yourself, and frequently write down your own thoughts, not, indeed, with a view to publish them, but for your own improvement in biblical knowledge." (Nathan Bangs. *Letters to Young Ministers of the Gospel, on the Importance and Method of Study*. New-York, NY: N. Bangs & J. Emory, 1826, 16-19)

Bangs mentions apologetics, the ability to "Defend the Sacred Scriptures" from any kind of hostile criticism. "The revelation of God's word has been assailed and continues to be assailed by malice, by ingenuity, by sarcasm, and in a word, by all the strength of human genius, learning, and depravity. This hydra of opposition must be encountered, and driven from the field" in a way consistent with our faith. The reading he recommends for this purpose is extensive, including works of world, national, and general history, as well as a thorough grounding in the literature of Methodism. In addition to these positive endorsements, Bangs advises his readers on authors to avoid and others of no great value. He strongly advocates for preachers to be knowledgeable and prayerfully committed regarding their church's ongoing ministries in the world. All this must be a supplement to knowledge of Scripture and not its replacement. Everything a preacher studies should advance the main objective of the ministerial calling. "What is the object which a conscientious minister proposes to himself? It is the salvation of himself and those who hear him. Every branch of knowledge, therefore, after which you may seek, must be laid under contribution for the attainment of the primary and ultimate object." (Nathan Bangs. *Letters to Young Ministers of the Gospel, on the Importance and Method of Study*. New York, NY: N. Bangs & J. Emory, 1826, 19&20; 16.)

Bangs' *Letters* lives up to its title by focusing on the kinds of things a preacher needs to study, why each area matters to preachers, and how best to go about that study. This emphasis leaves many dimensions of a pastor's life unaddressed, but it does offer an abundance of useful resources designed to equip pastors for their central task. Among the subjects he writes about are topics in the Bible itself, such as prophecy, miracles, and Geography; Philosophy and Rhetoric; Poetry and Languages. Studies like these illuminate the world of Scripture and the world to which Scripture speaks. Some of them, especially Philosophy and Rhetoric, clarify understanding and improve expression. Poetry gives a preacher different "voices" to convey a message, and enables a richness of one's own voice. Biblical languages allow for clarity and depth for understanding a text. For each area of study, Bangs recommends reliable scholars and methods to assist preachers in making the most of their available time. He also cautions against the dangers and effects of self-serving uses of study.

Scripture itself gives examples of the contributions of context. The Book of Acts shows Luke, its author, to be highly conversant in the geography, customs, and organization of the places where Peter, Paul, and others ministered. Paul's letters reveal a sophisticated use of the language, ideas, and rhetoric of Gentile society, to which he is called to preach. Revelation uses a vast array of symbols and allusions, carefully chosen to offer hope to a persecuted Church. All the Biblical writers had the capacity to receive and transmit God's inspired word, in their own time and for all time, not robotically, but with the Spirit working through their distinctive personalities, experiences, and gifts.

Through all of this, Bangs is clear that Scripture itself, the one called to proclaim it, and the way of salvation it contains, must always remain paramount. Finally, he preacher's perspective must be eternal:

> You must connect he [sic] present and future worlds together – let your thoughts stretch themselves far 'beyond the bounds of time and space' - and recollect that that is to be your future residence – that your business in this world is to fit yourself, and persuade others to fit themselves, for that eternal state." (Nathan Bangs. Letters to Young Ministers of the Gospel on the Importance and Method of Study. New-York, NY: N. Bangs & J. Emory, 1826, 177.

Before long, as church publications multiplied and educational institutions grew and flourished across these lands, advice on what and how to study became formalized and eventually mandated. Some preachers would take degrees at Wesleyan University in Connecticut or Victoria in Ontario, or any of the many others that expressed Methodism's thirst for learning and instinct for competition with other denominations. As the movement fragmented, many of the newer denominations built their own schools, such as Chili Seminary (Free Methodist) and Wilberforce University (African Methodist Episcopal). Circuit riders like Wilbur Fisk (Methodist Episcopal), Daniel Payne (African Methodist Episcopal), and Samuel Nelles (Wesleyan, Canada) became presidents or faculty members of such institutions. Egerton Ryerson (Methodist, Canada) and James Finley (Methodist Episcopal) were instrumental in founding universities (Victoria, Ontario; Ohio Wesleyan).

At the same time schools and courses of study were gaining favor and showing promise, there remained a need for the same informal methods that had served so well in equipping vast numbers of "self-educated preachers." James Porter published a manual in 1879 for those who would read and study on their own and with informal or self-chosen mentoring. He wrote his handbook for "itinerant preachers whose opportunities for preparatory education were limited," and who found most of the available literature inaccessible. "They desire a work in English that will be more simple and practical, covering the whole ground from actual experience, and speaking kind and encouraging words to unfortunate brothers who have not enjoyed many educational privileges." He also hoped his book would be of help to "Local preachers, Exhorters, and other speakers" for whom little help was available; that his book would provide encouragement and help them "to speak in the best possible manner." He believed his target readership was "a very large one." (James Porter. *Hints to Self-Educated Ministers (etc.)*. New York: Phillips & Hunt; Cincinnati: Walden & Stowe, 1879, 3&4.)

While Wesleyan tradition churches and entrepreneurial leaders were establishing colleges at a mighty rate, there would also be a persistent skepticism about perceived dangers in formal, university or college preparation of pastors and others. While a strain of anti-intellectualism certainly contributed to this skepticism, there was also a recognition of secular bias in Western higher education. The suspicion that this secularism was inimical to the churches and their aims for Christian higher education has been vindicated by subsequent developments. Several (though certainly not all) of the institutions established in our tradition have either separated themselves from their parent denominations or minimized their influence. This has come in stages, over time, while other schools have been founded or reformed in order to regain the original vision. "The great abuse of learning in higher literary institutions in Europe and America, had filled many of our members not only with indifference towards it, but with prejudice against it." While this skepticism provided a necessary – indeed prophetic - critique, it did little to quell the proliferation of Methodist and other church related schools. (S.P. Spreng. *The Life and Labors of John Seybert, First Bishop of the Evangelical Association*. Cleveland, OH: Lauer & Mattill, 1888, 229. In the twentieth-century, widespread mistrust of denominational and secular institutions prompted Henry Clay Morrison and others to establish Asbury College and Asbury Theological Seminary as alternatives for students seeking a traditional education. Others have followed. Asbury has been particularly effective in this regard, providing for the preparation of pastors from many Wesleyan (and other) denominations.

In spite of these differing approaches to ministerial education, the one constant, universal reality behind it all was the ubiquitous desire for learning. Very few needed John Wesley's warning aimed at preachers who had little or no "taste for reading: "Contract a taste for it by use or return to trade." (John Wesley, quoted in Brian G. Hedges, "John Wesley on the Discipline of Reading," brianghedges/2013/10/john/wesley/on/discipline/of/reading.html., accessed 8/1/2024.

Another constant in Methodism's culture of mentoring were the reminders of the importance of the minister's calling. In his hints to self-educated ministers, William L. Harris echoes thoughts we have seen from Adam Clarke and Thomas Coke: "the most solemn and important duties which any man can undertake, are involved in the office and work of a minister of the Gospel. ... to him is committed the wealth of instrumentalities for the salvation of the world..." (William L. Harris, Introduction, James Porter. *Hints to Self-Educated Ministers (etc.)*. New York, NY: Phillips & Hunt; Cincinnati, OH: Walden & Stowe, 1879, 7.) Across the generations, preachers have needed to hear this and take it to heart, in order to counter self-doubt, and the disregard of "opposers" they have inevitably encountered. As with so many insights and realities related to ministry, it has always been essential to turn to Scripture for wisdom that rises above the false wisdom of the world. After Scripture, but also critically necessary, is the support of leaders, mentors, and the "endless line of splendor" in our tradition. That procession – part of the relay race of faith that merges into the "great cloud of witnesses," (Hebrews 12:1, NIV) continues to remind us of what actually matters in life. Here we have an excellent reason to celebrate and draw inspiration from All Saints Day. This should also remind us never to recite the Apostles' Creed absent mindedly – for many reasons, but in this context, because being part of "the communion of saints" is an indispensable blessing.

Harris knew the benefits of formal education for the training of pastors, but he also knew the realities that made that kind of training difficult or impossible:

> "the amount of preparatory study which one called to the ministry should accomplish before beginning his work, may not be always the same, and must be largely determined by the particular circumstances of each case." William L. Harris, Introduction, James Porter. Hints to Self-Educated Ministers etc.). New York, NY: Phillip & Hunt; Cincinnati: Walden & Stowe, 1879, 10.)

Given the distinctive personality, experience, and ministry setting of each minister, the best preparation for each ministry may vary dramatically from one to another. Everyone who has served as a district superintendent or presiding elder has seen how pastors with different kinds and amounts of formal education have served well in well-chosen appointments. Education can be extremely helpful to one who is called and motivated to serve, but education alone guarantees nothing. Even so, James Porter offers very useful advice that is broadly applicable. For example, "Preachers should seek to know something with regard to all subjects, and all branches of business." This may seem impractical, until we consider that we often learn on a need know basis.

Bishop Thomas Morris, from his vantage point in the mid-nineteenth-century, takes us back to what it was like to study and prepare sermons on frontier circuits in an earlier time, highlighting the unconventional but determined way the preachers of Methodism gained the education they needed for effective ministry:

> In this part of our employment we were rather embarrassed in cold weather. Home-room was scarce; and ... families were large. In many places where we were kindly entertained, a small cabin, consisting of one room, served for parlor, dining-room, kitchen,

bed-chamber, study, classroom, and chapel. Still, we did not neglect our books. After allowing a reasonable time for conversation, we resumed our studies. While the family were employed at their business, we read and wrote; and if they became so loquacious as to interrupt us much, we read aloud, and explained, to the mutual improvement of them and us. And we had more facilities for gaining knowledge than might, at first, be supposed. The Bible, and most of the standard works which we have now, we had then, and made good use of them, being at that time but little affected with the extended variety of light reading which now diverts the mind and heart from more important things. And owing to our peculiar mode of circulating books, these standard works got into the hands of all the preachers, and many of the members, together with a sufficient number of literary works to answer the purpose. To all these we applied ourselves diligently. In the winter, those whose eyes could bear it, read much at night. If they could obtain a lamp or candle, well; if not, they split boards and old fence-rails to splinters, and throwing in a piece at a time, read by the blazing light. And in warm weather we took for our study the shade of a tree; or, if the musketos [sic] became very troublesome, the preacher might occasionally be seen up in the fork, or on a large limb of a beech tree among the boughs, where those insects suffered him to pursue his studies in peace. We also read much on horseback, occasionally closing the book, and reflecting on its contents; to which mode of study our long, lonesome rides were admirably adapted. But what rendered our studies most profitable, was the daily opportunity afforded us of turning immediately to practical, useful account all the knowledge we gained from books, conversation, and meditation. The consequence of the whole was, many of the Methodist preachers who entered the work with very limited education, became not only grammarians, historians, philosophers, and orators, but

Thomas Morris

what was much better, profound theologians and able ministers of the New Testament. When self-styled competent ministers of certain Churches, brought up in holy things, on the ground that we were uneducated and ignorant men, we referred them to the hundreds and thousands converted to God under our ministry, living epistles, known and read of all men. Some, not satisfied with this answer, and self-confident in the support of their supposed orthodoxy, especially considering they were from the college, and we from the woods, provoked some of our preachers to public discussion of questions in controversy between them and us; but the result before the people seldom or never failed to help our cause at the expense of their own. (T. A. Morris. Miscellany (Etc.). Cincinnati: L. Swormstedt & A. Poe, 1854, 250-252.)

George Peck laid out his early plan for study, and included some of the obstacles he sometimes encountered:

The books for our district were stored at Norwich. I took an early opportunity to visit the place, and fill my saddle-bags with books for sale and for use.

The [Methodist Episcopal] General Conference of 1816 had planned a course of reading and study for preachers on trial in the Conference, and the presiding elder had furnished me with a list of the books named. The young men were to be examined in their studies, not annually, but when they came up for admission into the Conference. I selected Wesley's Sermons and Fletcher's Checks as the principle work of the year, and tasked myself with a certain number of pages daily. If I gained any time I employed it to the best advantage in my power in other studies. My method was to study the allotted portion of Wesley in the morning, while yet at the house where I had spent the previous night; then, mounting my horse, I rode on to my next appointment, reflecting as I went on what I had read, and studying my sermon. On reaching my next stopping-place I passed a few minutes in conversation, and then got out my copy of Fletcher and studied as long as other duties permitted. Thus I read a portion daily in both Wesley and Fletcher till I had gone through them with close attention. They were more precious to me than gold. ...

I found immediate use for the edge tools with which I was thus made acquainted. It was a time of controversy and debate. Every preacher was expected to be perpetually in line of battle, ready for either attack or defense; and when sundry zealous opposers of the Methodists thought to win an easy victory over "the boy," they found that they could not stand before John Fletcher. ...

Peck's methods were his own, modified by season and circumstance. Other circuit riders had their own ways, but the one constant was intentional learning. Peck would no doubt have appreciated the privacy of the preachers' rooms some Methodists managed to include in their homes.

> I was obliged to sit down with my book in the same room with the family where I chanced to be, the children noisy, the adults full of talk, and all manner of domestic operations in progress. Sometimes I would be assailed with questions, designed to draw me into the conversational current, but l contrived to bring out my answers so slowly, and sometimes so much at random, as to make the impression that my attention was not to be diverted. The good people soon learned my ways, and when I opened my book they usually left me to myself; but there were still difficulties in the way. (George Peck. The Life and Times of George Peck, D.D. New York, NY: Nelson & Phillips; Cincinnati, OH, 1874, 73-75.)

How different were Nathan Bangs' accommodations at one point during his early ministry in Canada:

> The next day ... I rode ten miles and preached in the house of an Indian woman, the widow of a French Canadian, who had left her considerable property. She was a good, simple-hearted, earnest creature, and reminded me of the Shunamite, for she prepared for me, in an upper room, a bed, a table, a chair, and a candlestick. In this room I preached, and ate, and slept, and no one was allowed to enter it in my absence, except to keep it in order. She never asked me to sit at the table with her, deeming herself unworthy, but prepared my food, and put it on the table in my room. She considered herself highly honoured by having the Gospel preached in her house, and she treated me in this way during all my stay in this country. When I parted with her the next day after my first visit, in shaking hands she left a dollar in my palm. It was much needed, for I was nearly out of money. (Egerton Ryerson. Canadian Methodism (etc.). Toronto, ON: William Briggs, 1882, 50 &51.)

HUMILITY

In *The Sacred Hour*, Ohio circuit rider Maxwell Gaddis shares the experience of a young woman who had the spiritual depth and humility to turn away from this world's empty promises to the only promise that actually brings happiness:

> My heart was filed with pride and vanity, but God only knows the bitterness of heart I experienced at times. My conscience condemned me for the course I was pursuing. Finding that Fashion made slaves of all her votaries, I turned from her shrine in disgust, resolving to seek for happiness in fame. But, alas! I soon proved that all these combined were unable to bring happiness and peace to the soul. At last, I turned my weary, aching heart to seek for rest in the wounds of Jesus. After a struggle of many weeks to understand the way of faith, I obtained relief sometime in January, 1852. But still the evidence of my acceptance with God was not as clear and satisfactory as I desired it should be. Glory be to God! On the 13th of May, 1852, at the sweet hour of sunset, while reading and praying over a work called "Faith and its Effects," I grasped the promise – 'He that believeth shall be saved, and instantly light from on high shone into my soul. I was happy.' (Maxwell Pierson Gaddis, The Sacred Hour, Cincinnati, OH: Methodist Book Concern, For the Author, 1863, 28&29.)

THE TWO WAYS

Wesley wanted to avoid or minimize conflict within Methodism and between Methodists and other traditions. Nevertheless, a kind of flagship "controversy ... arose in this country between us and other denominations, but more particularly Wesley and George Whitefield, whom Nathan Bangs called "two great and good men." In North America, the conflict came to rage between orthodox Presbyterians on the one side, and Methodists on the other. Books were written, sermons were preached and debates held as to the leading strategy for evangelism and spirituality between Calvinists and Methodists.

Military officers in an increasingly divided society found it difficult to carry on their normal daily routine and relationships within institutions such as West Point and their surrounding communities. The family of future general Emory Upton combined within itself a strict form of Methodism, together with abolitionism and participation in the underground railroad. Emory attended Charles G. Finney's Oberlin College, picking up strands of revivalism and abolitionism.

ENCOURAGEMENT

Bishop Joseph Long wrote letters to pastors and church leaders to encourage them to live out and deepen their faith. His letters flowed from "a very sympathetic and grateful heart," reflecting his own experiences and inspired vision for the Church. In one of these he writes of a journey that included a camp meeting in Ohio. In this letter he pictures an entire life spent in ministry:

> On the 27th day of August 9 [1845] I started on a journey for the West and attended a camp meeting in the so-called Black Swamp, Sandusky County, Ohio. To my great joy I here met a number of my old friends, well-known ministerial brethren, of whom several, by the grace of God, were largely instrumental in my conversion and subsequent reception into the Evangelical Association. This quickened my spirit and rejoiced my soul. It was a great enjoyment to see these faithful old heroes, once more in the pulpit and to listen to their unctuous and powerful preaching. It reminded me very vividly of ties long past, especially the days of my youth, when the plain and weighty words of these dear men of God so often penetrated my heart. I also met a few who, in former times, traveled with me on circuits and devoted the strength of their younger years and the flower of their lives, together with a great portion of their earthly possessions, to the promotion of the work of the Lord and they were compelled by physical infirmities, to accept a local relation. They now serve God in the circle of their families, friends and acquaintances and partly in temporal poverty during the rest of their wearisome earthly days, waiting in patience for the summons: "Call the laborers and give them their hire." (R. Yeakel. Bishop Joseph Long: The Peerless Preacher of the Evangelical Association. Cleveland, OH: Thomas & Matill, 1897, 146.)

REAFFIRMING SHARED BELIEFS, VALUES, PURPOSE

One key formative factor in the lives of preachers and lay people alike was and remains the rapidly growing number of Wesleyan colleges, universities, and seminaries across the continent. These temporary communities of faith and learning aimed to reinforce foundational understandings, experiences, and values consistent with those of the church.

The production of a vast array of books, magazines, and tracts made people familiar with the purpose of the church, and these generally held principles taught in Sunday Schools, class meetings and sermons. Those same beliefs were shared in camp meetings and quarterly conferences. People's clarity on Methodist beliefs and values was sharpened by conversations and even public debates with representatives of other traditions.

PERSONAL MESSAGES

> When, in March, 1844, Bishop Joseph Long and his colleague, along with a few of the older ministers had prepared the first course of study for young ministers, he appended, in his peculiar style, the following excellent admonitory remarks: "In order to make a beneficial use of the above plan of study, we recommend that each one begin and continue his studies regularly, and to this end arrange his time in such manner as will enable him to have his special hours for his studies. The early hour of the day should be devoted to the study of the Holy Scriptures, and then the other studies follow in regular order, pursuing them perseveringly. We advise particularly to commence early in the morning, and not sit up unnecessarily late in the evening." (R Yeakel. Bishop Joseph Long: The Peerless Preacher of the Evangelical Association. Cleveland, OH: Thomas & Matill, 1897, 147.)

WORSHIP, FELLOWSHIP, RENEWAL

Charles Giles, a Methodist Episcopal preacher and presiding elder, recalled a time of memorable fellowship in connection with a camp meeting:

> By the interchange of thoughts on the way, our journey was made pleasant and profitable: with bounding thoughts we moved along over the rough road, reflecting on the past, and cogitating on the events to come. So the time passed away till we arrived at the place we were so anxious to gain. (Charles Giles. Pioneer. New-York, NY: Lane & Sandford, 1844, 95.)

Camp Meetings, and travels to and from camp meetings, brought preachers and lay people together from across considerable regions, where they shared in the encouragement of worship, fellowship, and mutually upbuilding conversation – what John Wesley called "holy conferencing." Canada's first camp meeting took place in 1805, at Adolphustown, on the Bay of Quinte Circuit in Upper Canada [Ontario]. Led by circuit riders Nathan Bangs, William Case, and Henry Ryan, this gathering brought people together from across that wilderness territory to experience the powerful presence of God in their midst, in a way that would transform their lives and communities. This camp meeting would follow the general pattern developed in the late eighteenth-century and brought to almost universal public notice at Cane Ridge in 1801. At this early time the largest body of Methodists, the Methodist Episcopal Church, spanned the U.S. – Canadian border. Bangs began his career in Canada and later became well known as a writer, publisher, and missionary executive in the States. Case served most of his life in Canada and became a well-known missionary to indigenous people there. Ryan became a presiding elder and somewhat combative leader of a breakaway movement in Canada. Abel Stevens' rendition of Bangs' extended account of this event is well worth reading because of its foundational place in camp meeting history and its representation of what was already becoming typical of camp meetings generally.

> Its announcement beforehand excited great interest far and near. Whole families prepared for a pilgrimage to the ground. Processions of wagons and of foot passengers wended along the highways. With two of his fellow evangelists our itinerant [Bangs] had to take his course from a remote appointment through a range of forest thirty miles in extent. They hastened forward, conversing on religious themes, praying or singing, and eager with expectation of the moral battle-scene about to open. ... The exer-

cises began with singing, prayer, and a short sermon.... Several exhortations followed, and after an intermission of about twenty minutes another sermon was delivered.... Some lively exhortations again followed, and the Spirit of the Lord seemed to move among the people. After an interruption of an hour and a half, a prayer meeting was held, and toward its close the power of God descended upon the assembly, and songs of victory and praise resounded through the forest. The battle thus opened, the exercises continued with preaching, exhorting, and singing, until midnight, when the people retired to their booths. The night was clear and serene, and the scene being new to us, a peculiar solemnity rested upon all minds. The lights glowing among the trees and above the tents, and the voice of prayer and praise mingling and ascending into the star-lit night, altogether inspired the heart with emotions better felt than described. During this day six persons passed from death to life.

At five o'clock Saturday [the next] morning a prayer meeting was held, and at ten o'clock a sermon was preached.... At this time the congregation had increased to perhaps twenty-five hundred, and the people of God were seated together on logs near the stand, while a crowd were standing in a semicircle around them. During the sermon I felt an unusual sense of the divine presence and thought I could see a cloud of divine glory resting upon the congregation. The circle of spectators unconsciously fell back, step by step until quite a space was opened between them and those who were seated. The preacher stopped and said, "Take it and go on." "No, I replied, "I rise not to preach." I immediately descended from the stand among the hearers; the rest of the preachers all spontaneously followed me, and we went among the people, exhorting the impenitent and comforting the distressed; for while Christians were filled with "joy unspeakable and full of glory," many a sinner was weeping and praying in the surrounding crowd. These we collected together in little groups, and exhorted God's people to join in prayer for them, and not to leave them until he should save their souls. O what a scene of tears and prayers was this! I suppose that not less than a dozen little praying circles were thus formed in the course of a few minutes. It was truly affecting to see parents weeping over their children, neighbors exhorting their unrepentant neighbors to repent, while all, old and young, were awe-struck. The wicked looked on with silent amazement while they beheld some of their companions struck down by the mighty power of God, and heard his people pray for them. The mingled voices of prayer and praise were heard afar off, and produced a solemn awe apparently upon all minds. As the sun was setting, struck by the grandeur of the spectacle and the religious interest of the crowd, a preacher mounted the stand and proclaimed for his text, "Behold, he cometh with clouds, and every eye shall see him." The meeting continued all night. During this time some forty persons were converted or sanctified.

Sunday was a high point of camp meetings, where a harvest was brought in and people were aware that the gathering would soon come to a close.

On Sabbath morning, as the natural sun arose in splendor, darting its rays through the forest, we presented ourselves before its Maker, and poured out our songs of thanksgiving to Lord of the universe. We felt that our early sacrifices were accepted, for the "Sun of righteousness" shone upon our souls and made all within us rejoice....

After breakfast, a host being now on the ground, we held a lovefeast. The interest and excitement were so great and the crowd so large that while some assembled around the stand, a preacher mounted a wagon at a distance and addressed a separate congregation. The impression of the Word was universal, the power of the Spirit was manifest throughout the whole encampment, and almost every tent was a scene of prayer. At noon the Lord's Supper was administered to multitudes, while other multitudes looked on with astonishment and tears. ...

Perhaps the strongest part of this account is its concluding picture of participants leaving the camp meeting. It is here that we sense their grief in having to return to normal. Yet they will never be the same. The camp meeting experience, centered in a transforming encounter with God, goes with them, and the camp ground itself, along with others across North America, remains holy ground.

I will not attempt to describe the parting scene, for it was indescribable. The preachers, about to disperse to their distant and hard fields of labor, hung upon each other's necks weeping and yet rejoicing. Christians from remote settlements, who had here formed holy friendships which they expected would survive in heaven, parted probably to meet no more on earth, but in joyful hope of reunion above. They wept, prayed, sang, shouted aloud, and had at last to break away from one another as by force. As the hosts marched off in different directions the songs of victory rolled along the highways.

Bangs goes on to describe the ongoing effects of this gathering, long after the event itself is over, as people, congregations and communities are touched by its radiant energy.

> Great was the good that followed. A general revival of religion spread around the circuits, especially that of the Bay of Quinte, on which this meeting was held. I returned to Augusta circuit and renewed my labors, somewhat worn, but full of faith and the Holy Ghost.

Notice that he mentions "circuits;" his own appointment was to a circuit beyond the one where this gathering was held. Even more to the point of this study, camp meetings were among the means of grace – in this case, the extraordinary means of grace, which repeatedly renewed Methodists' connection to their original Biblical and Wesleyan identity and purpose. At camp meetings, preachers and lay participants encountered God in ways that refreshed their spiritual lives and reminded them of their central beliefs and values. These events centered on group experiences of worship even as they strengthened all the constituent individuals and groups that comprised the movement – families, communities, classes, local churches, circuits, districts, and conferences. They were particularly well designed for recruiting, mentoring, equipping, and motivating preachers. Held outdoors, away from ordinary responsibilities and distractions, in ever widening circles of fellowship, fostering cooperative working relationships, and upholding a shared vision of life in Christ, camp meetings were ideal reflections of, and contributors to Christian life among Methodists. Wherever else they might go, the campground remained a powerful, memorable context for mentoring.

The best known of these gatherings followed Cane Ridge and spread across the Appalachians and into Ohio and Ontario. But they also made their way into New England, and New York, transforming the spiritual landscape everywhere they went. One of these, which was remembered as "very successful," was held in East Bethany in western New York in 1809, the year before the Genesee Conference of the Methodist Episcopal Church was organized. Since East Bethany was just outside Batavia, center of settlement for the western part of the state, the influence of this camp meeting would have radiated in every direction over that region. (George Peck. *Early Methodism within the Bounds of the Old Genesee Conference (etc.)*. York, NY: Carlton & Porter, 1860, 239.)

Camp Meetings not only reinforced the Methodist way for those already in the family. At their best they extended and enlarged the family. Their commitment to evangelism and community building could transcend ethnic and even language barriers. On several occasions, German and English speakers united in camp meetings where common purpose made possible the challenge of ministering in less than familiar settings. The responses of preachers and people alike were similar to those at single language meetings. African American Methodists sometimes attended camp meetings along with white participants. This became a feature of holiness meetings late in the nineteenth century, though attempts to normalize and expand this practice fell before persistent prejudice. African Americans also developed their own camp meetings, some of them still flourishing today. (Minuette Floyd. *A Place to Worship: African American Camp Meetings in the Carolinas*. Columbia, SC: University of South Carolina Press, 2018.)

Like all human institutions, our churches and ministries – even means of grace intended as conduits of the Spirit – often fell far short of their God-given potential. But they sometimes succeeded admirably, for their own time and in passing on the baton of faith. AME Evangelist Jarena Lee recounted her experience with a Delaware camp meeting:

> I left Philadelphia for Lewistown, Delaware to attend a camp meeting of the African Methodist Episcopal connexion, of which I was a member, to be held in Gov. Paynter's woods. There was [sic] immense large congregations, and a greater display of God's power I never saw. The people came from all parts, without dis-

tinction of size, sex, or color, and the display of God's power commenced from singing. ... There appeared to be a great union with the white friends. ... Right Rev. Bishop Allen was present. The ministry were all for me, and the Elder gave me an appointment, and the Governor with a great concourse came to hear the weak female. ... After I took my text, it appeared to me as if I had nothing to do but open my mouth, and the Lord filled it, consequently I was much encouraged: It was an immense assembly of people. (Jarena Lee, Giving an Account of Her Call to Preach the Gospel [revised]. Philadelphia, PA: Printed and Published for the Author, 1849, blog posted July 29, 2018,"Women and Work in the 19C United States of America: Evangelist Jerena Lee (etc.), n.p. (First page in selection.) Accessed 9-14-2024.

Richard Allen

Another early A.M.E preacher, David Smith, left this similar account of a shorter (quarterly?) meeting in Little York, PA:

> The meeting was held in a school house; we commenced the service at 11A.M. The power of the Lord was so wonderfully poured out upon the assembly, that the meeting did not break up until 3P.M. Here I saw the slaves and their masters singing, shouting and praising God together. All seemed to be one in Christ Jesus; there was no distinction as to the rich or poor, bond or free, but all were melted into sweet communion with the spirit [sic] and united in Christian fellowship; and to my mind they could have befittingly sang [sic] this blessed hymn:
>
>> Blessed be the dear uniting love
>> That will not let us part
>> Our bodies may far off remove, We still are one in heart.
>> (David Smith. Biography of Rev. David Smith, of the
>> A.M.E. Church (etc.). n.c: Dodo (reprint}, orig. 1888, 10.)

Another example is the surprising role of camp meetings in bringing together indigenous people and people of European ancestry in North America. While relationships of this kind were fraught with difficulties and were unable to stop racist violence, abuse, injustice, and systematic expropriation of native lands, they could, for a time and in limited situations, demonstrate the unifying and transforming capability of Christ.

This potential, while far from universally realized, did make a major contribution to Methodism in Canada. Less than twenty years after Canada's first camp meeting, one of its organizers, William Case, led another camp meeting at Ancaster, near Hamilton, Upper Canada, at the western end of Lake Ontario.. Here is an account of that event by a participant who was converted there, Keh-ke-wa-guo-na-ba, Rev. Peter Jones, a Mississauga Ojibway:

> I was prompted by curiosity to go and see how the Methodists worshipped the Great Spirit in the wilderness:

> On arriving at the encampment, I was immediately struck with the solemnity of the people, several of whom were engaged in singing and prayer. Some strange feeling came over my mind, and I was led to believe that the Supreme Being was in the midst of his people who were now engaged in worshipping him. We pitched our tent upon the ground allotted to us, it was made of course linen cloth. The encampment contained about two acres enclosed by a brush fence. The tents were pitched within this circle, all the underbrush was taken away, whilst the larger trees were left standing, forming a most beautiful shade. There were three gates leading into the encampment. During each night the whole place was illuminated with firestands, which had a very imposing appearance amongst the trees and leaves. The people came from different parts of the country, some ten, some twenty,

Peter Jones

and some even fifty miles in their wagons, with their sons and daughters, for the purpose of presenting them to the Lord for conversion. I should judge there were about a thousand persons on the ground. The Rev. William Case being the Presiding Elder, had the general oversight of the encampment. There were a number of ministers present, who alternately delivered powerful discourses to the listening multitude, from what is called a Preacher's stand.

William Case

This description shows how standardized camp grounds had become. The familiar pattern would appear, with local variations, across the continent. (See B.W. Gorham. *Camp Meeting Manual (etc.)*. Boston, MA: H.V. Degen, 1854.) Peter Jones goes on to describe what he experienced at Ancaster:

> At the sound of the horn we went and took our seats in front of the stand from which a sermon was delivered. After this there was a prayer meeting in which all who felt disposed took part in praying for penitents. The next day, Saturday, 2nd of June, several sermons were preached, and prayer meetings were held during the intervals. By this time, I began to feel very sick in my heart, but did not make my feelings known. On Sabbath, there was a great concourse of people who came from the adjoining settlements, and many discourses were delivered, some of which deeply impressed my mind, as I could understand most of what was being said. I thought the black-coats [ministers] knew all that was in my heart, and that I was the person addressed. The burden of my soul began still to increase, and my heart said, "What must I do to be saved?" for I saw myself to be in the gall of bitterness and in the bond of iniquity. The more I understood the plan of salvation by our Lord Jesus Christ, the more I was convinced of the truth of the Christian religion and of my need for salvation. In spite of my old Indian heart, tears flowed down my cheeks at the

remembrance of my sins. I saw many of the white people powerfully awakened, and heard them crying aloud for mercy, whilst others stood and gazed, and some even laughed and mocked. ...

Monday brought another round of "discourses," causing Peter to weep and struggle, afraid that someone "might see [him] weeping like an old woman, as all my countrymen consider this to be beneath the dignity of an Indian brave." His "anguish of soul" was certainly his own, and distinctively that of a First Nations man, but it also ran parallel to the inner struggles of many who came under conviction. Finally, "fully convinced that if [he] did not find mercy from the Lord Jesus" he "certainly should be lost forever," he sought the prayers of believers –actually, they sought to pray for him - there at the meeting.

> On arriving at the prayer meeting, I found my sister apparently as happy as she could be; she came to me and began to weep over me and to exhort me to give my heart to God, telling me how she had found the Lord. These words came with power to my poor sinking heart, and I fell upon my knees and cried to God for mercy. My sister prayed for me as well as other good people, and especially Mr. Stoney, whose zeal for my salvation I shall never forget.

Chapter 7

Passing the Baton from Here

The conclusion of all this was a divine breakthrough that would bring him great joy and a preacher's calling.

> At the dawn of the day I was enabled to cast myself wholly upon the Lord, and to claim the atoning blood of Jesus, and He, as my all sufficient Saviour, who had borne all my sins in His own body on the cross. That very instant my burden was removed, joy unspeakable filled my heart, and I could say "Abba Father." The love of God being now shed abroad in my heart, I loved Him intensely, and praised Him in the midst of the people. Every thing now appeared in a new light, and all the works of God seemed to unite with me in uttering the praises of the Lord. The people, the trees of the woods, the gentle winds, the warbling notes of the birds, and the approaching sun, all declared the power and the goodness of the Great Spirit. And what was I that I should not raise my voice in giving glory to God, who had done such great things for me!

Parallel to some of Jones' experience was the conversion of Mary Apess, a Pequot Indian and Methodist, whose husband William was also a Pequot and a Methodist preacher. Their story is a compelling account of New England life, especially in its portrayal of ethnicity and religion, including the place of camp meetings, early in the nineteenth-century:

> One day upon the campground, there was a light from heaven shone into my soul, above the brightness of the sun. I lost sight of all earthly things – heaven was open to my view, and the glory of the upper world beamed upon my soul. My body of clay was all that hindered my flying up to meet Jesus in the air. How long I remained in this happy frame of mind I do not know. But when

I came to my recollection, my Christian friends were around me singing the sweet songs if heaven; and I thought I was in the suburbs of glory. And when I saw them, they looked like angels, for they were praising God. I felt the love of God like a river flowing into my soul." Some time later she went to another camp meeting, seeking the gracious gift of sanctification. "...before the meeting closed, God in Christ showed himself mighty to save and strong to deliver. I felt the mighty power of God again, like electric fire, go through every part of me, cleansing me throughout soul, flesh, and spirit. I felt now that I was purified, sanctified, and justified." (Barry O'Connell, ed. A Son of the Forest and other Writings, by William Apess, a Pequot. Amherst, MA: University of Massachusetts Press, 1997, 82&83.)

Peter Cartwright had a comparable experience at his camp meeting conversion at Cane Ridge:

Peter Cartwright

Divine light flashed all round me, unspeakable joy sprung up in my soul. I rose to my feet, opened my eyes, and it really seemed as if I was in heaven; the trees, the leaves on them, and everything seemed, and I really thought were, praising God. My mother raised the shout, my Christian friends crowded around me and joined me in praising God.... (W.P. Strickland, ed. Autobiography of Peter Cartwright (etc.). New York, NY: Carlton & Porter, 1857, 37&38.)

The baton was being successfully passed, from camp meeting to camp meeting. God's redeeming love was "shed abroad" and returned in the form of prayer and praise. It was also passing from person to person, in this case from Peter's Jones' sister and Mr. Stoney (with others) to Peter. But the handing on of faith completes its mission only when the receiver carries it forward, which is exactly what Peter does; what camp meetings were designed to do. The word is meant to accomplish its purpose (Isaiah 55:11).

The dynamic involved in passing the baton of faith is this: "We love because he first loved us." (I John 4:19, NIV) What follows in Peter Jones conversion account is the overflowing love that originated in God and extended through Peter to everyone around him.

> My heart was now drawn out in love and compassion for all people, especially for my parents, brothers, sisters, and countrymen, for whose conversion I prayed, that they might also find this great salvation. ...
>
> Before the meeting closed ... a fellowship meeting was held. The Rev. W. Case requested all those who had experienced the blessing of justification to stand up, and a goodly number rose, amongst whom were my sister Mary and myself. When elder Case recognized me, he exclaimed, - Glory to God, there stands a son of Augustus Jones, of the Grand River, amongst the converts, now is the door opened for the work of conversion amongst his nation!" Peter Jones. Life and Journals of Keh-ke-wa-guo-na-ba (Rev. Peter Jones,) Wesleyan Missionary. Toronto: Anson Green, 1860, 9-14.)

As preacher, translator, writer, missionary, and spokesman for Indigenous People, Peter Jones would fulfill the vision of William Case and the original vision of the whole Methodist movement, through camp meetings and other kinds of outreach that brought whites and native people together in the family of God.

His camp meeting experience at Ancaster, and everything that followed, illustrates Methodism's highly successful way of passing the baton of faith. This kind of mountain top experience was unforgettable, motivating, and sharable, whether by testimony or a return to a campground.

Henry Benson told of another camp meeting that brought Indigenous people and settlers together. In this case, the setting was the Ozark Mountains, and the native people were Choctaws, forced from their ancestral lands back east. Benson wrote: "Our camp meeting was small, about "one hundred and fifty souls" on Sunday. Although they were far from any large, established communities, their camp meeting resembled in essential ways similar outdoor gatherings across the continent. Prayer and preaching, love feast and communion (using "wild grapes which were found upon a forest tree") were part of the meeting, all in an atmosphere of traditional Methodist fellowship. The gathering lasted for several days. Most who attended were poor. Settlers, as well as Choctaws, had traveled west and would travel farther. Upon closing, the worship of God had crossed imposing barriers to bring them together. "We then separated, not again to meet till summoned to stand before the tribunal of God...." (Henry Benson. *Life among the Choctaws*. Cincinnati, OH: L. Swormstedt & A. Poe, 1860, 143&146.)

Henry Benson

Camp meetings flourished throughout North America, in nearly every demographic. Ohio circuit rider James Finley told the story as it unfolded among settlers and Indians in his part of the country.

> But few can look upon a camp meeting scene and not be moved. Such a scene as is presented by an encampment at night, to one who has never witnessed anything like it before, must be impressive. To look upon the long ranges of tents surrounding a large area, in each corner of which fires are lighted up, and then from tent and tree to see innumerable lamps hung out, casting their lights among the branches and illuminating all the ground.... Then the sound of the trumpet, and the gathering together of thousands, who pass to and fro with lights and torches, all has a tendency to awaken the most solemn reflections. And when the holy song rises from a thousand voices, and floats out upon the stillness of the night, the listener must feel that surely such a place is holy ground. These camp meetings were scenes of special mercy to thousands, and many who came to curse remained to pray for salvation and seek an interest in the blessed Savior. (W.P. Strickland, ed. Autobiography of the Rev. James B, Finley (etc.). Cincinnati: Methodist Book Concern, for the author, 1856, 345.)

We are fortunate to have many examples of preaching, exhorting, testimony, and autobiography, from indigenous writers, in the States and in Canada. One of these was by a Wyandotte called Between the Logs. It took place at a quarterly meeting in Northeast Ohio, where "about two hundred Indians were encamped on the ground."

> My brothers and sisters, I do not rise this morning to tell you the feats of my past life as a warrior or hunter, or the feats of my ancestors; but I rise to tell you of the sweetness of religion, and the unspeakable joy I feel in laboring in its cause. Here, under these lofty oaks – for here once stood an Indian village – is the place that gave me birth. They are my fostering parents; for beneath their lofty and spreading branches I spent my juvenile years, in all the vanities and follies of Indian youth. Among the groves of the forest I have spent the whole career of my life. But in all this time, I was ignorant and in gross darkness. I had not at that time heard the name of Jesus, nor did my tongue learn to lisp his praise. My mind had not conceived an object so dear – a name so precious – the sound of which now makes my soul expand, and warms my heart with a flame of love. Brethren, my feelings overwhelm me at this time – they will not allow me to say much. But suffer me to add, that under these shady groves I am determined to finish my course, laboring in the cause of my divine Master. I humbly confess my life is not perfect; that I am still liable to err, and feel a proneness to evil. But I desire to do my Master's will, and meet you and all the friends of Jesus in our Father's home above. (D.W. Clark, ed. Life among the Indians ... by James B. Finley. Cincinnati, OH: Jennings & Graham; n.d., 347&348.)

Preachers who ministered together at camp meetings grew stronger through their camaraderie and teamwork. They prayed together, learned from each other, and found a great synergy in their different gifts, styles, and personalities. George Cole once employed his writing skills in a song about the preachers at a large Connecticut camp meeting. With appreciation and with humor he drew a word picture of each preacher on the ground, highlighting their memorable traits. (Elbert Osborn. *Passages in the Life and Ministry of Elbert Osborn (etc,)*. New-York, NY: Conference Office, 1847, 102-104.)

Camp meetings continue in many forms and localities, long after their heyday, among many denominations and no denomination at all. In her book of photos and text, Minuette Floyd describes the role of a cluster of African American Methodist camp meetings operating today in rural North and South Carolina. "Camp meetings allow participants to stop the whirlwind of daily activity, look one another in the eye, and focus on things that really matter." In a world that often devotes time and energy to the frenetic and frivolous, "the biggest shift in priorities is the one that allows participants to connect with the divine." (Minuette Floyd. *A Place to Worship: African American Camp Meetings in the Carolinas.* Columbia, SC; University of South Carolina Press, 2018, 33.) Camp meetings offer opportunities to reflect deeply on the Word, to reorient our lives around God, to put aside the world's distractions, and to reconnect with companions on our journey through the blessings and obstacles we encounter in life.

GRACE AND PEACE

As in the New Testament era, letters connected the connection. John Wesley sent and received an abundance of letters across Britain and Ireland, and across the Atlantic to and from North America. Leaders of the rapidly growing movement on this continent, between conferences and between visits, kept in touch in the same way. Below are portions of letters from Freeborn Garrettson concerning his concern for and ministry with Methodists in Nova Scotia. These letters (or portions) are not intended to tell a complete story, but rather to demonstrate how letters functioned and the purposes they served. Parallels with New Testament Letters will become immediately clear.

First, the setting, provided by Nathan Bangs:

> I remain your sincere, though unworthy servant, in the bonds of the powerful gospel of Christ.

> We have already seen the manner in which Mr. Garrettson was employed in calling the preachers together, and the opinion expressed by Dr. Coke of his diligence and activity, his meekness and love. The preachers, about sixty in number, assembled in Baltimore, December 25th, 1784, and held what had been designated the "Christmas conference." ...

At the conclusion of the revolutionary war, a number of persons who still retained their attachment to the British government removed to the province of Nova Scotia. Among those emigrants were some who had been members of the Methodist society in this country; others had emigrated from Europe. These were as sheep without a shepherd. They therefore expressed a strong desire to have Methodist missionaries sent among them. ... Mr. Garrettson volunteered his services for Nova Scotia. While preparing for this enterprise, he wrote the following letters, one of which appears to be addressed to members of some former charge, and the other to a respected friend: -

My dearly beloved friends and brethren, - Peace and consolation attend you forever, through Jesus Christ, Amen! I had great expectation of paying you a visit before I took my departure to some other quarter of my Master's vineyard; but had not had an opportunity, being confined to other places. I send this epistle, hoping it will, in some sense, supply my lack of service. Through the mercy of our God I enjoy health of body; and blessed be his dear name, I think my love and zeal for his glory are as great as ever; desiring to spend and be spent in the best of causes, not counting my life dear, so I can win souls, and at last stand blameless before the throne of my God, not having my own righteousness, but a righteousness through the faith of the Son of God.

You know very well I was among you with tears and fasting; labouring both night and day, and, glory be to God, I hope not altogether in vain. 'ye were once darkness, but now are ye light in the Lord; walk as children of the light.' When I shall be among you again, I know not, being straitened between two, whether to go out into the wilderness or to tarry with the children of the kingdom. It is the most pleasing to nature to tarry, but having a great sense of the deplorable condition thousands of souls are in, I feel a willingness to tread unbeaten paths in the wilderness, and call home hundreds and thousands of the lost sheep of the house of Israel, who now (as you once did) sit in darkness, that we all may be of one fold, feeding in one pasture, under one great Shepherd. ...

I shall now close with an address to you in the several stations you occupy in the church of God. Some of you God has set apart to speak in his name: O that you may do it faithfully! To the leaders I would say, keep the life and power of God in your souls, that your prayers and admonitions may have the happy effect of kindling all around you the flames of holy, pure love; then will you long for your class day to come. The private members I would enjoin to love each other, and to bear each other's burdens: be watchful, sober; train up your children in the fear of God, and be as burning lights to all around you; then will you force the heathen world to say, 'see how these Christians love one another!' You that are young men and women, be sober minded, and be not unequally yoked together with unbelievers.... I earnestly exhort you all to receive with kindness, and esteem highly those who labour among you in word and doctrine; they watch for your souls, as they that must give an account, that they may do it with joy. God has already in his wisdom seen fit to remove some from among you into eternity, I hope, to surround his glorious throne.

I now commend you to the fatherly goodness of Jehovah, praying and beseeching him to keep you all by the power of the Spirit, that if I never enjoy your company here, I may eternally enjoy it in heaven. I desire the prayers of all my dear friends and children, that I may stand fast in the faith, and finish my course with comfort. May we all meet to be crowned with an eternal crown! Friends meet and part here, but there we shall meet never to part more. Our sorrows will be wiped away; the wicked will cease from meddling, and our weary souls will forever be at rest; to which happy place may God in his infinite mercy grant to bring us all, for the sake of his dear Son. Amen.

F. Garrettson

In part of a second, shorter letter from roughly the same time, Garrettson expresses his hope and intention for a life of usefulness and humility: "Blessed be God, my mind is sweetly drawn out in the work of the ministry, and I hope I shall ever be little and mean in my own eyes, and that I may ever be rising higher in the divine image." (Nathan Bangs. *The Life of the Rev. Freeborn Garrettson (etc.)*. New-York, NY: T. Mason & G. Lane, 1839, 135-140.).

In the first letter, Garrettson includes several elements that are familiar to us from various New Testament Letters. Although some of these sound apostolic, Garrettson was not writing as a bishop. He begins with a greeting and a reference to his relationship to his readers. He assures them of his good health and gives the reason for his inability to visit them. He writes about the way his calling as a minister can take him away from friends, confirming his attachment to them even as he justifies his missionary journey, taking ownership of his "willingness to tread unbeaten paths in the wilderness." He describes the spiritual situation he hopes to address, compares it to the experience of his readers, and relates it to spiritual aims he has for himself.

In his fourth paragraph, he speaks to different groups within his readers' community, taking us back to Letters in the New Testament, especially the Pastorals and I John. He places all that he says in the context of the way of salvation, his own ultimate destiny, and theirs. He also emphasizes the importance of prayer. In the second letter, we find a moving statement of his spiritual goal of humility.

Like the New Testament Letters, these contain several inspiring, memorable lines:

> I feel a willingness to tread unbeaten paths in the wilderness.
>
> Keep the life and power of God in your souls.
>
> Friends meet and part here, but there we shall meet never to part more.

SCRIPTURE, STUDY

Inspiring accounts of circuit riders' sometimes herculean efforts to gain an education demonstrate their eagerness to learn and their awareness of the importance of learning to success in their work. For some this meant learning to read and write. For others it meant taking a deep dive into the writings of John Wesley, John Fletcher, and Adam Clarke. Still others would somehow learn the ancient Biblical languages or the skills required for composing hymns or teaching children. Some studied in formal classrooms, while others would seek out tutors in the vicinity of their appointments. Some made astounding progress, even meriting faculty or administrative positions in universities and colleges.

John Fletcher   Adam Clarke

All grew in their own vocations and in their ability to strengthen their churches' ministry. In this chapter we can only lift up a few examples.

One of these was Daniel A. Payne, preacher and bishop in the African Methodist Episcopal Church. Bishop Payne recorded the way his pursuit of learning began:

> Several weeks after this event [his conversion], ... I was in my humble chamber, pouring out my prayers into the listenlng ears of the Saviour, when I felt as if the hands of a man were pressing my two shoulders and a voice speaking within my soul saying: "I have set you apart to educate thyself in order that thou mayest be an educator of thy people." The impression was irresistible and divine; it gave a new direction to my thoughts and efforts. ...
>
> After this circumstances [sic] I resolved to devote every moment of leisure to the study of books, and every cent to the purchase of them." (C.S. Smith, Daniel A. Payne. Recollections of Seventy Years. Nashville, TN: A.M.E. Sunday School Union, 1888, 19.)

For William Hanby, the overarching purpose of his life and ministry was: "...that I may stand fast in the faith...." Wesleyans of German ethnicity developed their own tradition, passing the baton of faith by means of camp meetings and all the ways available to them, especially in the middle states, westward into Ohio and the Midwest, and through upstate New York and into Ontario. In many ways the churches of these groups paralleled each other and carried on similar ministries, including camp meetings and the theological and spiritual life they shared in the revival. The German groups also shared a strong commitment to education. William Hanby was a bishop of the United Brethren in Christ for whom education and ministry went hand in hand. At various times he served as treasurer of his denomination's publishing house, editor and contributor for its publication, the *Religious Telescope*, denominational historian, writer and compiler of hymns, a founder of Otterbein University, an abolitionist and leader of the underground railroad. His was not an easy life, yet when he died in 1880, his last words were, "I'm in the midst of glory." (Paul Rodes Koontz. *The Bishops, Church of the United Brethren in Christ.* Dayton, OH: Otterbein, 1950, I:332-348.b)

Bishop John Seybert made a trek across the Alleghanys that should forever symbolize the commitment of these churches to education, for ministers and laity alike. Individual preachers carried Bibles and other books with them on their circuits. They were the primary distribution system for their publishing houses. The books they carried, read, and sold brought spiritual sustenance, news, literacy, and encouragement wherever they went. They represented their connections when living representatives were thin on the ground, giving people a common language to express common ideas. BIshop Seybert's trek recognized the great need for these books on the frontier, and he was determined to meet that need. In time there would be branch or independent book concerns for the various denominations in New York, Cincinnati, Pittsburgh, Toronto, Halifax, Baltimore, Dayton, New Berlin, PA; Cleveland, Nashville, Chicago, and other strategically placed cities. Bishop Seybert's massive consignment illustrated the drive behind all of this.

Following annual conference, he made the journey from New Berlin, PA, where the Evangelical Publishing House was then located, west to Ohio.

Before leaving for the Ohio conference, the Bishop ordered the largest consignment of books ever issued from the Publishing House at one time. And this in 1841, in a Church that has been accused of being indifferent, if not opposed, to matters of culture and education. Seybert's order called for twenty-three thousand seven hundred and twenty-five volumes, which he intended to take with him on his trip to the Ohio conference. Their weight was twenty-five hundred pounds, and their cost, including a small quantity for Illinois, amounted to $4,306.25. ... In closing his order, he remarked: "You will probably think I have entirely overshot the mark, in ordering so many books. But if you were as well acquainted with the scarcity of books in the West as I am, you would judge differently."

John Seybert

So great was Bishop Seybert's anxiety to have the families, schools and churches supplied with proper literature, that he undertook to forward these books and distribute them himself, mostly in Ohio, but also in Indiana and Illinois. He shipped them to the West per canal, and then distributed and sold them to the ministers and laity, taking all the financial risks himself. Though he lost no money in the operation, neither did he gain any. It was done solely in the interests of the Church. He was a far-seeing man, who fully appreciated the value and importance of education and intelligence. He not only wanted the preachers to be studious, but also the laity, and he provided a liberal assortment of juvenile literature. All impressions to the contrary notwithstanding, Seybert thoroughly believed that intelligence should be fostered by the Church. (S.P. Spreng. The Life and Labors of John Seybert, First Bishop of the Evangelical Association. Cleveland, OH: Lauer & Matill, 1888, 227-229; cf. 2387239; For more on Bishop Seybert: J. Steven O'Malley, John Seybert and the Evangelical Heritage (etc.). Lexington, KY: Emeth, 2008.

The passion to advance the cause of education was part of the general passion for saving souls, no matter how remote and difficult to reach they might be. Evangelical Association preacher William Yost demonstrated his undying commitment to such a ministry when he reached a new appointment. The "out appointment" on this charge prompted people in the larger congregation to advise their new pastor against making the arduous journey and investing his time and energy on this unproductive effort.

William Yost

North of Mahoning Valley [Pennsylvania], across a steep mountain, there is a small, stony valley nestling down amidst the rocky ledges. Here a few families eked out a scanty livelihood. Some of them were members of our church. On account of its isolated and inconvenient location, the neighborhood was difficult of access, the road leading to it over the mountain, exceedingly stony and hard to travel. Some of the brethren of the church were of the opinion that I ought to drop this appointment; that the journey was precarious to my horse, and liable to work injury to my buggy, and, moreover, would not pay in the end. The congregations were exceedingly small, consisting of seven or eight hearers, of whom three were deaf and dumb people. I filled an appointment here, and upon that occasion a German, who had been an earnest seeker after pardon, had come seven miles across the mountain to attend. He was gloriously saved, and returned to his home rejoicing. I decided, thereupon, that these isolated ones of God's children ought not to be neglected, whatever the consequences to myself might be. (William Yost. Reminiscences. Cleveland, OH: Publishing House of the Evangelical Association, 1911, 83&84.)

As in the case of Bishop Seybert, solid Christian education was important for everyone, as evidenced by ambitious Sunday School programs, but also by the growth of Church sponsored higher education. In *The Christian Pastorate*, Daniel Kidder gave what became the standard view of a Methodist pastor's duty in promoting Christian higher education among the laity. His approach fit the democratic ethos and evangelistic purpose of Methodism while avoiding anti-intellectualism.

Kidder expressed the view that "all the best schools and school systems of modern times are an outgrowth of Christianity." He emphasized not the growth of secularism at the expense of faith, but rather a synergy in which the academy and the church supported each other. Therefore, he believed, "Christian ministers of the present and of the future should cherish a lively interest in education, and manifest it in all appropriate ways, and not to do so will be to forfeit many opportunities of enlarging their influence usefulness." This attitude and involvement would result in "favorably influencing the educational agencies by which they are surrounded, and of enabling young persons of their acquaintance to profit by them in the largest degree...." Among the specific ways to accomplish this was to use their influence with parents "to induce young people to commence a career of study and self-discipline" and help them "to discriminate in favor of those educational institutions in which direct Christian influences are exerted." The pastoral concern at work here is by no means a thing of the past but remains viable today:

> Many persons fail to consider properly the responsibility of selecting the right institutions and instruction for their children. They make their choice a matter of accident or mere temporary convenience, whereas their children are to receive but one education for life, and upon that education their happiness, their character, their future position in society, and their welfare in the world to come, will necessarily, in a great degree, depend.(Daniel P. Kidder. The Christian Pastorate (etc.). Cincinnati, OH: Hitchcock & Walden; New York, NY: Carlton & Lanahan, 1871, 515-518.)

Education was important in the African-American Methodist churches as well. Early in the history of the African Methodist Episcopal Zion Church, Bishop Christopher Rush exemplified the usefulness of education for the church's leaders. Elected bishop in 1828, he served for 24 years in that capacity. Blindness cut his episcopal service short. Loss of his vision made difficult or impossible many of the responsibilities of the episcopate, but his church continued to depend upon his experience and the wisdom for which he was known. J.W. Hood wrote:

Christopher Rush

> His intellectual faculties were deep-seated, strong, and vigorous; as a reasoner he was clear and cogent; as a contestant he was insuperable; as a theologian he was profound. His fund of knowledge was vast and varied; his mental ability and general knowledge were so ample that he was ever prepared to hold sway with public criticism on all popular and great questions of the day. Although he was debarred by the prejudice of his caste from collegiate training, yet by his extraordinary work of self his scholarly attainments astonished all that came in contact with him. (J.W. Hood. One Hundred Years of the African Methodist Episcopal Zion Church (etc.), New York, NY: A. M. E. Zion Book Concern, 1898, 168 &169.)

Another example from the AME Zion fold is B.F. Wheeler, whose studies show a determination that is the essence of perseverance. To prepare for his calling in ministry, he began studying at Oberlin College in 1877. His desire to learn, however, was not matched by his ability to pay for his education.

> The hardest pecuniary struggles of his life were experienced while at Oberlin in trying to pay his own way through school with what money he could earn during the summer vacation of two and a half months. It often happened that on returning to school by the time he paid up expenses and debts of the preceding year he would not have money enough to matriculate. But he worked for his board, sawing wood in the middle of winter from four o'clock in the morning, by candle light, until day; and by getting credit for his room rent and other necessary expenses he would pull

through the school year. For months he would be without even a penny with which to send a postal card home. ... He never told any of his friends at home or elsewhere of his dreadfully straitened circumstances. He now regards those days of adversity as not among the least agencies in fitting him for the stern realities of life.

When he later graduated from Lincoln University, he gave the class day address in Greek, and while pursuing his theology degree, also at Lincoln, he served as a tutor in Greek. He eventually earned Bachelor of Arts, Doctor of Sacred Theology, and Bachelor of Divinity degrees. (J.W. Hood. *One Hundred Years of the African Methodist Episcopal Zion Church (etc.)*. New York, NY: A..M.E. Zion Book Concern, 1895, 398&399.)

Asa Shinn had one of the most dramatic transitions imaginable in his education. He began his ministry, at age 20, with practically no education at all.

It was related by the venerable John Collins, that at one of his appointments, on the first round of his circuit, in 1801, Mr. Shinn, for the first time, met with a family clock! He had commenced services, in a private house; and after being for some time disconcerted by the ticking noise, when the time piece struck the hour, he was nearly brought to a stand, with astonishment. After the congregation had retired, he earnestly besought his host to tell him the nature and uses of the article. This he did, and at his request, he opened it, and exhibited its wheels, and weights, and pendulum, and explained to the interested inquirer the mechanical principles involved. (Ancell H. Bassett. History of the Methodist Protestant Church (etc.). Pittsburgh: James Robison; Baltimore: J.C. Dulaney, 1882, 410.)

Later in his ministry Asa Shinn would be a respected leader in his denomination and the author of challenging books of philosophical theology. His story is amazing, but by no means unique. The starting and ending points are particular to each individual, but their onward and upward trajectories are surprisingly common.

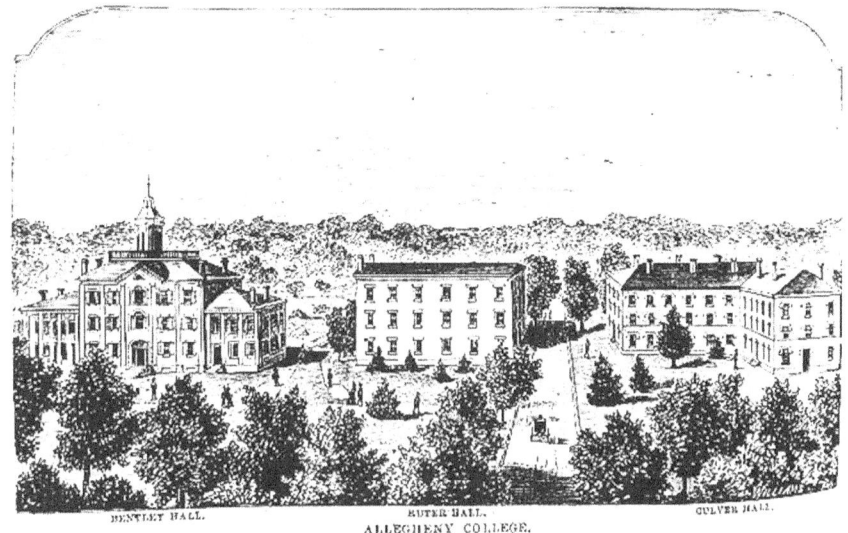

Allegheny College

Another dramatic educational journey was that of Martin Ruter.

After beginning his ministry on circuits in New England and Montreal, Ruter moved into a ministry focused on education. He was in 1820 appointed to head the new Book Concern in Cincinnati, and at various times served as Book Agent in Cincinnati, pastor in Pittsburgh and president of Augusta College in Kentucky and Allegheny College in Pennsylvania. After Texas established itself as a republic, Ruter volunteered to serve there as a pioneer missionary, educator, and author. (Nolan Harmon, Gen Ed. *The Encyclopedia of World Methodism.* Nashville, TN: 1974, 2: 2058&2059.)

One of the most effective evangelists in nineteenth-century Methodism was Maggie Newton Van Cott, the first woman licensed to preach in the Methodist Episcopal Church. Her eloquence and the impact of her preaching were widely known, receiving lavish praise, without the benefit of formal theological education. But rather than arguing against the importance of education for ministry, her gifts and power reveal an astounding capacity to gather and mobilize extraordinary wisdom and expression in the course of ordinary living. At a time when a woman in the pulpit often brought a negative response, instead there was abundant acclaim, much of it expressed in superlatives, of which this is one example, from *Zion's Herald*, April 9, 1870:

> Like a woman, she speaks from the heart, and, by means of a vivid imagination, pictures before the audience the scenes she wishes to present, and then, with the happiest tact, gives point to her lessons so as to lead men to Christ. ... she stands before the audience self-possessed, and like a skillful player on an instrument, ready to evoke any tune she may choose. Like all great leaders of men, she has the power of attaching to her, as with 'hooks of steel,' whole troops of people. She has many of the qualities that distinguish Henry Ward Beecher – bold, imaginative, electrical, often carrying an audience into the wildest enthusiasm by a single dash of her wand. ... having been operating in this vicinity for six months, her enduring popularity is evinced by the fact that several Churches ask for her as their pastor. (John O. Foster. Life and Labors of Mrs, Maggie Newton Van Cott (etc.). Cincinnati: Hitchcock & Walden, 1872, 331&332).

Bishop Gilbert Haven made it clear that, like so many of great preachers of that century, hers was not a conventional theological education. Yet she was powerfully effective with the informal preparation she picked up along the way.

> Her learning is not of the schools. She knows little about theology as a science, probably nothing, scholars being judges. She never had the least "theological education," so called, which is often an education without theology. She never was trained in public speaking. She prepares no discourses, in the usual sense of pulpit preparation. Yet, Many fish are caught by this skillful fisher of men who abide in their new grace, and will grow in it unto eternal life. She is, without doubt, to-day, the most popular, most laborious, and most successful preacher in the Methodist Episcopal Church. She has more calls, does more work, and wins more souls to Christ than any of her brothers. She does this by her genius and her faith. (Gilbert Haven, Introduction, John O. Foster. Life and Labors of Mrs. Maggie Newton Van Cott (etc.). Cincinnati: Hitchcock & Walden, 1872, xxiii.)

Gilbert Haven   Maggie Newton VanCott

HUMILITY

John Seybert, the first bishop of the Evangelical Association, who was an example of the humility Paul described in Jesus, sought to imitate in his own life, and found in some of the Christians in Philippi. One who knew Bishop Seybert well said," I have never found another such friendly, benevolent, humble-looking Protestant preacher, possessing withal such a Christ-like spirit as this man. His dress, manners, conversation and disposition indicated a humble, sincere Christian and true ambassador of Jesus Christ." (S.P. Spreng. *The Life and Labors of John Seybert, First Bishop of the Evangelical Association*. Cleveland, OH: Lauer & Mattill, 1888, 58.)

John Sensel, a blacksmith turned preacher under the influence of Seybert's ministry, often repeated a saying that helped him and his fellow preachers keep God on the throne in case any of them assumed that position by becoming overly harsh in their preaching. He said, "without grace, no sermon." In other words, no preacher should elevate himself so as to preach judgement, looking down on their listeners. A sermon should not descend to mere moralism, but should offer the grace needed to accomplish any task. (S.P. Spreng. *The Life and Labors of John Seybert, First Bishop of the Evangelical Association*. Cleveland, OH: Lauer & Mattill, 1888, 86.)

Methodist Episcopal Bishop Thomas Morris gathered in one volume, articles on a variety of subjects which he had published in scattered places. Humility, along with related subjects, is a prominent theme in this collection. For example, he writes, "Inordinate self-esteem, haughtiness of spirit, and insolent manners, constitute pride, and are sad proofs of the fall of man. Of all the features of the carnal mind, pride is one of the most prominent and unseemly." To wiser people, pride comes across as "contemptible," in spite of its common occurrence in people of every kind and social position. Morris calls pride a "moral disease," deserving "more pity than indignation." (T. A. Morris. *Miscellany (etc.)*. Cincinnati, OH: L. Swornstedt & A. Poe, 1854, 75&76.)

"Humility," on the other hand, "is freedom from pride...." It is "of gracious origin, belongs not to our fallen nature, but to 'the new man,' and is one of the fairest ornaments of the Christian character." The humility he holds before his readers should not be confused with false humility, a counterfeit which places oneself "below what he knows to be the truth...." This he calls "voluntary humility," or humility designed to impress, "whereas genuine humility is modest, unassuming, not disposed to intrude its subject into public notice unnecessarily." His perspective on humility is rooted in Paul's Letters and the example and teaching of Jesus, and was ideal wisdom to share with all Christians, especially pastors. (T. A. Morris. *Miscellany (etc.)*. Cincinnati, OH: L. Swormstedt & A. Poe, 1854, 77&78.)

Bishop Morris gives "loquacity" as a sign of *lack* of humility: "Loquacity, which, according to Walker, means "too much talk," is a fault as disagreeable as it is common." He is clear that loquacity "is not restricted to either sex," but is equally "objectionable, because it savors of vanity. It indicates that the speaker wishes to bring himself into notice by a display of words. And, consequently, that he presumes upon his own intelligence, and upon the ignorance of others, as if they knew nothing till he enlightened them." (T. A. Morris. *Miscellany (etc.)*. Cincinnati, OH: L. Swormstedt & A. Poe, 1854, 131&132.) This behavior is surely not exclusive to preachers, but neither does it exclude preachers. I once interviewed a prospective pastor regarding potential appointment. The question was, "What is the first thing you would do in your new appointment?" the answer: "listen and learn." The appointment was fixed and was a success.

Morris notes, "Let it not be supposed that talkative characters are peculiar to this age or country. Paul said, "there are many unruly and vain talkers, and deceivers, especially they of the circumcision, ...whose mouths must be stopped." And he instructed Titus to "rebuke them sharply." The bishop also mentions the polar opposite of loquacity, which he calls "taciturnity, or habitual silence." Loquacity speaks when it should be silent; taciturnity is silent when it should speak. The solution: "there is, between the two extremes of loquacity and taciturnity, a happy medium; that of speaking on a sensible subject, at the right time, and in a proper manner, so as to accomplish some good purpose."(T.A. Morris. *Miscellany (etc.)*. Cincinnati, OH: L. Swormstedt & A. Poe, 1854, 132; 134&135; Titus 1:10 &11 cf. "The Tongue," 135-137.)

THE TWO WAYS

Thomas Morris' handling of pride and humility has much in common with Biblical and early Christian lists of two ways. Limitations on his essays made it necessary to cover only one pair of vice/virtue opposites, but the importance and clarity of other issues addressed were much the same. Morris has a parallel and related contrast concerning ways people deal with fashion in choosing their way through life. There are "dupes of *fashion*," whose lives are dominated by fashion's influence, and there are others who are free to spend their lives making life better for others. The pursuit of fashion does not square well with Christian charity or humility. It skews our priorities by distracting us, focusing our minds on things of this world rather than on "things above" and inclines us to value people accordingly. (T. A. Morris. *Miscellany (etc.)*. Cincinnati, OH: L. Swormstedt & A. Poe, 1854, 129; Colossians 3: 1&2, NIV; James 2: 1-8; Matthew 6: 25-34.)

Morris sees the good and evil in life as a kind of tug of war that must and will be won by "the cause of Christ, even though that cause is vigorously opposed by formidable foes." He lists many of those foes, and then says, "the array of opposition looks fearful; but 'he that is for us is greater than all that can be against us, and, ... he will go before us, and fight our battles for us.'" No matter how things may look, to Christ and those who stand with him, "the ranks of the devil must give way, and break into general confusion...." (T.A. Morris. *Miscellany (etc.)*. Cincinnati: L. Swormstedt & A. Poe, 1854, 168&170.) The way of life and the way of death are locked in battle in every generation – not merely lists but decisions, forces, and cosmic powers. In our own time, we very much need the bishop's faith, confidence, and determination.

This contest between two ways was accompanied by a theological and evangelistic struggle over God's intentions in his plan for the salvation of humanity. Since the way of salvation was central to Wesley's theology and the mission of his movement, it was essential that his preachers got it right.

And because the issues at stake were foundational to both parties in this debate, the contest was bound to be long and loud. This was the contest between Wesleyans and Calvinists, particularly as pertained to beginning as "a difference ... between two great and good men," Wesley and George Whitefield (Nathan Bangs. *A History of the Methodist Episcopal Church*. New-York, NY: T. Mason & G. Lane, 1840, III:1.)

At the heart of this debate were radically different interpretations of certain passages in Paul's letters. A clear, straightforward Scripture expressing the Wesleyan position is: "God wants everyone to be saved and to fully understand the truth." (I Timothy 2:4, ESV) A statement offering apparent support to the Calvinist position is: "For he chose us in him before the creation of the world to be holy and blameless in his sight. In love he predestined us for adoption to sonship through Jesus Christ, in accordance with his pleasure and will...." (Ephesians 1:4&5, NIV) The first passage speaks from and encourages a compassion that is universal, directed toward "everyone." The second speaks from the same divine love, but is made subservient to a powerful choice made "before the creation of the world." The origin of love remains God. The recipients are part of a select company, chosen long before they could respond. It would remain for the Wesleyans to explain that God's loving choice was intended for all who would, by grace-empowered freedom, choose to accept that love and cooperate with that universally available grace.

Nathan Bangs pointed out the dramatic difference in evangelistic outcomes for the churches that followed these conflicting paths:

> Had he [Whitefield] followed in the track of Wesley, and adopted his enlarged views of the Divine goodness in the work of redemption by Jesus Christ, instead of the narrow views of Calvin respecting unconditional election and reprobation ... he had achieved a victory in the name of his divine Master much more enduring and beneficial in its effects upon the interests of true religion. Let the history of the two men, and the results of their labors, decide the truth of this remark. Whitefield was "a burning and shining light," but "the people rejoiced in his light" for a short season only; while Wesley blazed in the symbolical heavens as a star of the first magnitude.... (Nathan Bangs. A History of the Methodist Episcopal Church. New-York, NY: T, Mason & G. Lane, 1839, I: 29&30.

Looking back at the first half off the nineteenth-century, American Baptist historian Winthrop Hudson underscored Bangs' comment when he said, "the decades immediately preceding the civil war witnessed the triumph of the distinctive emphases of Methodism," not only within its own growing institutions, but "in practically all the denominations." (Winthrop S. Hudson. *Religion in America*. New York, NY: Macmillan; London, UK: Collier Macmillan, 1987 (4th ed.), 168.)/

The starkness of Calvinist doctrine is plain in the wording of its standard articulation:

> Some men and angels are predestinated unto everlasting life, and others fore-ordained to everlasting death.

> These angels and men, thus predestinated and fore-ordained, are particularly and unchangeably designed; and their number is so certain and definite that it cannot be either increased or diminished. (The Constitution of the Presbyterian Church in the United States of America (etc.), Philadelphia, PA: Presbyterian Board

of Publication, 1939, 27&28.).

The conflict between Wesleyans and Calvinists over predestination and related teachings would manifest itself in numerous books, articles, tracts, sermons, and debates. Some of the public expression of this conflict could get pretty contentious, as in Peter Cartwright's *Autobiography* and *Fifty Years as a Presiding Elder*.

Cartwright included in his *Autobiography* a humorous encounter with "a high-strung predestinarian," who "believed, or professed to believe, that God had decreed everything that comes to pass." This general determinism was part of the Calvinist Confession, providing the background for the more specific doctrine of predestination:

> "God from all eternity did by the most wise and holy counsel of his own will, freely and unchangeably ordain whatsoever comes to pass...." After introducing myself to him, he presently bristled up for an argument. I told him I had not come to debate, but to invite him to the Savior. He said he could not receive any thing from me, for he cordially despised the Methodists. I told him if God had decreed all things, he had decreed that there should be Methodists, and that they should believe precisely as they did, any that they were raised up by the decree of God to torment him before his time, and that he must be a great simpleton to suppose that the Methodists could do or believe any thing but what they did; and now, my dear sir, you must be a vile wretch to want to break the decrees of God, and wish to exterminate the Methodists; that if his doctrine was true, the Methodists were as certainly fulfilling the glorious decrees of God, which were founded in truth and righteousness, as the angels around the burning throne; and several admonitions I gave him, and, by the by, he had some feeling on the subject. I talked kindly and prayed with him, and left.
>
> After I left he began to think on the topics of conversation, and the more he thought the more his mind became perplexed about these eternal decrees. When he would sit down, or ride, or walk the road, he would soliloquise on the subject.
>
> Thus he went on till his family became alarmed, thinking he was deranged. The little settlement, also, was fearful that he had lost

his balance of mind.

> At length ... He called the neighbors to come and pray for him, and, after a long and sore conflict with the devil and his decrees, it pleased God to give him religion, and almost all his family were converted and joined the Methodist Church, and walked worthy of their high and holy calling. (W.P. Strickland, ed. Autobiography of Peter Cartwright (etc.). Cincinnati, OH: Jennings & Graham; New York, NY: Eaton & Mains, n.d. 331&332; The Constitution of the Presbyterian Church in the United States of America (etc.). Philadelphia, PA: Presbyterian Board of Publication, 1839, 25.)

Cartwright's second book includes an extended tirade against Calvinism, which displays the depth of his theological and pastoral outrage over the deception and damage it was causing. A brief excerpt will suffice to convey the extent of the antipathy he felt:

> But the Kentuckians possessed too much good sense to be long hoodwinked with a doctrine so detestable, so abominable, and so derogatory to the character of God; and as a filthy snail will always leave slime behind, so has it happened to the filthy reptile, Calvinism. Men became provoked that they had been so long charmed with the heresy; had, like silly people, parted with their money to support a nest of Calvinistic drones, whose constant cry in plain English was: "we can do nothing; all that is, is right; God fore-ordains whatever comes to pass," etc. (W. S. Hooper, ed. Fifty Years as a Presiding Elder, by Rev. Peter Cartwright (etc.). Cincinnati, OH: Jennings & Graham; New York, NY: Eaton & Mains, n.d., 140-141.)

The emotional horsepower in these statements was, or seemed, justified not only as a defense of the truth of God's character, but a championing of his rescue mission for humanity. Sadly, this division between Wesleyans and Calvinists accentuated the larger picture of division in the Church universal. Yet there was too much at stake to soft pedal the differences. Calvinist and Wesleyan churches were trying to attract people in the same communities. When someone crossed a boundary, they were often enthusiastic about their new church family and happy to explain their choice. One example is I. Smith, who on title page of his book identifies himself as "for some years a member of the close-communion Calvinist Baptist Church." In his book he delivers his *Reasons for Becoming a Methodist.*

While Calvinism is most often associated with Presbyterian and Reformed Churches, there were, and continue to be, others. Today there are Calvinists in Baptist and Anglican churches, and there have even been Calvinistic Methodist churches tracing roots back to George Whitefield, though to most Methodists the name embodies a stark contradiction. Likewise, there have been Free Will Baptists, and Presbyterians in the tradition of Charles Finney, whose theology resembled that of many Presbyterians who led the great Cane Ridge Camp Meeting, either a radically modified Calvinism, or a borrowed or incipient Wesleyan/Arminianism. The "Calvinism of the older denominations was becoming so diluted as to be unrecognizable." (Winthrop S. Hudson. *Religion in America.* New York, NY: Macmillan; London, UK: Collier Macmillan, 1987 (4th ed.), 168&169.)

The more brother Smith "heard and studied upon the subject, the more [he] was convinced that it was dangerous, in its tendency, and contrary to the experience and common sense of all men, and without foundation tn the Scriptures." He came to support open communion and a variety of modes of baptism. Regarding predestination, he came to see man as created "in the image of God," with "the power of choice, or the ability to choose between good and evil...." He adopted the Methodist view that "Christ gave himself a ransom for all," not "only for the elect," and "that life and salvation are freely offered to every man," along with "grace sufficient to enable him to receive the offer of life and be saved." He joined the Methodists in affirming "that God never did, and never will bring any irresistible influence to bear upon any person to insure their salvation...." (I. Smith. *Reasons for Becoming a Methodist.* Boston, MA: Published for the Author by G.C. Rand, 1853, 21; 34; 36&37.)

Theologian Laurence Kean countered a Calvinist named Samuel Pelton by disputing Pelton's *The Absurdities of Methodism.* Kean clarifies the actual positions of Methodism on relevant doctrinal issues and systematically argues for Methodism's stance against

Calvinist detractors. Kean carefully relates the history of the doctrines he opposes and dismantles the Calvinists' reasoning. Not everyone needs or wants this much detail in making the comparisons, but the Church needs to have it in order to maintain the accuracy of its teaching and then to adapt its doctrine to its audience. This extensive background and depth gives reliable guidance and confidence to people in local churches, and credibility to pastors and all who represent the church in the public square. This book emerged from and extended such a debate. The author made his purpose clear when he said,

> I hope the following work will not only prove the truth, and disprove errors, laid to the charge of Methodism; but also breathe a spirit of seriousness, and an affectionate concern for the instruction of ignorance, the removal of error, and the salvation of precious souls. I hope the observations made, are not only intellectual and doctrinal, but calculated, by the blessing of God, to subserve the interests of pure and undefiled Christianity; directing the attentive reader to Christ, and encouraging his humble confidence in the mercy of God, through the great Mediator. (Laurence Kean. A Plain and Positive Refutation of the Rev. Samuel Pelton's Unjust and Unfounded Charges, entitled "the Absurdities of Methodism" (etc.). New York, NY: J. & J. Harper, 1823, 6.)

Not surprisingly, the Methodist understanding of election and predestination shows up un sermons, such as one by D.D. Davidson, published in 1854. Here the preacher clarifies from several key passages in the New Testament Letters,that God's election was first of his Son, then "to invite and draw sinners into a state of union with Jesus Christ, by the preaching of the word, and the operation of the Holy Spirit." God calls and empowers people to respond in faith to that call, but those he calls have the grace-empowered ability to reject God's offer. Salvation belongs to "those who embrace it ... because of their obedience to the invitation." (W.P. Strickland, ed. *Practical Sermons on Various Subjects, by Rev. D.D. Davisson (etc.)*. Cincinnati, OH: 1854, 100&101.

A sermon by James Floy, on "Salvation – Mysterious and Glorious," celebrates neither a God who chooses among people he foreknows to be worthy, nor a capricious God, who saves for no reason beyond the inscrutable designs of his own power, but rather the God who loves and seeks to save everyone who will accept and live by his universal offer of salvation.

This is the God who transforms us by the synergy of grace and faith toward a destiny far greater than any we could ever imagine or create for ourselves.

> It [Salvation] stops not to inquire about the degree of the sinner's guilt, or the extent of his iniquity. As the Saviour, when on earth he healed the lepers, unstopped the ears of the deaf, and on the sightless eyeball poured the day, asked no questions as to the virulence or the duration of the malady; so salvation is offered ... to every outcast on this side of the caverns of damnation. (Davis W. Clark, ed. The Methodist Episcopal Pulpit (etc.). New-York, NY: Lane & Scott, 1850, 81.)

In Canada, where William Black, supported by John Wesley himself, had contended for the Methodist Gospel in the Maritimes, Methodism's message was the same. For Wesley,

> Only God's grace could save totally undeserving humanity; only God could justify, that is, make acceptable. But God had repeatedly promised, through Christ's new covenant, that all who had faith and humbly sought grace would be saved. The Scriptures clearly promised that this grace was universally available. The notion that only a few preordained elect had been chosen for salvation was, to Wesley, logically and Scripturally absurd. ... Wesley went so far as to claim that these Calvinist doctrines of election were placed in the path of human salvation by the devil. (Neil Semple. The Lord's Dominion: The History of Canadian Methodism. Montreal, QC & Kingston, ON; London, UK & Buffalo, NY: McGill-Queens University Press, 1996, 15 .)

Nathan Bangs devoted one of his many books to this debate. *The Reformer Reformed* is a part of his engagement, already well under way, with a Calvinist who has published "a vindication of the doctrine of divine decrees." Bangs goes into exhaustive detail to strengthen and clarify his Methodist arguments and decisively refute his opponent. Bangs is confident in his position: "we submit, without any anxiety, the decision of the question to those whom bigotry has not eaten up their candour." The depth of Bangs' research, the energy in his words, and the effect of his repartee testify to the importance of the matter at hand - for him and for his church. (Nathan Bangs. *The Reformer Reformed (etc.)*. New-York, NY: John C. Totten, 1818, 99.)

Wilbur Fisk added his voice to the chorus of Wesleyan scholars and pastors with his *Calvinistic Controversy,* published with *A Sermon on Predestination and Election.* He acknowledged in his sermon that he was walking onto a well-plowed field.

Wilbur Fisk

> By doing this, much that is new cannot be expected. The whole ground of this controversy has been examined and re-examined; and the various arguments, on both sides, have been urged and opposed by the most able polemics in philosophy and theology. The most, therefore, that can now be expected, is to a concise view of the subject, in a form and manner suited to the present state of the controversy, and to the circumstances of the present congregation. (Wilbur Fisk. Calvinistic controversy, Embracing A Sermon on Predestination and Election (etc.). New – York, NY: T. Mason & G. Lane, 1837, 7.)

Yet plow he did, because as long as God's people were beset by the perennial falsehoods of Calvinism, the record would need to be set straight and Scriptural doctrine vindicated. The same needs remain with us today. Also, Fisk challenges us to argue truthfully and effectively, while maintaining a respectful, charitable attitude:

> It is hoped, at least, that the subject may be investigated in the spirit of Christianity; and that there will be no loss of brotherly and Christian candour.... Yet, in a desire to give no offense, I must not suppress the truth, nor neglect to so often point out, as I am able, the absurdity of error, and its unprofitable influence on the minds of those who propagate or receive it. The truth should be spoken, but it should be spoken in love.

A sample of Fisk's extended argument in the sermon draws out one implication of Calvinist determinism. In this case the Calvinist disputant tried to soften their message by focusing only on predestination to heaven and passing over its unavoidable implication:

> All ... who hold to the unconditional election of a part of mankind to eternal life, must, to be consistent with themselves, take into their creed the "horrible decree" of reprobation. They must believe that in the ages of eternity God determined to create men and angels for the express purpose to damn them for eternity! That for doing as they were impelled to do, by the irresistible decree of Jehovah, they must lie down for ever, under the scalding vials of his vengeance in the pit of hell! To state this doctrine in its true character is enough to chill one's blood – and we are drawn by all that is rational within us, to turn away from such a God with horror, as from the presence of an almighty Tyrant. (Wilbur Fisk. Calvinistic Controversy, Embracing a Sermon on Predestination and Election (etc.). New York, NY: T. Mason & G. Lane, 1837, 7&8; 41&42.)

Fisk's example of careful, persistent, Scriptural, and logical argument is worthy of taking seriously in its own right and carrying forward into a new era.

Another nineteenth-century work in this area is R.S. Foster's *Objections to Calvinism as It Is*. As with Nathan Bangs' and Laurence Kean's earlier books, this one is responding to a Calvinist writer. An introduction by Matthew Simpson provides a historical context for Foster's presentation of the issues. The authors of these books represent the highest expressions of the teaching office of the church. Nathan Bangs was a prolific author, publisher, and mission executive. Wilbur Fisk was a university professor and first president of Wesleyan University. He was elected bishop but was unable to serve for reasons

Randolph Foster

of health. Randolph S. Foster was an author and academic who was at one point President at Northwestern University and eventually a bishop. Foster wrote the most influential book on the theology of sanctification in his lifetime and was a leader in the Holiness Movement. Their role in teaching the content of Christian faith has roots going back to the Apostles and early episcopacy and also resembles the role currently envisioned for bishops in The Global Methodist Church.

Foster explained his reason for entering this fray:

> The Church, of which he [the author] is a humble and obscure minister, had been long and grievously assailed by one of the principle organs of a sister denomination – her doctrines and usages held up to public odium, as perverted by the pen of misrepresentation – her influence for piety questioned, and whatever was peculiar to her organization ridiculed and calumniated. And this ungenerous course was commenced and pursued by an accredited champion, at a time when peace and Christian union had long existed – against remonstrances on our part, and published depredations of the consequences which were certain to ensue. We endured for a time. But this only seemed to whet the envenomed appetite of an adversary who seemed intent to devour us. The greater our reluctance, the greater his ferocity. It now seemed, that to remain longer - silent would not only be a reproach to ourselves – a matter which, alone considered, gave us little concern – but must, also, weaken the force, if not peril the interests, of truth itself. It was under such circumstances that the substance of what is contained in this volume was given to the public, through one of the journals of our Church, in a series of letters, addressed to the reverend gentleman [N.L. Rice] who seemed so anxious to discuss our respective differences. This is our apology, if any is necessary, for sending to the public a volume which, it may be, some unacquainted with the facts might conclude was uncalled for. Truth and Religion required it. The time had come when the real issues needed to be stated, and truth vindicated.

Only a concern for "Truth and Religion" could prompt yet another Methodist scholar to critically work through once again the wilderness of strained logic by which Calvinists seek to render their doctrine Scriptural and make it conform both to the character of God and the good sense of his people.

> It has been no pleasure, [he writes,] but, on the contrary, extremely painful to me, to make the plain statements contained in the foregoing pages. Nothing but a provocation, which it would have been unchristian to endure longer, could have induced it – unchristian, because truth and righteousness were suffering, and likely to suffer more by silence. We would have been content to let the controversy slumber, leaving truth to work out error by a peaceable process, which it was doing, rather than to have caused the least pain to a single disciple of Christ – much more, rather than to involve two large Christian bodies in unpleasant conflict. ... but nothing would do but controversy. We, therefore, reluctantly yielded to the necessity. (R.S. Foster. Objections to Calvinism As It Is (etc.). Cincinnati: Printed for the Author, Methodist Book Concern, 1850, 13 & 14; 309.)

Calvinism was waning, and perhaps without the oxygen of debate would have continued to decline, but it was not to be, as we have seen in the twentieth and twenty-first-centuries. Meanwhile, the standard of truth was held aloft for generations and the baton of faith handed on.

Methodist apologists believed that the picture of God drawn by Calvinist theology was more like a hideous, capricious monster than the loving God we know in Christ. Such a God might be feared or hated, but surely not loved. They saw predestination as taking away hope.

AFFIRMING SHARED BELIEFS, VALUES, PURPOSE

John Thomas Mitchell expressed his dying experience by saying, "I am going home to rest. The port is in sight. You and I have often sung together here on earth, but we'll sing up yonder. My peace flows as a river. I have a desire to depart and be with Christ. To a ministerial brother he said, 'I am unspeakably happy.'"

"To a member of the conference who visited him frequently during his sickness" Octavius Mason repeated the famous dying words of John Wesley, "the best of all is, God is with us."

George Maley said, as he was dying, "'the gospel which I have preached to others supports me now. The world is empty; religion is my only trust. I have an unfaltering trust in the merits of Christ.' As death approached his countenance was lighted up with heavenly radiance...."

An important and moving genre of Methodist writing in the late nineteenth-century focused on the last moments and words of preachers and others. Often those who were dying wanted to convey messages to colleagues in the ministry, reaffirming the truth of their purpose and calling. Others shared visions of what lay just beyond this present life. Though some might expect these accounts to be sorrowful or morose, they are generally inspiring and victorious - just the kind of reading to brighten and encourage someone who may be living through a difficult time. They reinforce basic convictions and address universal human fears with assurances of eternal life.

These, and hundreds more, are accounts of ministers of the Methodist Episcopal Church, gathered by Maxwell Gaddis, mainly, but not exclusively from Ohio. Bishop W.M. Weekley made a collection from his own United Brethren Church. Like Addis, he wrote not to depress, but to inspire. Weekley said in his foreword,

"As I searched out these testimonies, I found in them a blessing for my own heart" and wanted others to know that blessing. His hope was "that all who may chance to read this booklet may be strengthened in the faith, and helped in a life of consecration."

Examples from his collection:

> William Turner spoke these words to those who were with him in his dying moments: "Tell my brethren that it is all well. The gospel that l preached to others comforts my own heart. I am enjoying heights and depths of the love of God that I never realized before. Oh, it is wonderful! "

Bishop Jacob Erb: "For sixty years, in consecutive order, he attended the sessions of Pennsylvania Conference. When the time of the sixty-first drew near, and he saw that he would be too feeble to attend, he addressed a fatherly letter to his brethren to be read in open conference. In closing he said: "My faith in God is strong, my confidence in his word unshaken, and I know by personal experience that there is a power in true religion. The future of a blessed life is to me full of hope and promise. God is my refuge and strength."

J.W. Fulkerson said, "the more of the Bible we have woven into our lives the richer our experience, and the brighter our hope of heaven. If I had my life to live over I should spend it in the Church of the United Brethren in Christ. The name is sweeter to me now than ever before."

An earlier collection by Davis Clark included Wilbur Fisk, Methodist preacher and first president of Wesleyan University. Like the thoughtful theologian he was, Fisk devoted some of his last moments to reflecting at length on death, resurrection, and eternal life. Here is what he said about heaven and Sabbath:

> "Perhaps," said Mrs. Fisk, "the Lord will take you to his rest this day."
>
> "Then I can worship," was his answer, "with the Sabbath-keeping band in heaven; but I cannot here."
>
> On being reminded that he always loved the Sabbath,
>
> "Yes," he replied, "and though it was a day of toil for me, yet I loved my work. To me the Sabbath has been an emblem of that promised rest. O, that rest is sweet. It is glorious.

Through his hymns and his prominence in the Methodist movement, Charles Wesley has from the beginning held a significant place in its culture and worship. The story of Charles' transition between worlds followed naturally from his ministry, and especially his hymn writing. "To prepare for it has been the leading business of the greater part of his life. He expected it therefore, not with alarm, but with hope and desire. His treasure and his heart were already in heaven; and the abiding consciousness which he had of his title to the future inheritance, resulting from his filial relation to God, and of his meetness for it, through the sanctifying power of the Holy Ghost, filled him with adoring thankfulness. (Maxwell Pierson Gaddis. *Last Words and Old-Time Memories*. New York, NY & Pittsburgh, PA: Phillips & Hunt; Cincinnati & Chicago: Walden & Stowe, 1880, 212; 224; W.M. Weekley. *From*

Life to Life: How Our Preachers Die. Dayton, OH: Otterbein, 1918. 19; 27 & 28; 68; Davis W. Clarke. *Death-bed Scenes; or, Dying with and without Religion.* New York, NY: Carlton & Porter, 1851, 208; 220.)

The most powerful means of upholding shared beliefs, were class and camp meetings, reinforced by the distribution of Methodist literature. Each of these is described in some detail elsewhere in the book. Each one conveys grace and discipline to anyone willing to participate, in a form adaptable to nearly every way of life.

ENCOURAGEMENT

One form of encouragement can be found in teamwork among those engaged in a difficult but important task or mission. By itself, that teamwork may not be enough to sustain all the members of a team when they are hard pressed in their work, but without it, little of any value can be accomplished.

As early as 1800, the explosive power of camp meetings overspread the Appalachian frontier. People who had experienced one camp meeting, and who knew the Divine Source of its power, could look ahead to others. Preachers who had spoken or organized a camp meeting, who had known the intense camaraderie among the leaders there, could likewise anticipate other such gatherings, as their movement ... spread through all the settlements of the western country; and such was the eagerness of the people to attend, that the roads were literally crowded with those that were pressing their way to the groves; so much so that entire neighborhoods would be forsaken, for a season, of their inhabitants.

Historian and camp meeting organizer and preacher Nathan Bangs, wrote about some of the Methodist preachers of that day:

> Among the traveling preachers who entered into this work in those days, we may mention William Burke, John Sale, Benjamin Lakin, and Henry Smith, with a number of others, whose zealous efforts contributed greatly to spread the gospel in these new settlements. Mr. [Bishop] McKendree was the life and soul of this army of itinerants. Wherever he went, both by precept and example, he aroused the lukewarm to diligence, confirmed those who stood in the faith, and alarmed the fears of careless sinners by his

powerful appeals to their consciences. (Nathan Bangs. A History of the Methodist Episcopal Church. New-York, NY: T. Mason & G. Lane, 1839, 2: 110&111.)

This continued the ministry of Francis Asbury, which had already begun, when, as early as 1786, the Methodist preachers had penetrated the wilderness beyond the Alleghany mountains, and "had gradually extended their labors from year to year, being led on and encouraged in their work both by the example and precept of bishop Asbury, who was generally in the foremost ranks when danger and hardship were to be encountered and endured." (Nathan Bangs. *A History of the Methodist Episcopal Church*. New-York, NY: T. Mason & G. Lane, 1839, 2: 111.

Encouragement came in many forms, two of which were the grateful words and generosity of those who were especially blessed by a preacher's ministry. John Seybert received such encouragement when he took the courageous step of preaching in English "for the first time in his life. He had a congregation that was almost exclusively English. How could he serve them in their own language, much as he desire to do so, was the question." Seybert had no idea that his desire would be answered by a new Pentecost.

After talking a while in German, he ventured to say a few words in English. No sooner had he begun this, than the power of God came upon the people, and the effort was as blessed as it was stammering and imperfect. And really, it "went" better than he imagined it would. An English brother afterwards came up and gave him some money for salary. He seemed very well pleased, and encouraged him. He thanked God and took courage. (S.P. Spreng. *The Life and Labors of John Seybert, First Bishop of the Evangelical Association*. Cleveland, OH: Lauer & Mattill, 1888, 59&60; cf. 79, where after a sermon, someone gave Seybert the dollar he needed to buy an important book.)

We have focused mainly on ways pastors, especially those in apostolic or supervisory roles, have given and received encouragement for ministry. Daniel P. Kidder, in The Christian Pastorate (1871), reminded readers that the relationship between a pastor and congregation should be "reciprocal." We saw reciprocity in the Letters of the New Testament, especially between Paul and his readers. They prayed for each other, encouraged each other, communicated with each other, and saw each other as coworkers. We saw the way Christian love and encouragement flowed within a congregation. Now we see how encouragement must move back and forth between pastor and congregation, and how much it matters that a pastor be fueled by the love and spiritual support of the church.

One form of encouragement we should note is found in biographies, which by praising the character and accomplishments of earlier Methodist preachers and exemplary laity, these writings uphold the purpose of their movement and encourage a newer generation to emulate past heroes of the faith:

Freeborn Garrettson

IN MEMORY OF THE LATE VENERABLE FREEBORN GARRETTSON.

Full fifty years the cross he bore, In heat and cold, in war and strife;

In perils oft, in days of yore, Nor counted dear his valued life,
 So he might gain the heavenly prize - A crown of glory in the skies!

At home, abroad, by night and day, - 'In labors more abundant,' too, he did not fear what man could say, But gave to all their, righteous due, While he proclaimed the living word, The counsel of his faithful Lord.

Sound in the doctrines of the cross,- A friend to truth in error's night, - Bold in the great Redeemer's cause, He saw the aliens put to flight; Nor lived to see that glory gone, Which first upon our Israel shone.

But Moses-like, on Pisgah's height, He view'd the promise from afar; Which ushers in the glorious day, When night and shadows flee away.

(George Coles. My First Seven Years in America. New-York, NY: Carlton & Phillips, 1852, 313-314.)

James Finley preserved for us the sad story of Francis Poythress, an early circuit rider who fell prey to depression, a message offered to discourage anyone from following the tragic steps Brother Poythress took. He was a preacher of considerable accomplishments. But his accomplishments did not save him. Instead they drove him to attempt too much, while neglecting what should have been empowering resources of grace. To understand the path Poythress traveled, we need to see the powerful means of grace the early pioneer preachers could be to each other. Since Finley was one of them, his witness is especially important:

> The pioneers of Methodism in that part of Western Virginia and the western territory suffered many privations, and underwent much toil and labor, preaching in forts and cabins, sleeping on straw, bear and buffalo skins, living on bear meat, venison, and wild turkeys, traveling over mountains and through solitary valleys, and, sometimes, lying on the cold ground; receiving but a scanty support, barely enough to keep soul and body together, with coarse, home-made apparel;

Such was the context of ministry in what was, in 1800, the American West. This was where Methodist preachers found the people who would make up the frontier circuits of that heroic age. Next Finley describes the resources these preachers were to each other. His description matches Nathan Bangs' account of people leaving the first camp meeting in Canada (1805) and what those who had gathered there meant to each other.

> The best of all was, their labors were owned and blessed of God, and they were like a band of brothers, having one purpose and end in view, the glory of God and the salvation of immortal souls. When the preachers met from their different and distant fields of labor, they had a feast of love and friendship; and when the parted, they wept and embraced each other as brothers beloved. Such was the spirit of primitive Methodist preachers. (W.P. Strickland,

ed. Sketches of Western Methodism (etc.), by Rev. James B. Finley, Cincinnati, OH: Methodist Book Concern, for the author, 1856, 58.)

Poythress was one of the "band of brothers," those heroic preachers in the Appalachian forests. Through the 1790s Poythress was assigned to multiple circuits and districts that were large and remote, requiring much and offering little to sustain him.

> In the year 1800 he was sent to a district in North Carolina, embracing fifteen circuits. His removal to a new field, among strangers, and the subjection, if possible, to greater hardships than he had endured on his former fields, alone and friendless, without a companion, save the companionship which he found at different and distant points among his brethren, preyed heavily upon his system, shattering his nerves, and making fearful inroads upon a mind naturally of a too contemplative, if not somber cast, and seasons of gloom and darkness gathered around him. He should at once have desisted, and sought that rest and society for which he so much longed, among the friends and companions of his youth; but, alas! The necessity that rested in those days upon a Methodist preacher, stern as fate, kept him at his post and he toiled on till his shattered frame, like the broken strings of a harp, could only sigh to the winds that swept through it. And his mind ... became alike shattered and deranged. The next year he came back to Kentucky, but the light of the temple was gone, and the eye which shot the fires of genius and intelligence, now wildly stared upon the face of old, loving, long-tried friends as if they were strangers. Here he remained till death released him and sent his spirit home. Poor Poythress! Bravely didst thou toil and endure hardness on the well-fought field. A campaign of twenty-four years of incessant toil in the gloomy wilds of the west, away from friends and loved ones at home, proved too much for thy nature to bear. But thou art gone "where the wicked cease to trouble, and the weary are at rest." (W.P. Strickland, ed. Sketches of Western Methodism (etc.). Cincinnati, OH: Methodist Book Concern, for the Author, 1856, 131 & 132.

FELLOWSHIP, WORSHIP, RENEWAL

To an extent and in a form few of today's Methodists can imagine, early conferences were times for worship, fellowship, and transformation. "Revivals and conversions often occurred at conference and conferences functioned to sustain and cultivate the religious life." (Russell E. Richey. *The Methodist Conference in America: a History*. Nashville: Kingswood, 1996,

But a yearly gathering, no matter how well it fulfills its purpose, cannot by itself grow and shepherd the spiritual life of a church. Two extraordinary means of grace filled much of the space between general and annual conferences, and quarterly meetings. Class and camp meetings provided renewal and discipline needed to strengthen and deepen people's faith between conferences. Class meetings were essential to John Wesley's program for evangelical spirituality for the long haul. (Kevin Watson. *The Class Meeting (etc.)*. Franklin, TN: Seedbed, 2014, 19.) The class leader came to function as a "sub-pastor," both by encouraging spiritual growth along the way of salvation and sanctification, and exercising coordination and accountability. The class leader acted in concert with the pastor, much like the pastor did with the presiding elder and the presiding elder with the bishop. Effective as this system could be, even in that early, foundational time, Wesley was concerned that these meetings might lose their spiritual power. (Charles L. Goodell. *The Drillmaster of Methodism: Principles and Methods for the Class Leader* and *Pastor*. New York: Eaton & Mains; Cincinnati: Jennings & Pye, 1902, 5.).

More recently, David Lowes Watson has been a major part of the revival of Class Meetings, especially in the United Methodist Church, speaking and writing widely and working to reinstate this ministry after long years of neglect. He explored the history of class meetings and their leadership in other, especially African American Methodist churches and in World Methodism. Noting that in UM churches the ministry of class leader "has lapsed entirely in the great majority of congregations," he believed the tradition could still be revived as an essential part of rebuilding a culture of "faithful discipleship." He envisioned an arduous process of reconnecting with earlier and parallel traditions in a comprehensive, even elaborate, program which, if successful, would deepen and enliven the church , so that "We might even become 'Methodist' again." (David Lowes Watson. *Class Leaders (etc.).* Nashville, TN: Discipleship Resources, 1991, 64, 72, 59. His is a compelling vision, providing an extensive survey and rich understanding of the class meeting tradition, as well as an impressive means of reviving it. But there were elements in United Methodism that stood in the way, among them the absence of a shared denominational purpose. His method for recovery and, for most, reintroduction of this tradition also overlooked – could not have seen - the extent to which his church's organization and ethos were crumbling and could not carry the weight of his dream. What was needed was a church culture which much more resembled the movement and motivation of early Methodism. It would have to be simpler, more grass roots, and most of all, more like the transformative culture which birthed the classes.

Watson sees exactly what was and is at stake in creating, continuing, and now recovering the class meeting. It is, for all who accept the challenge, a matter of traditioning the New Testament faith of Wesley's original movement. Many things within ourselves and our world serve to dilute or even replace the baton of faith and weaken its transmission across time and space. Classes were designed to achieve, preserve, and convey depth, completeness, and permanence for the Wesleyan way of life. Watson agrees with Howard Snyder's statement that "the church must be 'a distinct, separate, countercultural covenant community,'" speaking and acting prophetically from within the Church. (David Lowes Watson. *The Early Methodist Class Meeting (etc.).* Nashville, TN: Discipleship Resources, 1992, 140.

The class meeting has been an important part of that traditioning process.

Wesley charged the early Methodists with a twofold traditioning of the gospel in the immediacy of their worldly context. They were to hand on the gospel within their community of faith and hand it over to the world. ... ...the early Methodists found themselves in the front line of service for the coming New Age of Jesus Christ as long as they held one another accountable for their discipleship. (David Lowes Watson. *The Early Methodist Class Meeting (etc.)*. Nashville, TN: Discipleship Resources, 1992, 144&145.)

Less well known are Wesley's Band meetings, which were and are smaller and more rigorous. Like the class meetings, band meetings are also experiencing a revival today. (Kevin M. Watson & Scott T. Kisker. *The Band Meeting (etc.)*. Franklin, TN: Seedbed, 2017) Efforts to renew both are strongly supported by the publisher Seedbed, though similar attempts have appeared from time to time throughout our history. (Charles L. Goodell. *The Drillmaster of Methodism: Principles and Methods for the Class Leader and Pastor.* New York: Eaton & Mains; Cincinnati: Jennings & Pye, 1902. David Lowes Watson. *Class Leaders.* Nashville, TN: Discipleship Resources, 1991; David Lowes Watson. *The Early Methodist Class MeetIng (etc.)*. Nashville: Discipleship Resources, 1992; John Atkinson. *The Class Leader (etc.)*. New York, N.Y: Nelson & Phillips; Cincinnati: Hitchcock & Walden, 1874.)

Perhaps the class meeting was so ubiquitous within Methodism, so much a part of its everyday life, that some began to take it for granted. This might account for the small number of books written to guide its practitioners or argue for usefulness. Thus John Atkinson wrote in 1874,

The class-meeting is a peculiar, conspicuous, and powerful agency of Methodism. Class leaders are invaluable and indispensable co-workers with the ministry. It is remarkable that an institution of such potency, and a class of laborers so numerous, gifted, and useful, have not received larger attention from Methodist writers. Only two or three small volumes and a few tracts, specifically devoted to this subject, are extant in the whole range of American Methodist publications.... (John Atkinson. *The Class Leader (etc.)*. New York, NY: Nelson & Phillips; Cincinnati: Jennings & Pye, 1874, 3.

Nearly three decades later, Charles Goodell could write, "The class meeting, like the church itself, has had its revival and declension; but in spite of all efforts to abolish it or to provide for it a substitute it still holds its place, second to none, as a means of grace in the development of a noble Christian character."

Goodell did take courage from a recent revival of interest in class meetings, centered in the New York City area, where he was serving. Yet as encouraging as that development was, there was too little change in the picture Atkinson had drawn, except by this time criticism had become more vocal and widespread: "Little has been published on the class meeting by our Book Concern for the last twenty-five years, and this book will therefore cover a field which is not touched by any recent publication." (Charles L. Goodell. *The Drillmaster of Methodism: Priniples and Methods for the Class Leader and Pastor*. New York, NY: Eaton & Mains; Cincinnati, OH: Jennings & Pye, 1902, 7 & 5.)

One relatively recent attempt to revive the class meeting is part of the Walk to Emmaus . Emmaus participants are urged to continue the renewal they experience on their Walk by faithful attendance at "group reunions." These reunion groups or "groupings" are intended to supplement larger "gatherings." While serving as Spiritual Director for my Emmaus Community, I discovered how difficult it could be to return to a practice that has fallen into disuse. While there were a few "groupings" or accountability groups active in our community, there were many members who had once attempted a group – perhaps even one that had prospered for a time - that eventually failed or faded away for a variety of reasons, while others had been enthusiastic about the idea, but could not turn theory into practice. In other words, some had tried groupings and found them difficult; others had seen groupings as difficult and did not try.

By his time Goodell felt it necessary to defend the class leaders' reputation and to clarify the original, essential, and enduring purpose of their work. There had long been prophetic voices who recognized the importance of class meetings and lamented their partial decline. The same appreciation and concern was expressed regarding camp meetings, which in nineteenth century North America saw both decline and renewal. The successful revival of camp meetings was staggering. (D. Gregory Van Dussen. *Camp Meetings: Power for the Road Ahead*. Lexington, KY: Emeth, 2022.)

Ohio circuit rider Maxwell P. Gaddis used biography, autobiography, and even *Last Words and Old-time Memories* to portray and convey the ethos of Methodism as he knew it in the nineteenth-century. But he had another way of accomplishing this task of passing the baton of faith. Late in his ministry, he wrote an unusual volume called *The Sacred Hour*, in which he sought to identify and explore the heart of worship. He did this by engaging with two young women to see what their radically transformed lives would look like and how their transformation might impact their world. He also set his own goal to live the most thoroughly consecrated Christian life possible: "I determined to be a Christian and work for God." [This he saw as a purely practical matter, to promote the POWER of Godliness – the life of Christ in the soul - I love to view religion on the practical side, as designed to operate by a few simple and grand truths, on the affections and habits of men. Blessed are the pure in heart, for they shall see God. Only a church,' focused on the light and love of Christ and nothing less, will "shine" forth with God's glory and accomplish God's purposes[5-9; 30.] It is this "burning desire which still] glows in my heart to be a co-worker with God,"- even as a "superannuate" (retiree). ...*my whole heart*, and whatever else I possess – are this day unreservedly given to God and to his service. ... My sole aim and purpose shall be to *good* – to *be useful*, and contribute all I can to make others happy." (Maxwell Pierson Gaddis. *The Sacred Hour. Cincinnati, OH: Methodist Book Concern,* 1856, 30)

Gundant ground for substantive unity. Jim Collins, in *How the Mighty Fall*, offers a pertinent perspective from the business world. He begins by asking how a large, successful organization loses its way in the marketplace, perhaps even plummeting into failure. His answers are extremely useful in understanding the decline and fall of the largest churches in the North American Methodist fold, The United Methodist Church and The United Church of Canada. Canada's United Church came from a 1925 merger of The Methodist Church with Congregationalists and a large number of Presbyterian churches. While this is different from the path through the twentieth-century taken by the largest American Methodist body, their overall patterns show similar trajectories and results. In the US, the northern Methodist Episcopal Church merged with the Methodist Episcopal Church South and the smaller Methodist Protestant Church in 1939 to form The Methodist Church. A parallel merger brought the Evangelical and United Brethren Churches together in 1946. Then, in 1968 these merged bodies joined to become The United Methodist Church. The UMC divided with the formation, by "disaffiliated" United Methodists, of The Global Methodist Church in 2022.

Collins believes "Decline can be avoided." If caught in time, it can even "be reversed," yet, "History shows, repeatedly, that the mighty can fall." From successful businesses to powerful empires, human institutions have often grown to greatness only to cave in under their own weight. Of course, all the while he is asking questions about this in the context of secular organizations, I am asking similar questions about churches and denominations. "How *do* the mighty fall? If some of the greatest companies in history can collapse from iconic to irrelevant, what might we learn by studying their demise, and how can others avoid their fate?"(Jim Collins, *How the Mighty Fall*. New York, NY: HarperCollins, 2009, xiv; 2&3; 20-23) The first stage is "hubris born of success virtually as an entitlement." The second is "the undisciplined pursuit of more – more scale, more growth, more acclaim, more of whatever those in power see as 'success.'" The third stage is "denial of risk or peril," In which continued signs of success mask warning signs. In the fourth stage, it becomes clear that the organization is in trouble and the response is "lurching for a quick salvation" in the shape of bold new directions, programs, creativity. "The longer a company remains in stage 4, repeatedly grasping for silver bullets, the more likely it will spiral downward" into stage 5, "irrelevance or death." Collins says," it is possible to skip a stage, although our research suggests that companies are likely to move through them in sequence."

It is not difficult to view the histories of the various Methodist denominations as passing through some of these stages. No doubt there will be readers who have already recognized at least one stage they have experienced. A complete study along these lines would be useful, but well beyond the scope of this book. It is important, however, and only fair, that we include Collins' hopeful findings. "For one thing, with a roadmap of decline in hand, institutions heading downhill might be able to apply the brakes early and reverse course. For another, we've found companies that recovered – in some cases, coming back even stronger – after having crashed down into the depths of Stage 4." (Jim Collins. *How the Mighty Fall (etc.)*. New York, NY: HarperCollins, 2009, xiv; 273; 20-25)

Among the fatal flaws of declining institutions is a displacement of its original purpose and fervor by "institutional self-perpetuation." Another is flailing around in search of something new – new direction, new leadership style, etc. Most important of all is loss of compelling purpose rooted in original vision.

If you cannot marshal a compelling answer to the question, "what would be lost, and how would the world be worse off, if we ceased to exist?" then perhaps capitulation is the wise path. But if you have a clear and inspired purpose built upon solid core values, then the noble course may be to fight on, to reverse decline, and to try to rekindle greatness. (Jim Collins. *How the Mighty Fall (etc.)*. New York, NY; HarperCollins, 2009, 111.)

Thus the Church is wise to seek renewal by a return to its foundational, "inspired purpose," whenever, and however often it wanders off course, loses its original energy, and finds itself mired in one of the stages of decline (especially, stage 4). In the case of Christianity, there is no possibility that our original vision is wrong, or no longer valid. There is, in other words, no hope to be found in replacing that vision with something new. And since we have – literally – an inspired purpose, we have recourse to the Source of that inspiration whenever it seems to weaken within us. (for relevant studies in the Methodist tradition, see David Hempton. *Methodism: Empire of the Spirit*. New Haven, CT & London, UK: Yale University Press, 2005; Kevin M. Watson. *Doctrine, Spirit, and Discipline: A History of the Wesleyan Tradition in the United States*. Grand Rapids: Zondervan Academic, 2024; *Old or New School Methodism: The Fragmentation of a Theological Tradition*. Oxford, UK; New York, NY: Oxford University Press, 2019; Neil Semple. *The Lord's Dominion: the History of Canadian Methodism*. Montreal, QC & Kingston, ON; London, UK & Buffalo, NY: McGill-Queens University Press,1996, 416-451.

Led by the Spirit of truth, essential Methodism will outlast separation. It is a part of our origination, our identity and purpose, that we dare not neglect. Toward the end of his life, Wesley said, "See that you never give place to one thought of separating from your brothers in Europe. Lose no opportunity of declaring to all men, that the Methodists are one people in all the world, and that it is their full determination so to continue." (Davis W. Clark. *Death-bed Scenes; or, Dying With and Without Religion (etc.)*. New York, NY: Carlton & Porter, 1851, 158.)

David F. Watson recently asked essentially the same question, and concluded that the traditioning that has kept the faith active and intact for so many generations gives us direction and hope now:

> How could this faith have survived so many attempts to destroy it, both from outside and within? Why hasn't Christianity simply collapsed under the weight of human sin? Why is it that, despite periods in which the church has capitulated to the spirit of the age, God continually calls us back to something more profound than a single generation can discern? Perhaps God has guided us across the ages because he loves us, and this gospel, the consensual tradition, the faith once delivered, teaches us how to be saved. That is God's will for us, after all – to be plucked out of the clutches of sin and death and receive new life, even into eternity.
>
> The God who so desires our salvation hasn't left us to our own devices to figure out how this might happen. The saving faith first delivered to the apostles has been entrusted to the saints, who have entrusted it to other saints, and so on, across the ages. Now it is our turn. The faith once delivered to the saints has been delivered to us. Generations to come will remember our witness, for better or worse. (David F. Watson. "To Contend for the Faith." Good News, May/June, 2024, 23.)

Behind and within this handing on of "the faith once for all delivered" is the love of God which "endures forever." (Jude v.3; Psalm 107:1, ESV)

Jesus assures us that even "the gates of hell shall not prevail against" the Church he has built to carry on his truth and love. (Matthew 16:18, ESV) From torture to corruption to ridicule, it seems that the adversary has used every possible weapon and obstacle against the Church. Yet its origin and source of power stand beyond this barrage. Every apparent, temporary defeat has been supplanted by reform and renewal. We in the Wesleyan movement, of all people, have a heritage that began and has continued with the overthrow of temporary defeat. We have every reason to pray for, work for, and anticipate a hopeful future.

Amid heroic advances and destructive detours, with help from a cloud of witnesses and blown off course by "every wind of doctrine" (Ephesians 4:14, ESV), the baton of faith has made its way into our hands, and soon into the hands of another generation. When we look across the expanses of time it has crossed and the storms it has weathered, we can still identify the path it has taken and the runners who have not let the baton drop. It has never lost its power to inspire and transform those who have graciously received it and generously passed it on. There have been times when the future has clouded over or when several runners have walked onto the track, ready to carry the baton down competing roads. We live in such a time. Yet we are not the first and we are not without guides. By "The Spirit of truth" we can listen with humility and discernment to the enduring message our predecessors have left us; we can still "hear what the Spirit says to the churches." (Revelation 2:7, NIV)

Where will the next runners take the Methodist baton of faith? Where will they come from? Will there be eager hands, ready to grasp the baton and run with it? Where will they find the wisdom and power for their road ahead? Will our generation prove worthy of the "endless line of splendor" we have inherited, and which we have now joined? Are the glory days relegated forever to the past, or can we still be "taken by surprise"?

Repeated experiences of major revivals at Asbury College and seminary argue strongly for surprise, (Mark Elliott, an observer/participant in the 2023 revival, used the term "spiritual spontaneous combustion," though the reliable leadership coming from those institutions tempers the surprise element. Certainly there are connections between the Asbury Revivals, Cane Ridge, Wesley's Revivals, and the ocean of camp meetings across nineteenth-century North America.

In all these, and many others extending across time and space, we see "fresh wind of God.'s Spirit" bringing "the restoration of God's people after a period of indifference and decline Mark R. Elliott. *Taken by Surprise: The Asbury Revival of 2023*. Franklin, TN: Seedbed, 2023, 5.)

Asbury has a long tradition of "spontaneous, student-generated" revivals. The academic and spiritually reflective environment there generates a genuine search for causes and effects that explain why either campus has needed or received a fresh outpouring of grace, the shape that has taken and the leadership it has provided. One key question has to be, "In what ways has this new revival strengthened the Church in its connection with God and the fulfillment of its mission?" Others must be, "Can the Church integrate its ongoing, multigenerational life and efforts with those of a student/academy – led, occasional movement?" "Are there connections that can be made with camp meetings and other evangelical ministries that might be mutually beneficial?" "Is there a way to move from ad hoc to reliable and connectional in way that will encourage the passing of the baton of faith across time and space?" (see also Robert J. Kanary. *Spontaneous Revivals: Asbury College, 1905-2006 (etc.)*

Amazon createspace, 2017; Robert E. Coleman & David A. Cyertson, eds. *One Divine Moment: The Account of the Asbury Revival of 1970*. Wilmore, KY: First Fruits, 2013.)

Meanwhile, the critical moment at which we now find ourselves is ideal for standing squarely on (not turning away from) our movement's past in order to gain a clear, motivating vision for the future. In an anthology called *The Next Methodism* we have facets of that vision, and the opportunity to "see with" these visionary authors and then shape what they and others are seeing for our own congregations, communities, and ministries.

Bill Arnold, in his chapter called "Embracing a Worldview Shaped by the Word" is calling for a future built on the core of Methodism's historic identity as we have seen it in the New Testament itself, in John Wesley, in the earliest Methodists in North

America, and in the present movement as it has tried to be faithful to its original purpose. The Bible is our foundational document and the lens through which we see and understand life itself. Methodism has nothing to give the world if it gives up that foundation and vision. But equipped with these, it will always be prepared to offer a hope-filled alternative to the deceptions and distractions the world is selling. The whole volume in which this chapter appears offers many important insights to help us make the right decisions and take the right steps to pass the baton of faith to new generations.

In the same book, Billy Abraham (sadly, now departed) reminds us of the great need for the church to be clear and united in its doctrine; the way it articulates, understands, teaches, proclaims, and practices its faith. We need to rely on the Spirit to guide our reflection and we must be clear on where we stand within the great tradition of orthodox Christianity, as authoritatively expressed in the great Creeds. We can never again allow novelty or cultural captivity to determine our faith or lead us off course. Abraham notes the ongoing value (for Global Methodists) of the Methodist Articles of Religion and the Confession of Faith of the Evangelical United Brethren, with this much needed proviso: "We need, of course, to excise the relevant anti-Catholic material."

Jonathan Powers' chapter on the future of worship provides welcome depth and richness in both the form and substance of "the central act of the church and the chief end of the Christian life." Without digressing into the well-worn issues and preferences of evangelical worship wars, he takes us to essentials of the way we connect the theological and spiritual realities of the faith to the way we approach the One who gives life and salvation.

James Thobaben's chapter on the future of sexual ethics in a reformed Methodism tackles the presenting moral issue which brought United Methodism to "irresolvable schism." He puts the subject in its proper context of holiness and purity in Scripture (Hebrews 12:14-17) and God's vision for the human family. He asks how we came to this point and what lessons we can learn from the experience. He compares the mainline Methodist withdrawal from traditional sexual ethics to the loss of Christian identity of United Methodist colleges – and how the two are related: "Not only would no UMC college prohibit premarital sex, tacit encouragement of such would occur in classrooms at almost all those schools. Similarly, these institutions would not prohibit or discourage homosexual relations." Where institutions have failed us, the one who has never ceased calling us; remains with us, leading us forward. Some of the smaller Methodist denominations, such as the Free Methodists, Wesleyans, and Nazarenes, have worked hard to retain the Christian identity of their colleges. If a larger body is going to have a meaningful presence in higher education, it will have to do the same. There is nothing to be gained by operating essentially secular colleges that are Methodist or Wesleyan in name only, no matter how excellent their early histories may have been. "A new Methodism must, therefore, find ways to prepare students to enter higher learning, develop Methodist universities that maintain a distinct Christian identity, and provide a vision of university life that involves a robust ethic of transformative service." (Kenneth J. Collins & Ryan N. Dunbar, eds. *The Next Methodism (etc.)*. Franklin, TN; Seedbed, 2021, 57, 9, 229, 285, 131. For more on Scriptural grounding, see also in the same book, chapters by Matt O'Reilly, 91-98; David F. Watson, 99-108; and Joel B. Green, 111-120.)

Again, where does the road lead for a new generation of Methodists seeking to be faithful to their mission as Methodist Christians? It must find us walking in solidarity with the great tradition that has always given us our identity and direction. We must find our strength in Christ and in the great cloud of witnesses he has given us as companions on this journey.

Beyond this, any attempt to answer great questions about the future in precise detail will surely fall far short, yet we have no reason to shrug our shoulders, step out of line, and walk away. Our heritage gives us endless reasons to hope. We have John Wesley's decision to preach to thousands outdoors; Freeborn Garrettson's "willingness to tread unbeaten paths in the wilderness;" John Seybert's shipments of thousands of books for pioneer families; Thomas Morris' humble leadership, and – a little closer to our own time – Margaret K. Henrichsen's refusal to give up on seven small churches. Of all the reasons our history offers, "the best of all is, God is with us."

It remains critically Important to seek our very best future by allowing that future, and issues of today that are challenging and even threatening Methodism, to continue their interaction with Scripture and with insightful moments and people of our movement's past.

Rural Maine in the mid-twentieth-century did not seem a likely place for small churches to flourish. To some, Margaret Henrichsen seemed an unlikely pastor to lead a group of "nearly deserted Methodist churches" back to life and a hopeful future. But this pastor had found spiritual strength in another church a few years earlier, and believed that with vision, love, and leadership, she and these small churches could offer to others the same strength she had found in and for them. While many were skeptical, she was able to get enough people to join in her experiment and she became the pastor of a seven church circuit.

Margaret Henrichsen's rescue mission with these seven churches demonstrated a characteristic she shared with the apostles and the early Methodist circuit riders. She loved the people and their churches. She loved the people who weren't in those churches – yet. She had a very Methodist passion for souls. Hers was a calling that would not accept the all too common conclusion that none of this matters very much. She was not distracted by negative conventional wisdom or easy defeat. It was easy to pass by small country churches that were closed and in disrepair; to dismiss them as romantic relics of a bygone age. Margaret saw beyond those surface impressions.

> I had seen day after day, the village children going by, growing up, children who had never been to church and knew no Sunday School, children to whom the Bible stories were almost unknown, children who had no real sense of a God who loved them and to whom they were accountable and responsible. The countryside seemed to be growing godless because no minister was there who cared!

The result of her ministry in those small seaside communities is clear in the vitality of their people, their churches, and her own life.

> I turned away to drive back home across this dear Maine land, passing one after another of the tiny buildings where we worship together, perfectly certain of one thing – that no matter how few in numbers the congregations I was called to serve, there are no little churches in the Kingdom of God. There is no such thing as a small church when it is a church of Jesus Christ. (Halford E. Luccock & Webb Garrison. Endless Line of Splendor. Evanston, IL: United Methodist Communications, 1975; Margaret K. Henrichsen. Seven Steeples. Boston, MA: Houghton Mifflin, 1953, 1; 238.)

Margaret Henrichsen gives us an example of the pattern we have seen concerning pastors' views of education for ministry, this time a perspective of a new, second career pastor on a rural circuit, in the mid-twentieth-century. Here she describes the books in her first parsonage:

> "You don't lack for books, do you?" was the comment of one of my neighbors when she came in. I certainly didn't lack for books. They were all over the place – three bookcases in the study, a large one in the hall, another at the head of the stairs, - a small one in my bedroom – and books on every table, along the edge of my desk, often in chairs, and occasionally on the floor. No, I didn't lack for books. I had had visions of long cozy winter evenings and days when one couldn't get out, and knowing I would be a long way from a library, and being very conscious of the need for resource material in connection with my studies and sermons, I had bought every book I could manage that seemed to be a necessary tool for the study course. (Margaret Henrichsen. Seven Steeples. Boston: Houghton Mifflin, 1953, 69&70.)

This is much more than one pastor's library. In fact, it immediately brings to mind the book collecting habits of nearly every pastor I have known over more than fifty years – myself included. There seems to be an insatiability for gathering important, useful books and making them part of us – extensions and resources of who we are and who we are becoming. That overflowing thirst for learning that has characterized pastoral leaders from the beginning, lives on undiminished today, a sign of clerical health we can hope lives in their congregations as well.

Along with reading, there are endless other opportunities for study - conferences, seminars, and retreats; covering general and cross disciplinary interests and targeted specializations. Pastors often gather with colleagues to share ideas and pray for one another. These gatherings may take place ecumenically or within traditions. All of these can be augmented and enriched by internet resources, including social media, or in traditional, face to face settings in churches, homes, retreat centers, or coffee houses.

For well over a century, pastors and seminarians, especially those in United Methodism and The United Church of Canada, have struggled over the nature and direction of theological education. Many seminaries and universities have become increasingly secular, adopting principles and approaches to doctrine and church life that resemble the secular academy and liberal social ethics of the surrounding culture more than the Christian tradition with its Biblical foundation. (Henry Clay Morrison. Autobiography of Bishop Henry Clay Morrison. Nashville, TN, Methodist Episcopal Church South, 1917; Thomas Oden. Requiem (etc.). Nashville, TN: Abingdon, 1995.)

One option that pretty much dooms its practitioners to failure is self-sufficient isolation; The preacher – the Christian, for that matter – who thinks they can get along without input from others, will lack the synergy of ideas, experience, and encouragement needed for long term, effective ministry. They will be neglecting the mutual mentoring that we have seen has been central in every generation of Christians, especially Methodist leadership, from New Testament times to our own. They may hold on as best they can to the baton of faith, but they will be more likely to let it slip from their hands and unlikely to effectively pass it on.

ENCOURAGEMENT

Mutual encouragement is at least as important as the sharing of practical and spiritual wisdom. Someone who is discouraged has, by definition, lost courage and hope. There are both discouragers and encouragers in our churches; people who drain the courage out of us, and others who pour courage in. Encouragement is a life-giving gift; Discouragement is a debilitating curse. Isolation in ministry leaves us open to, and relatively defenseless against, discouragement, but when we live and work together, encouraging each other, we have a grace-filled, renewing and renewable source of living and life-giving water to refresh our souls.

It takes an unshakable decision, followed and supported by determination and discipline, to give and seek encouragement, and to reject the discouragement that tries to take our hope away. Once we start to get discouraged, we need to see that discouragement for what it is, and we need to know where to find the antidote that will overcome its poison.

The need for encouragement is perhaps clearest and strongest when viewed from its polar opposite. Here we see it in one episode in the experience of Margaret Henrichsen's early ministry in Maine:

> These Down East folk are very slow to give encouragement. Many and many a week has passed without indication that my efforts to be a good pastor meant anything to anyone. Of all instruments the devil has at his command – and he certainly has quite a bag of tools – this one of making a person feel that he isn't really needed or wanted is the most dangerous, I verily believe. When sermons seemed flat and trite to me, and my spirits [sic] grew as brown as the mud and fog that were everywhere as the winter began to break up, the best cure was to go and call on someone like Effie. Yet even there self-distrust got in my way. I wondered if I were exploiting her helplessness because of my own need to be useful. But the glow in her dark eyes and the flush of pleasure on her face were reassuring. (Margaret Henricksen. Seven Steeples. Boston: Houghton Mifflin, 1953, 74.)

Discouragement is not to be found only in the devil's "bag of tools," or in the local culture of "Down East." It has been active just about everywhere, in individuals who do not seem to care and in shifts in attitudes and values across broad swaths of society. Discouragement has caused pastors to consider career change *for the wrong reasons* and reinforced a society-wide tendency toward loneliness. But within the body of Christ there are resources of Spirit-empowered, mutual strength available to build each other up and break away from downward spirals of discouragement. For those in the Methodist tradition there are opportunities for renewal of our original, life-giving purpose since the time of the Wesleys, and for all Christians there is the reality of Emmanuel, God with us.

THE TWO WAYS'

One choice handed down to us from the Wesleys and the circuit riders has undergone a kind of revival in recent decades: the conflict with a revived, muscular Calvinism. This reinvigorated Calvinism has been met, however, both by simple, pastoral restatement and, where something more stringent was needed, by strong and disciplined argument. An example of the former comes to us from Evangelical Association Bishop Samuel P Spreng, based on John 3:16 and Philippians 2:12&13:

> We can be saved if we will. We can be lost if we will. God does all that even God can do for us but he does not force us. He does not invade the rights of the human will. He leaves us free to choose.
>
> God works within us, creating the ability and the disposition, doing that which we ourselves cannot do, meeting us at the point of our helplessness, invigorating, graciously, our enfeebled powers, making it possible for us to will and to work. We on our part must act, must use the powers imparted to us by his [prevenient] grace. This is the beginning of salvation, or of our experience of conversion. (Samuel P. Spreng. What Evangelicals Believe. Cleveland, OH: Evangelical Publishing House, 1929, 100-101.)

A more aggressive, extended, philosophical response to the new Calvinism is Jerry Walls and Joseph Dongell's *Why I am Not a Calvinist*. This brings the theological and pastoral problems in Calvinism into clear focus, providing a compelling case against its determinism and views of limited atonement and predestination. It is hard to imagine a pastor in the Wesleyan tradition being ambivalent on the subject after reading their work. Roger Olsen's *Against Calvinism* can be compared to *Against Arminianism*, by Robert A. Peterson and with Calvinist author Michael Horton's

For Calvinism. Olsen is a Baptist Arminian, who, like Walls and Dongell, seeks to be fair and accurate in describing the Calvinist position, while making a compelling case against that position and equipping readers to stand, teach, and lead the churches on the solid ground of Arminian theology. (Jerry L. Walls & Joseph R. Dongell. *Why I Am Not a Calvinist*. Downers Grove, IL; InterVarsity, 2013; Roger E. Olsen. *Against Calvinism*.Grand Rapids, MI: Zondervan, 2011; Robert Peterson & Michael D. Williams. *Why I Am Not an Arminian*. Downers Grove, IL: InterVarsity, 2004; Michael Horton. *For Calvinism*. Grand Rapids, MI: Zondervan Academic, 2011.)

Jerry Walls has given us another powerful book on this vital subject, framed in a way that speaks with special clarity to Methodists. The title – *Does God Love Everyone?* – puts the matter into unmistakably clear focus. Walls cuts to the chase with a quote from Calvinist writer Arthur Pink: "When we say that God is sovereign [the foundational premise of the Calvinist view of God] in the exercise of His love, we mean that He loves whom He chooses. God does not love everybody." For Wesley, on the other hand, the foundational premise is the same as that of I John 4:8: "God is love." The best known and most memorized verse (albeit in different translations) in Scripture is John 3:!6, in which the central figures are God, who loves, and whoever believes. There is nothing said of God loving only a chosen few, or of people divinely created incapable of believing. In fact, what often comes across as the Calvinist fixation on God's sovereignty and power is so foreign to God's self-revelation as to be obviously artificial. While the Bible's portrayal of God's character is so clearly one of love, Walls points out the paucity of references to his love in Calvin's *Institutes*. In all of this magisterial work with its thousands of Scriptural references, there is no mention of I John 4:8 or John 3:16. This omission is what Walls refers to as "the blind spot of Calvinism." Not only is love the essence of God's character, but this love has a free, reciprocating object in his human creation. "...Love requires a free response." Citing the letter to the Laodiceans in Revelation, he sees in its message both God's love and the necessary place of humanity's freedom. Without both we are left with inescapable, purposeless tyranny. (Jerry L. Walls. *Does God Love* Everyone? Eugene, OR: Cascade, 2016, 3; 5; 77.)

There are times when weariness with this debate, alongside a desire for conciliation at any cost may tempt some to lose patience with the issue and even to believe it doesn't matter much any more. But for Methodism to be true to its message and for the essential truth of the gospel to be maintained, we will have to remain faithful to the Arminian heritage that comes to us from Scripture, through Wesley, the circuit riders, and today's tireless defenders and advocates of the truth.

The context in which this renewed issue has taken its current shape necessitates a restored clarity and new methods in our response. Both Canadian and American churches, especially from the late nineteenth-century on, have experienced a loss of consensus on the continuing value of revival, the atmosphere in which Methodism, including its Arminian gospel, grew and flourished. While some criticized revivals in general and camp meetings in particular for what they saw as emotionally excessive and out of sync with modern academic thinking or social conventions, actually, the theological issues remain, and even the methodology retains its usefulness, though, of course, the culture has changed.

Another factor that has changed Methodism's approach to Calvinism is ecumenism. From one vantage point, unity and harmonious interactions are obviously good, with abundant Scriptural warrant, for example, from Jesus' high priestly prayer in John 17 to Paul's eloquent appeal in Ephesians 4:

> Spare no efforts to make fast with the bonds of peace the unity which the Spirit gives. There is one body and one Spirit, just as there is one hope held out in God's call to you; one Lord, one faith, one baptism; one God and Father of all, who is over all and through all and in all. (Ephesians 4:3-6, REB)

Clearly rancor and mean spiritedness undermine any church or denomination. The same applies to interactions between and among churches or denominations. So how could ecumenism be a problem? The difficulty comes when our efforts to minimize conflict cause us to under value or disregard our distinctive identities, traditions, convictions, and commitments in order to achieve what may pass for unity. It is particularly problematic when unity seems to demand either that one group become less than it really is, or that one group intentionally overlook problems in what the other brings to the table.

Ecumenism among Wesleyans, to the extent that they are Wesleyan, and that their histories, traditions, gifts, and contributions are honored, remembered, and included in a cooperative, federated, or fully merged movement, can be and often is a very good thing. In that scenario, every participant is valued and all are blessed. Both Canadians and Americans can point to relevant examples. But there have been other examples where the contributions of smaller churches have been downplayed, disregarded, or forgotten in what some have called "a merger of a shark with its prey." Some readers may have an example or two in mind. Still, where two or more Wesleyan bodies honor each other, respect and incorporate each other fully in the life of their combined church or venture, there can be wonderful results. There is enough common ground for everyone to be deeply, genuinely rooted and nourished.

The situation can easily become more difficult and complicated when distinctly different traditions draw closer, and especially as they take steps toward merger. More to the point, how do Calvinists and Wesleyans achieve unity when some of their most strongly held beliefs are, or have been, radically at odds with each other? Can a "big tent" actually hold them both? Does one group need to relinquish its claim to the truth? Do they have to find a way to hold on to each position as an equal option, or must they turn their backs on both traditions, as though none of it matters anymore? Have the important questions been answered and problems resolved? Might they come back to haunt you once the excitement of the moment has passed? Is there a possibility so attractive that it outweighs the sacrifice you are contemplating? Are you giving up anything you will regret losing? Are there other possibilities that could make this new arrangement work?

The steps toward and within The United Church of Canada are particularly useful to illustrate these complex challenges. The 1925 merger included a sizable portion of a traditionally Calvinist body and the largest body of Wesleyans in the country. A century has passed since that combined reality began its life. Has the merged church fulfilled the dreams of its architects? Has the new denomination brought growth or decline? Have its attempts to sublimate, supersede, replace, or ignore traditional differences "worked?" Is the United Church now better positioned and equipped to serve and transform the world than were its constituent bodies? What has Canadian Methodism gained and lost by the merger? Have the smaller Methodist bodies succeeded in preserving a distinctive Wesleyan presence in Canada? (John Wilkins Sigsworth. *The Battle Was the Lord's: A History of the Free Methodist Church in Canada*. Wilmore, KY; First Fruits, 2016.) Would a Methodist from another part of the world, entering the country as an immigrant or visitor and looking to worship in a Methodist church, recognize the United Church as Methodist?

The situation South of the border looks quite different. The States, where some of the larger Methodist bodies merged or reunited more recently, and the merged bodies were all of the pan-Methodist tradition, have no equivalent to The United Church. Yet the more diverse collection of churches participating in the progressive ecumenical movement must come to terms with similar questions as those facing the United Church. In recent years, progressives in these churches have generally pursued common or parallel goals, though the older, institutional vision of merger has weakened. Have efforts to moderate or supersede denominational distinctives strengthened mainline Protestantism in the United States? Has Pluralism done more for the churches' outreach than orthodoxy? While reasons have been debated, it is far more

Metropolitan Methodist Church, Toronto (Now Metropolitan United Church of Canada)

than coincidental that these churches have been shrinking – often precipitously.

Meanwhile, traditionalists in these same denominations have dissented vigorously from the progressive directions of their churches, until sizable groups have found at least two ways out of their untenable situations. Some have made their way into what are often called "non-denominational" or "independent" churches – sometimes "megachurches." Often this has involved abandoning the historical identities of the churches they have left behind, as though they are no longer relevant. They may in this way free themselves from issues and leadership they rejected, but in the process they have likely given up much more. They have traded their old church for a new one, which feels new because it goes by a different name. They eventually realize the murkiness of their gains, and, perhaps, a bit more clarity on their losses. Another group makes an organized effort to depart with a clear sense of direction, into a new denomination of their own tradition, one that corrects the problems experienced in the old body, advances in a new direction consistent with its beliefs, values, and hopes, and is deeply rooted in the identity and purpose of its larger tradition. Such groups include The Anglican Church in North America, The Evangelical Presbyterian Church, and The Global Methodist Church.

There is also kind of relationship among theologically orthodox churches when they find enough in common to be able to learn from each other and work together without compromising their integrity. In this kind of relationship they may find themselves strengthened and enriched as they learn from each other's history and practice. This kind of ecumenism holds a special place in Methodism because of Wesley's eclectic sources. Among the traditions from which he drew were early (especially Eastern) Christianity (extended forward in Eastern Orthodoxy), Roman Catholicism (especially Thomas a Kempis), his own Anglican Church (which in his day was busily exploring its own roots), The Puritans, The Moravians, and Martin Luther.

Today it has been spiritually rewarding for me to continue Wesley's "mining" of ecumenical sources and fellowship, to which

I have gratefully added the Coptic Orthodox Church, especially through its modern writers, such as Pope Shenouda III and Matthew the Poor, and St. Mary and St. Moses Coptic Orthodox Church in North Tonawanda, New York. (as I did in *Transfiguration and Hope: a Conversation across Time and Space*. Eugene, OR: Wipf and Stock, 2018.)

All we are and do as Wesleyan Christians, must be soundly Biblical, "rooted and grounded in love," (Ephesians 3;17, ESV) and lived out faithfully within our historical and contemporary connexion. We must cherish and nurture our fellowship within the great tradition, and by grace we must press on, and invite others, to God's new creation, our destiny in glory. We will do all of this as we pass the baton of faith.

www.ingramcontent.com/pod-product-compliance
Lightning Source LLC
Chambersburg PA
CBHW070313230426
43663CB00011B/2119